Ship
Model
Building

THIRD EDITION
Revised and Enlarged

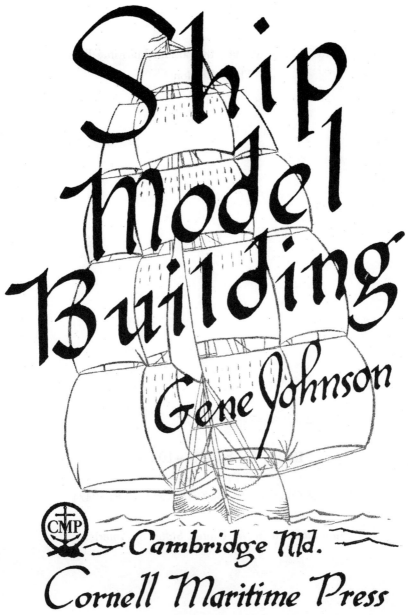

Ship Model Building

Gene Johnson

Cambridge Md.

Cornell Maritime Press

INCORPORATED

1961

ISBN 0—87033—101—9

Library of Congress Catalog Card Number: 61-17424

Manufactured in the United States of America

To My Wife
OLLIE
Without whose enthusiasm and unfailing assistance this volume could not have been completed.

INTRODUCTION

You don't have to be a tattooed Barnacle Bill to make a professional looking ship model. But many people who admire boats seem to think that it is a foregone conclusion that it must be too intricate a craft for the beginner.

This book is written because I know that model building is fun, and a hobby that any interested and intelligent person can enjoy who is willing to spend a little effort, time and patience on the process—especially during the preliminary stages. A table is the only necessary working space, and most of the tools actually needed are available in the average household.

The following pages give general construction information on various types of ships; the illustrations which suggest methods that are simple, but should be conducive to good results, do not apply to any one particular type of vessel. The hull illustrations, though, are the exception; the same basic work is required for all hulls: blocking, centering, profiling, shaping, and other operations.

No attempt has been made to adhere to any set scale, because ship models vary greatly in size; in fact, many of the drawings are purposely out of scale in order to get across certain points and ideas.

Be sure to take this fact into consideration before attempting any detail work. Keep the deck fixtures, fittings, etc., as conformable in scale to the ship as possible. It is difficult at first to realize how small—almost infinitesimal—most of the details will have to be. Tweezers will be constant companions for this work.

The most important advice in model building is this: *do not rush your work*. Before beginning construction, spread out the blueprints or kit assembly plans, and study the instructions carefully. Then study the general proportions, the lines of the hull, the superstructure, rigging, and rake of the masts. After you have formed a series of mental pictures of the various units and stages of construction, study the detail work. This does not mean, of course, that the beginner is expected to acquire understanding of the intricate rigging and other confusing details from the printed page: as with everything else, learning and understanding come from doing.

Check and compare all parts before assembling—especially the comparatively complicated sections where there are numbers of interrelated pieces. Model builder's cement is better than glue for the assembling of parts; it is quick-drying and will hold, regardless of temperature changes.

Kit assemblies contain a few stamped and molded fixtures of metal or fiber board; additional ones in graded sizes are obtainable at well-stocked department and novelty stores, and from ship model companies. Such places also carry supplies of balsa wood in sheets, blocks or strips of various sizes. This happens to be written at a time when governmental priorities are held on metal and balsa wood, but cardboard and fiber are being used extensively as substitutes. Check on the quality and thickness of the cardboard used for detail work.

It is a good idea to collect drawings and photographs of ships and ship details from newspapers and magazines. A little picture may save time and temper during some difficult stage in assembling.

It is interesting to see how the average model builder's respect for the craft increases as he progresses. Little by little, the cardboard used in earlier attempts is replaced by better materials, his workmanship improves, and his ships become more authentic. Running gear becomes workable, rudder and steering apparatus function correctly, blocks are provided with sheaves—in fact, he builds a real ship on a smaller scale.

I would like to say that the statements in the text are not meant to be entirely conclusive or dogmatic. As always, there are certain exceptions to almost every rule, and the builder who takes a real interest in the work will probably discover them and invent new and better ways.

The final word is a promise to the beginner, if he does follow instructions and gives attention to detail, that he will be sure to look at his first completed model with pleasant astonishment and say, "Did *I* make that?"

G. J.

PREFACE TO THE SECOND EDITION

This new printing gives me an opportunity—which I seized upon—to add a section on working ships, plus new working plans for two.

During the years, so many requests have come in for more information about the small trawler, or dragger, shown on p. 21, that it has now been my grateful pleasure to draw it up in complete detail—complete, as you will see, to the fishermen's gaffs and knives. May the model you make from it be so successful that its admirers almost smell the fish.

Also on a new plan sheet is that puffing little hard worker—the harbor tug. It is a universal favorite; people never seem to tire of watching them handle and dock long barges of box cars and other unwieldy cargo in swift tidal currents, or nosing the big ships in and out of their piers, or of hearing their hoarse whistle signals during a fog.

The more I see and hear about work ships, the more respect and liking I have for them. Besides tugs and fishing vessels, which include also beam trawlers, sealers, whalers, etc., they include freighters and other cargo carriers, tankers, sea trains, lumber carriers, ore colliers, dredgers, ferry boats, river steamers, and others too numerous to include here. They all present new and stimulating problems to the model builder; they are an exciting challenge to even the most expert and sensitive craftsman.

I have discovered, though, that this type of model invariably brings on such floods of comment and questions that it is a pretty good idea to learn as much as possible about its related industry, which of course dictated its unorthodox outlines and details. In a way almost mysterious, your alertness and knowledge will show through in your craftsmanship, and you will also be sure to inspire others to follow in your footsteps.

I take this opportunity to thank the kind model builders from here to New Zealand who have expressed pleasure in this volume.

G. J.
Eastchester, N. Y.

PREFACE TO THE THIRD EDITION

Well, here we are again—and never happier—to add another working ship or two to the book, plus something, this Centennial Year, to help commemorate our Civil War.

Also included are a few contemporary armaments, etc., that no doubt will attain historical value with the same speed as related designs in preceding editions. The next time, perhaps, we shall have something for navigating a newly discovered planetary ocean. Who dares say no?

One reason for including those strange-looking Civil War ironclads, the *Monitor* and the *Merrimac,* is because they are so different in design and structure from the many sailing vessels in these pages. Not only will they add historical value to your fleet, but they will give striking decorative contrast. Another reason is that they remind us of how revolutionary and modern they were in *their* time. In *The Great Democracies,* Winston Churchill wrote: "The combat of the *Merrimac* and the *Monitor* made the greatest change in sea-fighting since cannon fired by gunpowder had been mounted on ships about four hundred years before." *

Some details and features of a typical whaling vessel of the Moby Dick era are given in this new edition. If you ever have a chance to board one of these old whalers on public exhibition, do so by all means. And if you strike it on a raw, penetrating day, so much the better. Then you will get a fair idea of the incredibly tough, unglamorous existence of the crew. Try to imagine the cramped living conditions, the generally terrible food, the greasy, slippery decks, and the ever-present stench.

The ferryboats depicted here are the average river, or harbor, ferries for car and passenger use, usually of the double-ender type, meaning, obviously, that either end may serve as the bow.

For the naval craft enthusiast, there is a new ship weapon, recently declassified, that you will want to add to your most recent model of a naval vessel.

I hope sincerely that these new pages will give much added pleasure and information to all who are interested in the unusual type of ship. May your fleet keep growing!

---

* v. 4. *A History of the English Speaking Peoples,* Dodd, Mead & Co.

G. J.
Eastchester, N. Y.

TABLE OF CONTENTS

Ship Model Building

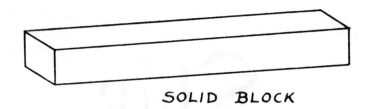

SOLID BLOCK

Plate 1

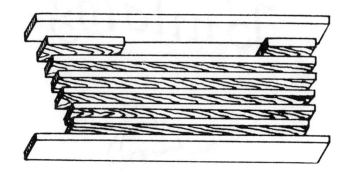

BUILT UP LONGITUDINAL SOLIDS

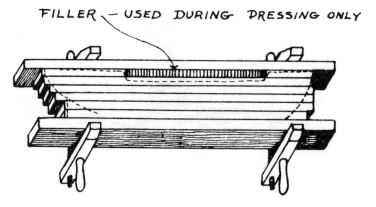

FILLER — USED DURING PRESSING ONLY

GLUED AND PLACED IN PRESS

HULL BLOCKS

SOLID BLOCKS. A solid block of wood is the simplest form possible for hull construction, and best in many respects for the beginner's first model. The unbroken surfaces simplify the tasks of measuring, marking, and squaring of template positions.

BUILT-UP SOLID BLOCKS. Hull blocks can also be made by gluing several layers of wood strips together. If you attempt this form, try to have the grain of all the strips of wood run in the same direction; then mark each piece so accurately that you won't be liable to make a mistake when gluing them together. These layers, or laminations, can be in a series of either horizontal or perpendicular strips, but, in my opinion, the horizontal pieces are more satisfactory. The block is easier to carve and shape, because a minimum of cross-grain cutting is necessary. Cross-grain cutting means cutting across the grain—as you would have to do if you rounded the end of a piece of wood. Your strips of wood can vary in thickness from thin plywood to material of one or two inches thick, depending upon the type of ship you are building, or, as is sometimes the case, the kinds of wood available. I have used several different woods for hull construction which are easy to carve and which have beautiful rich textures when left in their natural state—unpainted, except for a coat of shellac and a couple of coats of varnish—all finally rubbed down to a soft finish. These woods are: white wood, mahogany, and sugar pine, in the order named for surface beauty.

BUILT-UP HOLLOW BLOCKS. A third kind of hull block is constructed by gluing cut-out laminations together. For this type, the center portions of the strips are cut out with a coping saw; only the bottom piece and the pieces forming the fore and after decks are solid. The top piece has the greatest cut-out area, of course, and each consecutive lower strip has less excess material to be sawed out. Whenever the hull is built up of layers of wood, check the direction of the grain, use hot glue if possible and place temporary fillers where necessary to complete the solid block. These fillers help to distribute pressure evenly. Now place the block between two pieces of wood which are slightly longer than the block. Press tightly between vise or clamps. Allow to dry for at least twelve hours before removing pressure.

If your particular model does not call for raised fore and after decks, glue a thin sheet of balsa wood or cardboard over the top cut-out strip,

3

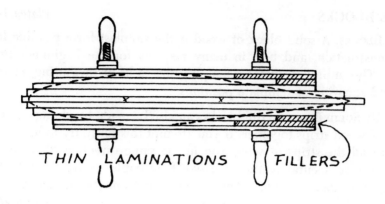

THIN LAMINATIONS   FILLERS

Plate 2

SIDE VIEW

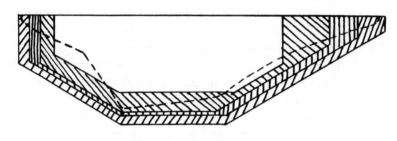

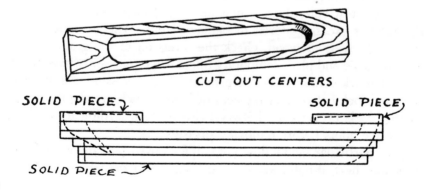

CUT OUT CENTERS

SOLID PIECE

SOLID PIECE

SOLID PIECE

4

so the ship will have a deck. However, this decking should not be placed until after the hull has been shaped. *(See the section on shaping, page 11.)* The reason for this is that in shaping the hull, the sheer line (the longitudinal line of the deck looking at the ship from the side) is never quite straight, which makes it necessary to remove a certain amount of wood throughout this area. This curve is very slight in some ships, in others more pronounced.

Foochow pole junk model made in China. (In the collection of The Mariners' Museum, Newport News, Va.)

5

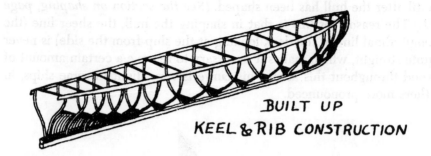

BUILT UP
KEEL & RIB CONSTRUCTION

Plate 3

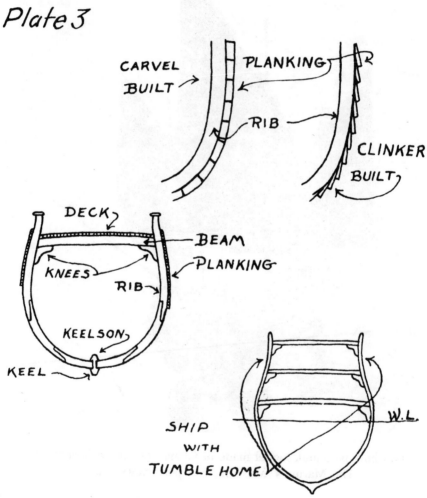

CARVEL BUILT → PLANKING ← RIB

CLINKER BUILT

DECK
BEAM
PLANKING
KNEES
RIB
KEELSON
KEEL

SHIP WITH TUMBLE HOME

W.L.

In this book the built-up model from keel and rib construction will not be dealt with except as another type of hull construction, for it is a problem for advanced model builders only. It is too complicated for the beginner, but, as experience grows, the goal becomes more attainable.

This type of construction requires a thorough knowledge of intricate ship construction plus the skill of a cabinet maker and the finger dexterity of a jeweler, but is the dream of every enthusiastic model builder, including myself. My own particular ambition is to construct a three-masted frigate of forty guns, and I hope to try my hand at it soon. To build a ship model from keel to truck with all gear complete and workable; to know that each and every part is a true reproduction of the original ship and that his own hands have carved and shaped each little piece and part to create such a work of beauty, must give a builder a marvelous sense of accomplishment. Such a model can rightly be called a work of art, and will, in all probability, find a place in some museum collection. But the knowledge of self-achievement and the confidence inspired will be the craftsman's greatest reward. It would be difficult to place a definite monetary value on a work of this kind, but some builders have sold models at very high prices.

I do not wish to convey the impression that this type of model is the only one that can qualify as a very fine piece of work. Some of the very best pieces that I have seen had solid or semi-solid hulls. The proportions and workmanship were as near perfection throughout as the scale allowed.

FISHING SMACK.

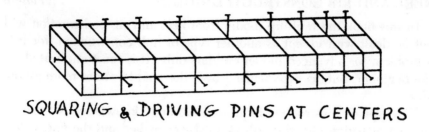

SQUARING & DRIVING PINS AT CENTERS

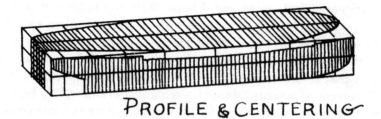

PROFILE & CENTERING

Plate 4

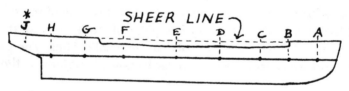

AFTER PROFILE CUTTING — SIDE

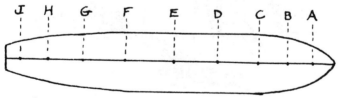

AFTER PROFILE CUTTING — TOP

These are important steps. Begin by being exact in all your measurements; then you will acquire the valuable habit of exactness and precision.

The term "blocking" means drawing a line around the wood block at the template positions and marking center lines of the block: on top, sides, ends and bottom, regardless of whether your block is solid or has been built-up. These lines should be drawn with a straight-edged instrument. The template positions are indicated on your working drawings or blueprints and the template lines should be drawn with a carpenter's try-square and should encircle the block and meet exactly.

Find exact centers of all intersections and drive pins ¼″ into the hull —or even deeper, if you think the profile cutting might possibly remove them. The illustration of the block shows one example where this procedure is not followed; the center portion of the last intersection at template position "J" on the sides will be removed in profile cutting; so drive the pin into the hull directly *above* the intersection, where you are positive it will remain. These pin-holes will prove to be valuable during the later work. The template or section lines will be lost after you do the profile cutting, but the pin-holes will remain and so centers are always available.

Good-looking hulls are achieved by being careful in this blocking, and by taking time with the profile cutting and shaping. *Profile cutting*, or roughing out, is the first step in the actual shaping of the hull; this process eliminates much of the excess wood. This work is generally done with a jig saw or a band saw plus the help of a medium-toothed rasp. An ordinary carpenter's coping saw will do, but the use of saw and rasp simplifies the work a great deal. If necessary, this can all be achieved with a knife but, of course, the work will take more time. Before cutting the profiles, some builders like to shade the hull area, or color it with crayon, so there will be no likelihood of cutting along misleading lines. This shading is not necessary if you are cutting with a knife, because then you have plenty of time to check your lines before beginning each cut or series of cuts. If you are using a saw, first do the profile cutting of the top and bottom; next, the profile cutting of the sides. Make sure that all pin-holes are still plainly visible. If they are not, replace them.

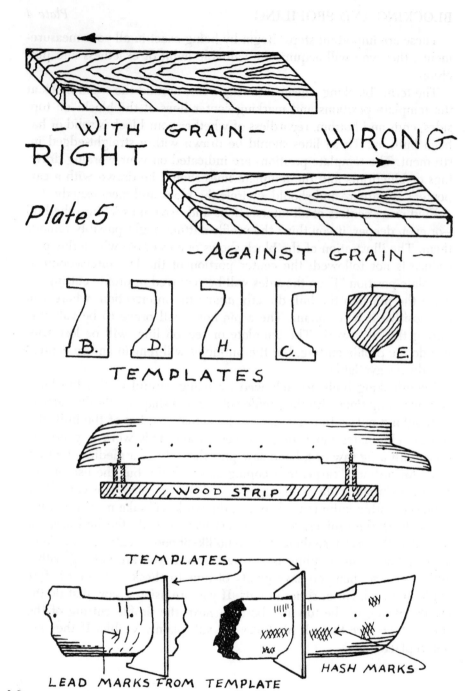

RIGHT — WITH GRAIN —

WRONG

— AGAINST GRAIN —

Plate 5

TEMPLATES

B.   D.   H.   C.   E.

WOOD STRIP

TEMPLATES

LEAD MARKS FROM TEMPLATE

HASH MARKS

10

Work with the grain of the wood *always*. Never cut or carve against the grain. Cutting with the grain does not remove too much wood nor does the wood have a tendency to split; as a result you will have a smoother and better flowing line and cut. Make all the templates of good stiff cardboard or thin metal, such as is found in cigarette tins. Your blueprints, or working drawings, will have the exact size of each template indicated, so all you have to do is to trace these drawings on your cardboard or metal and then cut them out. Needless to say, you must be exact here, both in the tracing and in the cutting of your templates. The number of templates necessary varies according to the type and size of model under construction. Mark each template, beginning with the bow, with a letter or numeral, according to the section it represents: A, B, C, D—1, 2, 3, 4, etc. The template should be clearly marked with its letter or numeral on both sides.

If you have a bench vise or machinist's vise at your disposal, it is a good idea to screw a narrow strip of wood on your hull, running from the fore deck to the after deck. The screw-holes can easily be filled in with plastic wood or putty after the shaping is finished. This strip can be held by the vise without injury to the hull as you do the shaping.

Now you are ready to carve and shape the hull. Have ready a sharp knife, spoke shave, rasp, or other available tools for this work. Also some sheets of coarse and fine sandpaper for the finishing. Have the templates at hand—correctly traced, cut and marked. Templates are half-section patterns, used to indicate hull contour at various points.

Shaping is exacting work. Go slowly and check frequently with the templates. Pencil "hash lines" are helpful at this stage to show the high spots, or the areas that have to be removed. Rubbing pencil-lead scrapings on the template edges is another good way of finding the high spots. Wherever the template comes in contact with the hull, the lead leaves a mark. When the template comes close to the top and bottom pin-holes—indicating the center lines of the hull—is the time to be most careful. Do not carve too closely. The last remnants of surface to be removed should be sandpapered off with the coarser paper, then given a light all-over sanding with the fine paper.

A suggestion: Temporary markings, at the keel pin-holes, speed up the work. Otherwise, you will have to count off the positions each time you use a template.

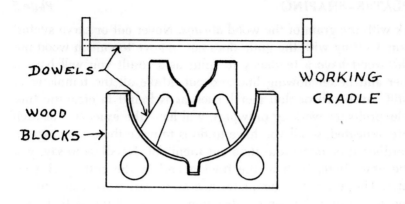

DOWELS

WOOD
BLOCKS →

WORKING
CRADLE

Plate 6

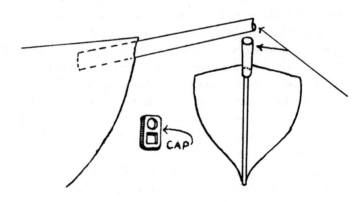

CAP

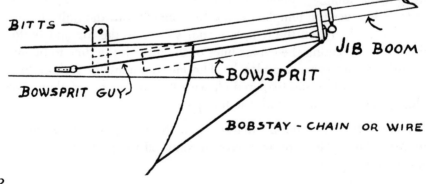

BITTS →

JIB BOOM

BOWSPRIT

BOWSPRIT GUY →

BOBSTAY - CHAIN OR WIRE

A cradle or temporary base of light wood should now be constructed, for the purpose of facilitating further work on the ship, also to protect the hull from unnecessary markings or possible damage. A cradle of this type allows more freedom of movement in the manipulating of the hull. Sometimes you will want to work with the ship bottom-side up, then you may want to tilt it this way or that in order to get at some particular spot. This shifting of the hull will be put to use quite soon, but it is in the later stages of work—during the placement of deck fixtures, super-structure, fitting and placing of the rigging—that it will prove its worth.

BOWSPRIT.—The bowsprit is not a difficult piece to shape, nor is it hard to place in the correct position. When using a solid or built-up block for the hull, drill a hole at the peak of the bow. This hole should be the size of the dowel or piece of wood you are going to use for your bow-sprit. The angle of the hole should correspond to the angle of bowsprit and hull, which will be given in the working drawings. Roughly shape the bowsprit, or, if you would rather, completely finish the shaping of it before setting into place; but do not cut it to exact length until you have glued it into the hull and it has had time to set firmly. Personally, I have found it best to rough-shape it first, then glue it into place and do the final shaping and cutting of length after it has dried. Usually the bowsprit is round for its entire length, with a slight tapering toward the cap, or outboard end.

Make the cap from a piece of thin wood; large enough to be pierced with two holes, a little smaller than the end of the bowsprit. One of these holes, it may be round or squared, should fit snugly over the end of the bowsprit. Shape the jib-boom before cutting the second hole, because this spar, when in its proper place, should fit the hole exactly.

The jib-boom is a round spar placed parallel with the bowsprit; it penetrates the upper hole in the cap and is over twice the length of the bowsprit, tapering almost to a point. The inboard end of the jib-boom may be attached to the deck by being fitted into a mooring post which is securely fastened to the hull; it may be fitted under a rail running between bitts; or locked into place by a bolt which penetrates the bitts and jib-boom. From the cap outward this jib-boom may have from one to four sheaves set into it, and from one to three bands or collars en-circling it. (*See* PLATE 88, *page 166.*)

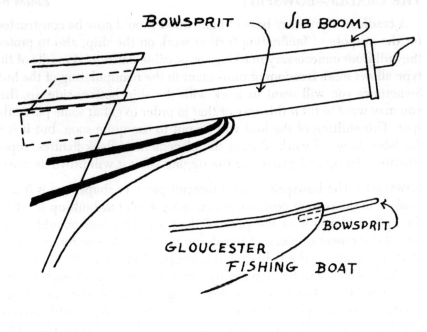

BOWSPRIT   JIB BOOM

BOWSPRIT

GLOUCESTER
FISHING BOAT

Plate 7

WHISKER BOOM

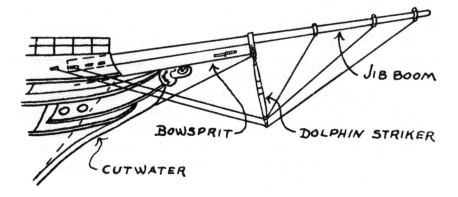

JIB BOOM

BOWSPRIT   DOLPHIN STRIKER

CUTWATER

Other parts of the bowsprit and jib-boom assembly are: the martingale, or dolphin striker, and a small spar, called a whisker boom. Sometimes the whisker boom is a single spar, tapering toward each end from the center, running at right angles to the bowsprit and fitted on the jib-boom next to the cap. In other cases whisker booms may consist of two shorter spars and be fastened on either side of, and to the cap. The dolphin striker is a similar short spar, fastened to the bottom of the cap with a fitting, and projecting downward and at an angle, slightly forward. Complete the building and fitting of cap, jib-boom, whiskers and martingale, but do not glue into place yet. Wrap these pieces in tissue paper and put away until time for final assembling.

Some ships, fishing schooners and other small sailing vessels, are equipped with stumps or short bowsprits and have no jib-booms.

THE *Half Moon.*

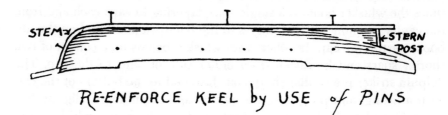

STEM

STERN POST

RE-ENFORCE KEEL by USE of PINS

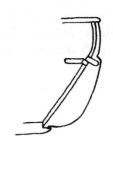

Plate 8

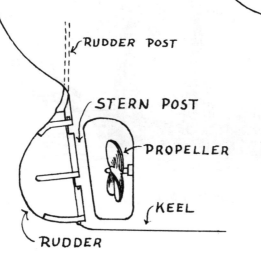

RUDDER POST

STERN POST

PROPELLER

KEEL

RUDDER

Now that the hull is shaped and the bowsprit is in place, turn the hull bottom-side up in its cradle. You are ready to attach the keel. Use a ruler to draw a line between all pin-holes along the bottom. This is the center line. Next, draw another line parallel to it, half the width of the keel. The keel width will be given in the blueprints or working drawings. This is the line you will follow when gluing on the keel.

In most kit assemblies, the keel consists of three pieces, although some sets use several. The principal pieces are: the keel proper, the sternpost or rudder block, and the stem, or bow piece. To strengthen the keel, drive a few pins through it into the hull at center, bow and stern. Do not use pins for very small models, as the keel is liable to split. When dry, trim and sandpaper so it becomes part of the hull. Fit the sternpost, and especially the stem, carefully into place before gluing.

RUDDER. The rudder can now be added to the hull. Rudder shapes vary greatly, but the general pattern is determined by the period, purpose and nationality of the ship. There are two general types: balanced, and unbalanced. All early rudders were unbalanced; the entire rudder was placed aft of the sternpost fittings (gudgeons and pintles). The balanced rudder is constructed so that a quarter of its surface area lies forward of the pivotal points; this type is often used for motor vessels requiring speed in maneuvering and ease in steering.

Rudders can be made of wood, metal or cardboard. If your model does not require a movable rudder, glue it directly to the sternpost. The gudgeon and pintle straps (described below) can be "painted on" after the general painting.

Movable, or workable rudders will have to be set on pivots so they can swing easily. These pivotal points, which are attached to the sternpost, are called pintles, or pins; gudgeons—the sockets fitting over them —are attached to the rudder. The top pin is threaded and a nut screwed into place, locking the rudder to the sternpost, but leaving it free to swing to port or starboard. A workable rudder is practicable only in hollow, or cut-out, hull models, unless the tiller bar is placed up on the deck. The following preliminary work for installing the mechanism should be done before the deck is glued in place.

Drill a hole through the stern hull bottom; run it parallel with and a little aft of the sternpost—this hole is for the rudder post to penetrate. Stiff, heavy wire is good material for the rudder post. The gudgeon

17

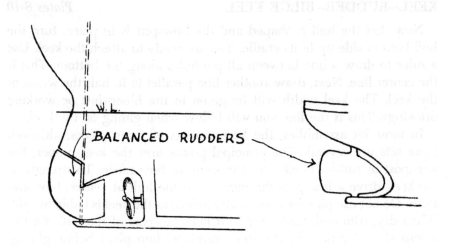

BALANCED RUDDERS

Plate 9

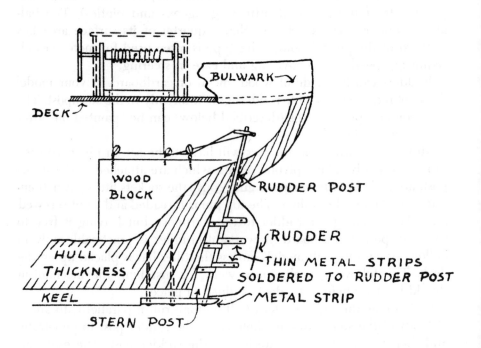

BULWARK

DECK

WOOD
BLOCK

RUDDER POST

HULL
THICKNESS

RUDDER

THIN METAL STRIPS
SOLDERED TO RUDDER POST

KEEL

METAL STRIP

STERN POST

straps can be cut from thin pieces of tin; pierce each one with at least one hole for attaching to the rudder.

Solder the gudgeon straps to the wire rudder post at the proper places. Cement the rudder and the rudder post together—strengthen further by driving small pins through the strap holes; snip pins off close to the strap, and clinch. When this is completed, pass the upper end of the rudder post through the hole drilled for it, letting the lower end rest in a shallow pivot hole bored into a metal strip fastened to the keel.

Now, after the addition of a tiller and tiller lines (or chains) plus the fitting and hooking up of steering apparatus, your model is finally going to have a workable rudder.

The tiller—a wooden crossbar, for leverage, to help swing the rudder—can be cemented firmly into place to the upper end of the rudder post.

Place a block of wood—the lower part shaped to conform to the hull —just forward of the rudder post; this will serve as a platform for the pulleys, placed as shown in the illustration: two on the port side and one to the starboard side.

Cut two 12″ lengths of linen thread and tie one end of each to an end of the tiller bar; cement the knots to hold. Feed the left (port) thread across to and through the pulley at starboard; likewise bring the right thread across the other thread, and pass it through the two port pulleys. Wind excess thread into two separate coils and lay them on the platform until they are needed for the later stages. (*See* STEERING ARRANGEMENTS, *page 85.*)

A few of the standard types of rudders are shown in the illustrations. In motor ships having a single propeller, the shaft penetrates the sternpost, and the rudder is placed somewhat beyond the propeller in order to allow clearance for both. In ships having two or more propellers, the rudder fits snugly against the sternpost except in the case of a balanced rudder.

BILGE KEEL. A bilge keel is an addition to the hull to help neutralize the "roll" of a vessel; a contrivance with which comparatively few ships are equipped. Some of the modern boats, and many Navy vessels have them. In model building, a bilge keel is constructed by gluing a rectangular strip of wood to the hull—well below the water line—at an angle of approximately 45°. It has an upward sweep at either end. If you are working on a small model, use pins merely as retainers to hold

19

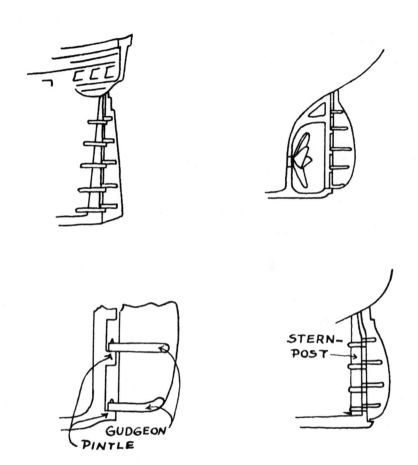

GUDGEON

PINTLE

STERN-POST →

Plate 10

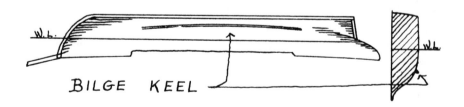

W.L.

BILGE KEEL

W.L.

the keel in place and give the curve you desire. If your model is large, and the keel heavy enough, drive the pins through the keel and into the hull. The greatest thickness of the bilge keel is throughout the center area. It tapers off toward each end. Sandpaper lightly, to give a rounded effect to the outer edge.

Detail—U.S.S. *Atlanta*. Forward house, port side, looking to starboard. Light Cruiser Class 51. (Courtesy Gibbs & Cox Inc. of New York.)

The cutwater is a triangular piece of wood, sometimes quite decorative, and often topped with a figurehead or other carved symbol. It is fitted between the stem and the bowsprit and attached to the stem. Most kit models have the cutwater and the stem combined to form one piece —the bow piece of the keel assembly.

In some of the early types of sailing vessels the bowsprit and cutwater piece were reinforced by a method of lashing called gammoning. It generally consisted of two lashings—an inner and outer gammoning. These were lashings of chain or heavy rope, with one end forming a loop which encircled the bowsprit, or was formed after passing through the slit in the cutwater. The free, or running, end of the rope was then threaded through the cutwater slit, passed over the bowsprit and back through the slit, etc., until the specified number of turns were completed.

FIGUREHEADS. The use of carved and decorated stems dates back to the earliest known watercraft. The first carvings were often symbolic, and were rather small. Religious emblems, animals, and busts predominated. Gradually the size and elaboration increased, until the use of full-length figures—or even groups—was not uncommon.

The figurehead is part of the cutwater, and can be built up on one end of it, or it can be made separately, and then fitted into place.

Make a drawing (copied or original) of the animal, figure, or whatever you are going to reproduce. Have some plastic wood and a few simple tools—small sharp knife, pointed nail file, and some toothpicks —handy. Set the cutwater in a vise, or other holder, in position for easiest possible modeling. This leaves both hands free to work, which is necessary, because speed is important.

Now press enough plastic wood around the end of the cutwater to rough-shape into the figure you want. Model with toothpicks and the pointed file; discard toothpicks for fresh ones as soon as any plastic wood sticks to them. Don't fuss with details; just try to get the simple angular planes of the figure in this first modeling. If you need depressions in these planes, make them definite, using the point or edge of the nail file. Work fast; if you find that you have tackled a larger mass of material than you can control while still pliable, lop off the excess before it dries. In fact, it is easier for some to build the figures up by

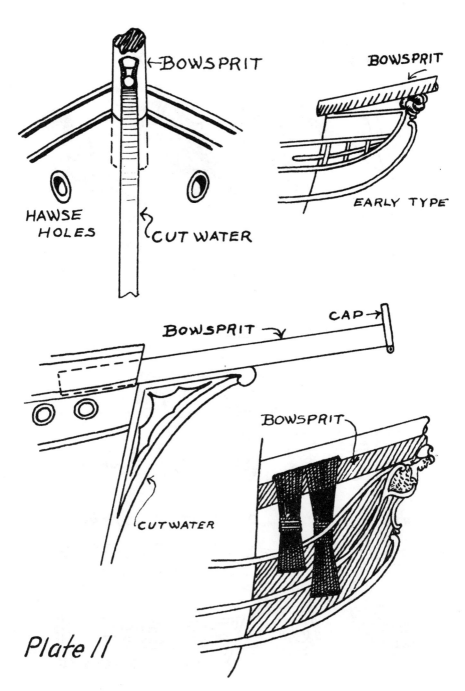

BOWSPRIT

HAWSE HOLES

CUT WATER

BOWSPRIT

EARLY TYPE

BOWSPRIT

CAP

CUTWATER

BOWSPRIT

Plate 11

23

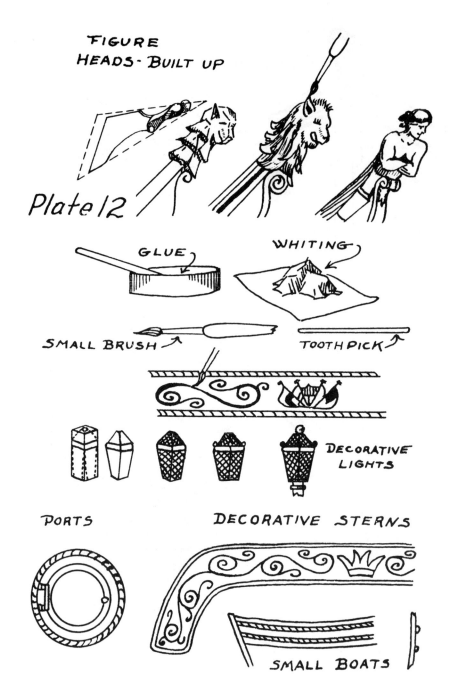

FIGURE
HEADS - BUILT UP

Plate 12

GLUE

WHITING

SMALL BRUSH

TOOTHPICK

DECORATIVE
LIGHTS

PORTS

DECORATIVE STERNS

SMALL BOATS

24

adding small portions at a time. After a few experiments you will know which is your way.

When you have acquired a fair rough-planed reproduction of your figurehead, set it aside to dry while you prepare for the next step. Assemble these materials: small brush, small mixing stick, some whiting, and a small receptacle (such as a cover) which contains a mixture of half a teaspoon of liquid glue, and three or four drops of water.

Stir a little whiting into the glue mixture with the stick. Keep adding whiting until you have a creamy paste thick enough not to run. The next step is to build up additional form and detail with this paste. Apply with the small brush, or with the toothpick, if you'd rather. Do not use too much of it in any one spot. When done, clean out the receptacle. Allow figure to dry hard. If a second application is needed, make a new glue mixture. Apply wherever you feel the figure needs additional building up. Let dry again. (Do not be too critical of your work. Viewed at this time, it is almost sure to appear crude, and not what you had hoped for. Don't let this get you down. After it has been placed and painted, you won't believe it's the same figure.) For a final finish, touch up with a knife to give sharpness to some angles; roundness to others. Then give it a coat of shellac.

For those having power units—and some knowledge of modeling—there is another method of shaping. Apply the plastic wood mass to the cutwater as before, and, with the fingers, shape into rough form. Allow to dry very hard. Profile-mark areas to be removed. Then, with cutters and burrs of the power unit, shape the figure into finished form. It may not be necessary to apply glue mixture. Dust well, and shellac.

OTHER DECORATIVE WORK. Some of the period ships had very decorative beaks (bow projections), and ornately carved poop decks with leaded windows. These decks were generally topped with decorative lanterns. All of this decorative work can be done with the whiting-and-glue paste —applied to the wood or cardboard where wanted. It gives a raised, or carved, effect to the design. The intricate scrollwork, etc., on sterns can also be done with this paste.

For long stretches of raised work, such as mouldings, strakes on small boats, decorative trim around portholes and other places, and even for the scrollwork, you can use string or thread saturated in glue, and applied directly where needed. Mark out the lines in pencil first, and use tweezers for the work.

Decorative lanterns add considerably to the general ornateness of these period ships. Shape a small rectangular block of wood, as shown in the illustration; glue old film to the sides. Drive a pin through the lantern from the top, allowing the head to jut out slightly. Paint a thin edge of glue-and-whiting paste along all the edges, covering the film seams and uniting the whole. Place a small drop of this paste at each upper corner, and add a drop to the pin-head, filling in around it. When this dries, paint to correspond to the other fixtures.

PROPELLERS
Plate 13

To make your own propellers, mold them to shape from plastic wood, carve from wood, or cut out the general three-blade shape from a flat piece of metal. Twist the blades into form. Heavy cardboard can be used for smaller models. Cut and bend to shape, shellac, and use pins to hold shape until the shellac dries.

Single-screw ships have the propeller shaft centering the hull, penetrating the sternpost. The propeller is fastened to the shaft at this point. Attach the propeller to the sternpost with a pin or small nail. To show a small portion of the shaft between the propeller and the sternpost, wrap the pin with a few turns of glued paper.

Twin- and multiple-screw models require additional propellers. Shafts and shaft supports are also necessary. Use a very thin dowel or a piece of heavy wire for the shaft; the supports can be carved out of small rectangular blocks of wood. The propeller shaft penetrates the support at its outer end—this end is called the shaft housing, and conforms to the shape of the shaft. In small models, do not try to have the shaft penetrate the support. Use two shaft pieces, and imbed them slightly into the ends of the housing. The shaft dowel should be fitted to the hull by an angle cut. A wire shaft can be imbedded directly into the hull at the proper place. Glue the ends into position at the housing. Make sure the shaft pieces are in a straight line, looking as though they penetrate the support. Now temporarily fasten the whole assembly into correct position, in order to check on the correctness of angle, straightness of shafts, and alignment of propellers and shafts. Both propellers should be the same depth from the water line, the same distance forward of the sternpost, and the same distance from the hull's perpendicular center line. When these points are correct, go ahead and glue into place permanently.

PROPELLERS

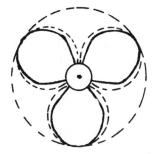

METAL-CARDBOARD LAY OUT

MOLD FROM PLASTIC WOOD

TWIST INTO SHAPE

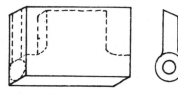

LAY OUT FOR SUPPORT

SHAFT & SUPPORT

Plate 13

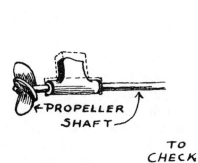

PROPELLER SHAFT

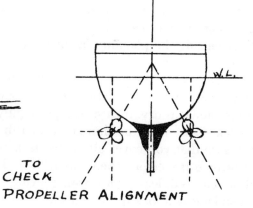

TO CHECK PROPELLER ALIGNMENT

It is a good idea to get your deck planking done at this early stage. Follow with a coat of shellac to protect the surface from glue, paint, finger marks, etc.

Deck planking can be simulated by scoring, or by cutting with a "V" gouge, which can be made from a nail. Leave a margin of approximately ¼" from the side of the hull, surrounding the entire deck area of the model. These margins are called the waterways, or scuppers, and are planking areas running parallel with the length of the ship. Mark out the areas that will be used for cabins, hatches, winches and other deck fixtures. Allow a little more space than is necessary, so that when these fixtures are placed there will be slight margins around them. This will give a neat and ship-shape appearance to the model. Do not plank these areas; allow them to remain blank. To draw the lines for the planking, use your original pin-holes as guides. Rule your deck space with straight parallel lines running fore and aft, leaving the fixture areas blank, as mentioned before. The lines can be evenly spaced, or varied slightly as to width. Scoring of lines is done only on small models. For this method use a sharp knife with a narrow point, and cut to a depth of not more than 1/16". For larger models use the "V"-gouge, and follow the lines, cutting a thin, shallow groove.

A continuous section of plank from bow to stern consists of several lengths of individual planks. To indicate the joinings of these various lengths, make right-angle cuts. Space them somewhat irregularly to avoid monotony. Do *not* use a gouge for this work; on the cross-grain surface of soft wood such an instrument will tear the wood instead of giving a clean-cut line. Do these short, cross cuts with a razor blade, and do not cut too deeply.

After cutting the planking, paint with two coats of shellac, thinned with a little alcohol, and allow to dry. If you prefer a little color and would like to have the planking a little more obvious, you can give the deck a wash with a thin mixture of umber and turpentine. First, be sure that the shellac is dry, then sandpaper lightly and remove all dust from the deck. Paint with the thin color, or rub the color on with a cloth, being sure that you cover all of the deck and that all of the planking cuts receive the color. Then rub with a clean cloth. All excess color will be removed, leaving a warm, glowing surface. The darker lines of the planking will look quite realistic.

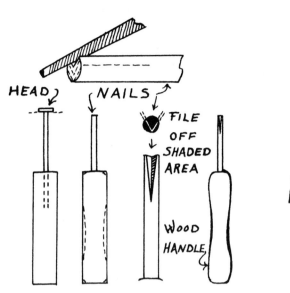

HEAD

NAILS

FILE OFF SHADED AREA

WOOD HANDLE

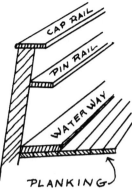

CAP RAIL

PIN RAIL

WATER WAY

PLANKING

Plate 14

VERY SHALLOW CUTS.

SIMULATING PLANKING

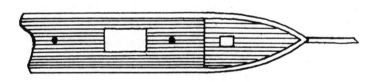

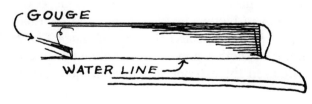

GOUGE

WATER LINE

Later on, you may wish to plank some of the deckhouses or cabins in this same manner. The planking of cabins can best and most easily be done before the cabins are cut out. Do the scoring or gouging of the walls after completing the layout and before you do other cutting of any kind.

BULWARKS *Plates 15-16*

The process of marking and cutting the right-angle niche for the bulwarks is simple. Draw the lines parallel with the length of the ship, one along the deck, and the other along the side. Be sure you do not cut deeper than the thickness of the bulwarks, which may be made of thin balsa sheets or of strips of cardboard cut a little longer than the hull of the ship. These bulwarks should fit flush with the hull. Bulwark and hull should fit together so as to present a surface which is unbroken except for the scupper drainage slots. These slots, or openings, allow water in the scuppers, or waterways, to run off. Try to cut the bulwark niche in two neat operations; first, cut from the side, and cut just deep enough to meet the next cut (your second operation) which you will make from the top. This should leave a clean right-angled niche into which the bulwarks will rest snugly.

For models having raised fore and after decks, the bulwarks have to be fitted to these decks. Where the bulwarks are continuous around the entire ship, fit the bow ends first; and allow bulwarks to run aft only to where the stern curvature begins. Then, from the port or starboard side, fit another piece, and continue around the stern to the opposite joint. Be sure to fit the bulwarks into the peak of the bow very carefully. You may have to join the two side pieces by cutting a slight angle from top to bottom in each. Glue, and set them into place, pressing firmly. Use pinch cocks (PLATE *135, page 230*) to hold them in place until dry. Another good way of holding in place is to use a cardboard retainer on the exterior side over the joint, firmly pinned to the hull.

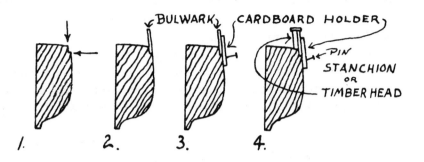

1.

2. BULWARK   CARDBOARD HOLDER

3.

4.   PIN
    STANCHION
    OR
    TIMBER HEAD

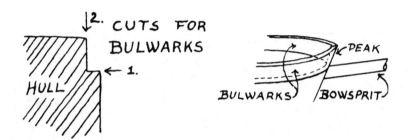

2. CUTS FOR
   BULWARKS
← 1.
HULL

PEAK
BULWARKS   BOWSPRIT

Plate 15

AFTER DECK

FORE DECK

CUTS IN FORE &
AFTER DECKS

31

The cardboard will follow the hull curve easily. You might need to apply both methods, because bulwarks are sometimes very obstinate in their tendency to straighten out.

Two of the most commonly used types of joints (or close fittings or junctures) are shown: butt joints and scarf joints. For small models the former type should be cut square and simply cemented together; for larger pieces that require reinforcing, use a staple made from a pin or wire.

Long pieces may be joined together by overlapping scarf joints. Cement is sufficient for joining small members, but larger ones should have pins driven into the joints from each side.

If you are using mortised stanchions, or timberheads, do not glue your bulwarks into place yet. See the following section on stanchions first.

Detail—U.S.S. *Atlanta*. Starboard side, looking aft and to port. Light Cruiser Class 51. (Courtesy Gibbs & Cox Inc. of New York.)

BULWARK CUT FOR ENTIRE
LENGTH OF SHIP.

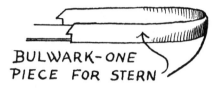

BULWARK-ONE
PIECE FOR STERN

TYPES OF JOINTS

STAPLE

BUTT
JOINT

Plate 16

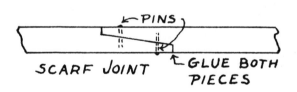

PINS

SCARF JOINT

GLUE BOTH
PIECES

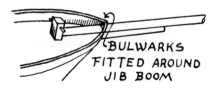

BULWARKS
FITTED AROUND
JIB BOOM

33

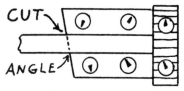
CUT
ANGLE

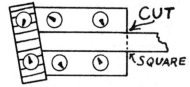
CUT
SQUARE

CARDBOARD JIG FOR STANCHIONS.

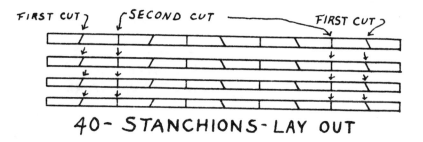

FIRST CUT   SECOND CUT   FIRST CUT

40 - STANCHIONS - LAY OUT

Plate 17

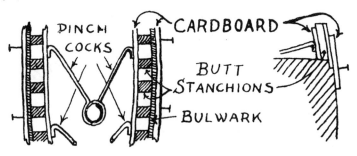

PINCH COCKS
CARDBOARD
BUTT STANCHIONS
BULWARK

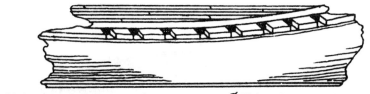

MORTISES CUT FOR STANCHIONS

The illustration shows a simple jig for cutting butt stanchions. It is easily made from stiff cardboard and held in place by tacks, thumbtacks, or small nails; and it will give you uniform stanchion lengths. Get the exact measurement of stanchion length from top of bulwark to deck; remember, the bottom of each stanchion, in order to fit the deck, must be cut at a slight angle. The depth and width of the stanchions will be governed by the scale of the model. Use rectangular lengths of balsa or pine if possible. Figure out the number of stanchions necessary—allowing for a few extras—and try to get them from as few rectangular strips as possible. If, for example, you require forty stanchions, you could use four lengths, getting ten stanchions out of each. Cut the end stanchions from each piece first—this will be the deck angle cut, giving you eight stanchions. Now change the jig stopper to the opposite end, and make the next cut a straight or right-angled cut, giving you sixteen stanchions; and so on, until you have them all cut. This makes them all as nearly alike as possible. Do not try to cut through in one motion unless the stanchions are very thin. Make two or more cuts with knife or razor blade, and do not press too heavily.

Mark the place for each stanchion on the deck or bulwark; glue, and set in place, keeping them all as straight as possible. Use a cardboard strip as a retainer, and place pinch cocks—outward pressure—to hold them in place until dry.

Mortises—Flare and Tumblehome Shapes. If your model requires mortises for stanchions, cut them out before setting the bulwarks into place. Mark the stanchion positions and cut the mortises to the depth needed. For absolute uniformity, use one stanchion for the marking of all these mortises.

Stanchions with either "flare" or "tumblehome" have to be cut to shape. There are several ways of cutting them. A time-saving method, and one of the easiest, is to lay out a double drawing of the stanchion on the end face of a rectangular block of wood just large enough for this purpose. The width of the stanchions will be taken into consideration when the individual ones are cut from the block.

First do the profile cutting much as you did for the hull. After profiling you have a double-shaped stanchion of considerable width. Now

35

LAYOUT ON BLOCK

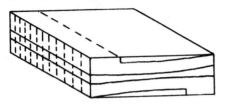

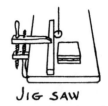

JIG SAW

THE ROUGHED-OUT STANCHION.

Plate 18

CHISEL

KERFS

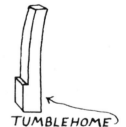

FLARE

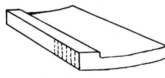

TUMBLEHOME

COPING SAW

36

cut out the excess wood between the stanchions; this gives you two wide stanchion blocks of correct contour, either flare or tumblehome. Mark off the width wanted, and cut out the individual stanchions. The profiling of these blocks can best be done with a jig saw; if the blocks are not too long, a coping saw can be used, and a simple miter box arranged so that the individual stanchions can be cut with an ordinary carpenter's saw

Another method of cutting out these shapes is to lay out a block the size of a single stanchion. Cut kerfs (saw slits) through the length of the block in the excess material; then use a chisel to remove this excess wood. Cut the individual pieces from this block, as mentioned above.

If you have no jig saw, or if, for some reason, you do not like the block method of cutting stanchions, there is another way of making them from a large sheet of wood. The thickness of the wood sheet must be the same as the width of your stanchions. Make a cardboard model, exact size, side view, of the stanchion you want. Use this cardboard piece to draw the number of stanchions you want on the sheet of wood. Lay them out in blocks of several pieces to the block. This will simplify cutting because these subdivided blocks can be cut out first, and are more easily handled than the large sheet. Cut out the individual stanchions from the subdivided blocks with a coping saw or jig saw.

Arrange them in a row. Split into groups that can be handled in a vise Hold firmly, and sandpaper them so all are alike. After they have been fitted into the mortises, glue, and set into place.

The bulwarks can now be glued and set in place also, and the proper retainer strips and pinch cocks arranged. The exterior holders in this case should be stronger than the ones previously described for bulwarks, because the bulwarks' natural tendency to detach themselves from the hull is now increased by the outward pressure of the inner pinch cocks. (*See* PLATE 17.)

Flare and tumblehome stanchions can also be cut as straight pieces. This saves time and cutting, but they will have to be shaped by bending into either flare or tumblehome form. For this process another type of jig can be built. It is simple in construction and takes very little time to make. Use a block for the base, lightly fastening a thin strip of wood near one end. Drill three holes through the strip and base, and insert bolts an inch longer than the combined thickness of base and strip,

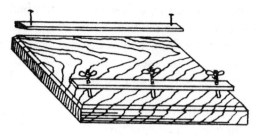

JIG for

CURVED STANCHIONS

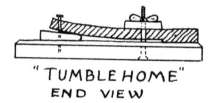

"TUMBLE HOME"
END VIEW

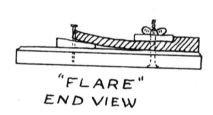

"FLARE"
END VIEW

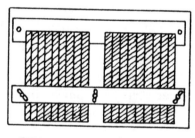

TOP VIEW

Plate 19

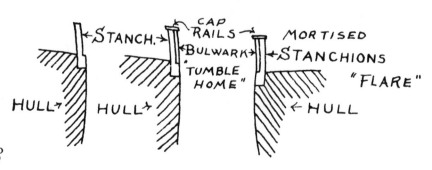

←STANCH.→ CAP RAILS → MORTISED
←BULWARK→ ←STANCHIONS
"TUMBLE "FLARE"
HOME"

HULL→ HULL→ ← HULL

equipped with washers and wing nuts. Remove the temporary fastenings from the strip to allow freedom of action up and down the bolts. The strip will form an anchorage when the wing nuts are screwed down tightly. A second strip of wood with a long bevel on the upper side, and with a nail in either end, completes the jig.

Place all the stanchions in a steam or hot-water bath; the length of time depends upon the size of the pieces. Twenty minutes to half an hour is sufficient for the average. To steam, put the pieces in a wire container suspended in a large receptacle which contains just enough water to keep from boiling dry. Keep covered while steaming. Remove and place pieces in the jig immediately. Screw down the anchor strip just enough to hold them in place while adjusting the beveled strip to give them the flare or tumblehome needed, plus a little for loss. Then turn down the wing nuts tightly, and allow to set for at least twelve hours. The pieces will set a little less than the full curve given them in the jig when they are removed.

Fit them to the mortises and glue into place as previously explained. The bulwarks and stanchions must be even, or flush at the top to accommodate the cap rail. If you find they come out a little uneven, trim them so that you will have no trouble in placing the rail.

THREE-MASTED SCHOONER.

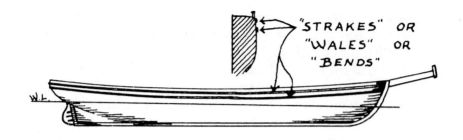

"STRAKES" OR "WALES" OR "BENDS"

W.L.

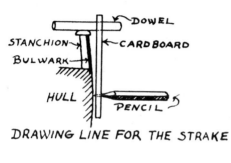

DOWEL

STANCHION — CARDBOARD

BULWARK

HULL

PENCIL

DRAWING LINE FOR THE STRAKE

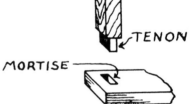

TENON

MORTISE

Plate 20

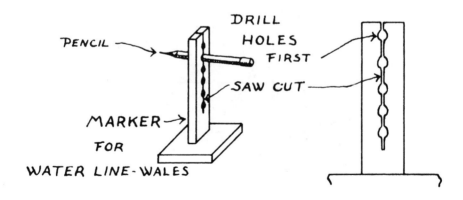

PENCIL

DRILL HOLES FIRST

SAW CUT

MARKER FOR WATER LINE - WALES

Strakes (or wales or bends) are chafing rails, or buffers, which run entirely around the ship at its greatest girth. They jut out from the hull and make the actual contact with the docks and landing piers, thereby protecting the hull from unnecessary friction, marred paint, and other minor damage.

Depending on the design, your model may require one, or several. To draw guide lines for the strakes so they will run parallel with the cap rail, construct a device as follows: force a pencil or dowel through one end of a rectangular piece of cardboard. Then, resting it on the cap rail, pierce or drill a small hole through the lower end of the cardboard at the proper strake level, as illustrated. Insert a pencil point through this lower hole, and slide the dowel along the rail.

Strakes can be made of very narrow strips of wood, or cut from cardboard. Use three pieces—one for the stern curvature, and the other two for continuation on either side to the bow peak—much the same as you subdivided the bulwarks. Draw a guide line on the hull at the correct position and glue the strips on, holding them in place with pinch cocks. If you have difficulty in holding the stern piece (which should be set first) in place, use a cardboard strip as a retainer, and drive pins into the hull. When dry, sandpaper lightly, giving the strip a rounded leading edge. Apply a coat of shellac.

WATER LINE. The water line can be drawn on the hull as follows: Construct a simple marker of two pieces of wood—one piece serving as a base block; the other a thin strip nailed or mortised to it in a perpendicular position. Drill a vertical row of holes (slightly smaller than the standard-size pencil) through it. Connect all the holes with a thin saw cut extending to ½″ below the lowest one. A pencil can now be held quite firmly in any of the holes. Other devices can be employed as pencil guides and supports for drawing on the proper water line: books, boxes. inkstand, etc.

The model may be placed keel up or down, but preferably up, because it is easier to hold firm and level this way. In most ships, the bow is a good deal higher above the water line than the stern, so, if you do work with the hull keel up, you will have to elevate the stern a trifle.

Place a temporary mark for your water line (indicated in your working drawings) on the stern or on the rudder post, and another on the stem, or bow piece; a straight line drawn between these two points will be the correct water line. Now, with your pencil firmly supported by your chosen device, draw a very faint line around the hull. (Move the device—*not* the hull!) If the finish point of the line does not meet the beginning line, adjust the hull until they do meet. Then draw a clearly defined line.

Many workers, including myself, like to deepen this line a little with a shallow "V" gouge, so that it will not become lost during the general painting of the hull. Quite often, after the over-all paint job on the hull is finished and dried, a stripe of a different color is added, separating the top paint (color above the water line) from the bottom paint. The slight, gouged-out depression is easy to follow, and makes a more neat and even striping possible.

Unless the specifications call for a definite color, top-paint can be of any color that is pleasing to the builder. Bottom-paint is usually referred to as "copper paint." It probably got its name from the early days when some ship bottoms were copper sheathed. Bottom-paint today is a reddish colored anti-fouling paint, and contains certain ingredients that discourage the growth of weeds and barnacles.

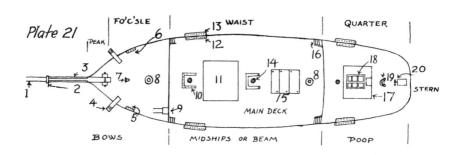

(1) Jib Boom   (2) Cap   (3) Bowsprit   (4) Catheads   (5) Port (*red*) (6) Starboard (*green*)   (7) Vent   (8) Capstan   (9) Companion   (10) Fife Rail   (11) Deck House   (12) Pin Rails   (13) Channels or Chains (14) Mast   (15) Main Hatch   (16) Stairs   (17) After Deck Housing (18) Skylight   (19) Binnacle   (20) Wheel

For those who feel the need of familiarizing themselves with the different parts of a sailing vessel, an illustration is introduced here showing the main subdivisions and the general arrangement aboard the average ship.

Some models will require fewer deck fittings than shown here, but most will use all of them—plus additional fixtures—depending on the type, the period, and the purpose of the ship. For instance, liners, tankers, cargo ships, cable ships, freighters, tugs and Naval vessels have all been designed to perform certain duties. They have been equipped with special deck fixtures for specific duties in addition to the fixtures and gear necessary for the operation of the ship.

Sometimes particular parts or pieces of a boat may go by more than one name, and are referred to at various times by their different terms. No doubt this is somewhat confusing to the beginner, but one soon gets to know all of them. In the drawings and text of this volume an effort has been made to indicate both terms when more than one name is used for any part.

A study of the drawing will equip the beginner with a better understanding of ships as a whole, and will serve as an introduction to other types. Use it as a reference whenever in doubt about portions or parts of sailing vessels. It will be of little service for other types of ships, except that it shows hull divisions. For these types of models the usual working drawings covering deck fixtures are adequate.

All ships' hulls are basically the same; there are minor differences in design (depending on the purpose of the ship) that alter the hull shape to some extent. The greatest difference from the average in hull construction appears in shallow-draft ships requiring fin keels and weighted keels, which give them lateral resistance and provide stability.

ARABIAN DHOW.

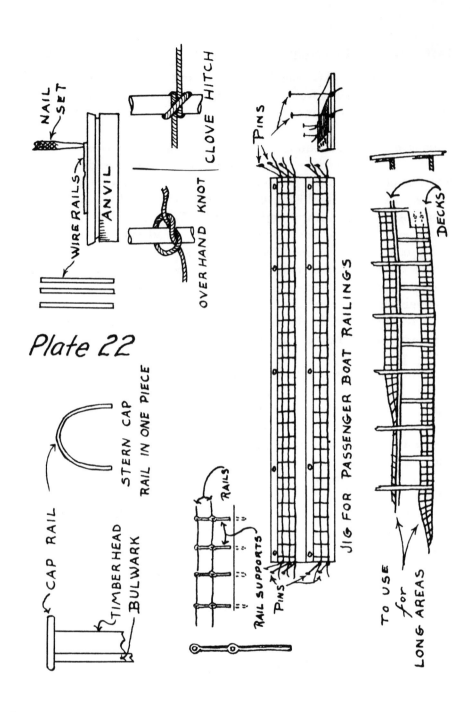

NAIL SET

WIRE RAILS

ANVIL

CLOVE HITCH

OVER HAND KNOT

Plate 22

CAP RAIL

STERN CAP

RAIL IN ONE PIECE

TIMBER HEAD

BULWARK

RAILS

RAIL SUPPORTS

PINS

PINS

JIG FOR PASSENGER BOAT RAILINGS

DECKS

TO USE for LONG AREAS

44

If your particular model calls for elaborate superstructures, you may prefer to leave all of the rail construction until later; but if the ship is a comparatively simple one, this can be your next step.

Cap rails are quite easy to make. Glue narrow strips of thin wood or cardboard to the tops of the bulwarks and stanchions. To avoid difficulties, cut the stern cap-rail piece to follow the stern curvature rather than to attempt bending the strips into this tight curve. For the sake of neatness, this piece should be cut just a little shorter (or longer) than the stern bulwark piece, so that the cap joints are not directly above the bulwark joints. The slight curve of the side cap rails should give you no trouble. The joint, or fitting, in the bows will have to be done carefully. It may be necessary to place a slight weight on all of the pieces, to hold them while drying. When completely dry, sandpaper very lightly to give slight rounded-edge effect. Dust off, and shellac.

RAIL SUPPORTS. Rail supports are not difficult to make, but they do take a little time, especially for models that need many of them, such as passenger ships, and some types of Naval vessels. The size of the model determines the scale of the railings; for instance, the use of common pins as rail supports would establish the model as a very large one. Pieces of fine wire, or splinters of bamboo or wood can be used for smaller ships. In cutting rail supports, try to get them uniform in length, and have plenty on hand when you begin to set them in place. Punch or drill holes at regular intervals in the deck. Set rail supports in the holes with a touch of glue, keeping them all at the same height—this saves extra work later on.

For pierced rail supports, use wire which has been flattened and drilled at the points through which the railing will pass. To prepare these: lay the wire supports on an anvil and, with a nail set, flatten out these spots. There will be two to four on each, depending on the size and type of boat. Then drill small holes through them. In order to keep the drill from slipping off the wire, make a slight depression in the center of each flat area with a center punch. This will also give you true center holes. File off any irregularities; then run either thread or wire through.

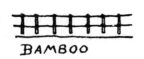

BAMBOO

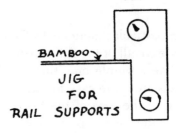

BAMBOO

JIG
FOR
RAIL SUPPORTS

D E C K

Plate23

QUARTER DECK

POOP

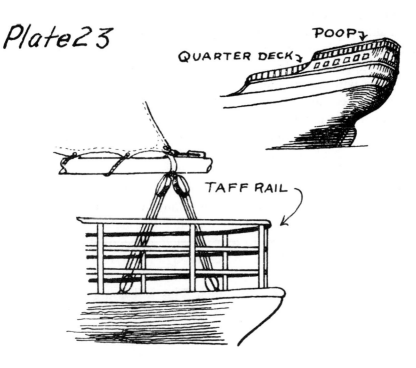

TAFF RAIL

46

For rail supports that are not pierced, there are two methods of fastening the rails. One way is to loop the thread in a clove hitch over each support; the other is to tie a simple overhand knot, enclosing the support. Both kinds should be strengthened with a touch of cement on the knots. After railing is completed and erected, give the threads a coat of shellac. This helps to increase and maintain tension, and makes them easier to paint later. Rails and supports are generally painted black or gray.

If you are building a liner or transport, you will need railings in quantity lots. Set up a jig for this work in the following manner: Cut a piece of cardboard at least 12" in length (for the base), and wide enough to accommodate two or three railing heights. Cement or tack two or three very narrow strips of cardboard to the base to serve as stoppers, thus making sure that all the supports are of even height. Drive pins at both ends of the jig for attaching the (thread) railings. Fasten the threads between these pins, keeping them taut. Have lots of rail supports ready—these can be of bamboo strips—and if you want to be certain of uniform length, use a jig similar to one for ladder treads, as shown on PLATE 28, page 58.

Insert these supports at regular intervals under the threads, and space according to scale. Apply cement where threads cross supports, and allow to dry. Apply a coat of shellac. After shellac has dried, long strips of this railing can be transferred from the jig directly into the proper place. For shorter lengths, cut the required sections from the long railings. These railings are cemented into place (1) behind the deck supports, (2) to the inboard side of the bulwarks and (3) to the deck at each rail support.

The rail around the deck of a vessel's stern is called the taffrail. According to the style and period of the ship it may have simple or decorative turned rail supports, or stanchions. They are topped with a heavy cap rail. For model taffrails, make rail supports of bamboo, railings of thread or wire. Top with a cap rail similar to the one used for bulwarks.

Handrails for ladders can be of wire, or thin bamboo splinters that are easily bent. If you use wire, solder all support joints, and also the point where the handrail meets deck rail support.

47

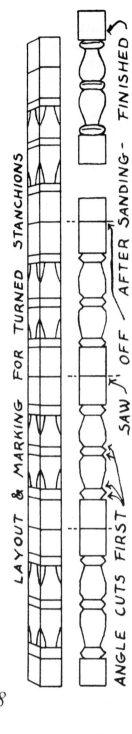

LAYOUT & MARKING FOR TURNED STANCHIONS

ANGLE CUTS FIRST — SAW ¼" OFF — AFTER SANDING - FINISHED

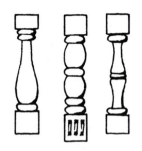

USING PASTE TO MAKE
TURNED STANCHIONS

Plate 24

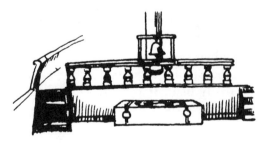

48

Occasionally you may work on models which call for turned stanchions, or balusters. These are heavy, sturdy uprights, shaped to give a decorative appearance. Topped with a handrail, they form straight or curved balustrades (depending on the deck contour), running along the fore and after decks facing the waist, or main deck. "Turned" stanchions (turned in a lathe) take quite a bit of time and effort for their execution, but are well worth it.

Do not attempt to execute this kind of stanchion to scale on the average small model—the size of each would be too tiny for detail work. Use ordinary bamboo rail supports set on a cardboard strip for a base, and topped with a narrow cardboard handrail. The general effect will be all right.

If you work on a slightly larger model, you may find that the rail supports are large enough for an attempted simulation of shaped pieces with the aid of a paste mixture. Prepare a mixture of glue, whiting and a few drops of water, a little thinner than that used on figureheads. (*See page* 25.) Using a toothpick, build up the effect you want with tiny applications of this paste. Do this work on the assembled balustrade, but before it is glued into place. Keep it simple and be careful not to overdo the effect.

The scale of some of the larger models permits decorative balusters bulky enough to shape individually. At best, however, they require delicate handling. Three methods for doing this shaping will be described here. Do not make them too ornate—keep the shapes simple.

Pieces 1″ or longer can be turned in a lathe (wood). The best way to begin is to make a model of the baluster you want out of a piece of scrap wood; then make reproductions of it. If you have no lathe and it is impossible to get the loan or use of one, the work will have to be done with a knife and razor blade.

Stanchions down to ½″ in length can be fashioned by this knife and razor-blade method.

Get a long rectangular strip of wood whose outside measurements are the same as those of the finished baluster. On this, mark the baluster lengths and the carving stations (or sections). The next step is to angle-cut at all carving stations—care should be taken not to cut too deeply.

After this the shaping and rounding of the turned parts can be done. When carving is finished, sandpaper with fine paper. Be careful not to lose the clean right-angle cuts forming the top and bottom cubes of the baluster. These stanchions can be glued directly to the deck—set in mortises or on a smaller base piece, which in turn is fastened to the deck. A handrail is glued along the upper ends to form a complete railing, or balustrade.

Another method for making turned stanchions is by the mold process, but is not recommended for those without some previous knowledge of plaster casting. Pieces (balusters) shorter than ¾" should not be done this way.

On a board, model a series of half-balusters out of clay or plasticine. As many as twelve can be done at a time. Place a cardboard retainer ½" to 1" high around the board to form walls. Pour plaster of Paris into the box up to the top. Give the box a few light taps occasionally to release air bubbles that may be trapped; be sure to do this before the plaster begins to set, or the bubbles will set with it, spoiling your efforts. When set and dry, remove the board and turn the plaster block over. Dig out the clay. Clean and dry the mold thoroughly, then apply a coat of shellac; avoid bubbles in the individual depressions. You should now have a perfect mold from which you can make several half-balusters at a time.

Place very thin tissue paper (so plastic wood will not adhere to the mold) over each individual hollow and fill the depression with plastic wood, packing it in firmly. If the area is not well packed you will not get a true reproduction of the model. After each half-mold has been filled, place small bent pieces of wire into the inner sides of both ends, and one in the center of each baluster. Later, these will help to hold the two halves together. When dry and hard, remove from the mold.

Now repeat the entire process up to the wire, which is omitted from these second halves. As each new half is filled, apply a drop of glue to each end of the fresh plastic wood. Then place a wired half on top and press together firmly. The placing of the two halves must be done with care and exactness, or the baluster will be worthless when removed. Allow to dry hard before removing from the mold. A little sandpapering and a coat of shellac are necessary to give them a finished look. Fasten to deck as described for the method before this. (*See* PLATE 25.)

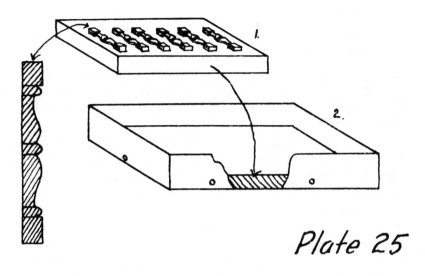

Plate 25

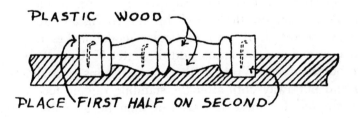

SMALL WIRES — — PLASTIC WOOD

3.

PLASTER OF PARIS MOLD

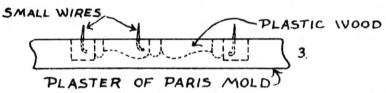

PLASTIC WOOD

PLACE FIRST HALF ON SECOND

Chainwales, or channels, are narrow flat ledges of timber, bolted edgewise to the outside of a ship's hull. They help to give additional spread to the shrouds and back stays. On sailing vessels that are equipped with them, they are placed on the sides of the hull opposite the masts; the forward ends begin directly opposite, or slightly forward, of the masts.

For model building, these channels can be built from thin strips of wood, long enough to accommodate the chain plates of the stays and shrouds belonging to their particular masts. Draw a line down the length of each channel, one-third of the way in from the outside edge. Drill holes, or make slots along the line—these are for the chain plates, or straps, to run through. These plates (or straps—or chains—or metal rods) are the anchorages for the standing rigging. Their lower ends are fastened to the hull by bolts. (Simulate the bolts by pins driven into the hull.) The plates lead up through single or double channels, and terminate in fittings which either enclose dead-eyes or are fastened directly to them.

Following is a time-saving suggestion you might like to try out. It can be used for models of any size, but is particularly helpful for the small ones having tiny, fragile channels. After drilling the holes or slots as mentioned above, split the channels lengthwise through these holes into inner and outer strips. Glue the inner pieces to the hull in their proper positions; then mark the outer strips with the initials of their respective positions—for example: *F.S.* (Fore, Starboard), *M.P.* (Main Port), etc.—so there will be no confusion later when the halves are matched. If your particular model makes use of double channels at one or more masts, add the letter *U* (Upper), or *L* (Lower) to the other initials. Wrap all the marked strips in a sheet of tissue paper and put away until after the standing rigging has been placed.

The shrouds for these models can then be assembled complete— from top mast loops to chain plates—as separate units, and fastened directly into place with small plate pins. As one can readily understand, considerable time and trouble is saved, because now, after the standing rigging is all set, the outer channel strips can just be glued into place, and held until dry with long pinch cocks.

This split-channel method facilitates the placing of all chain plates, regardless of the size of the model. It saves the worker from the tedious job of threading each plate through a hole or slot before fastening to the hull by pins. After all the chain plates have been fastened, the outer strips are glued into place.

All rigging has a tendency at some time or other to increase the tension, due to atmospheric conditions; this puts added strain on all fastenings and supports. On models 24″ or more in length, one can give added strength and permanency to the channels that enclose these supports by drilling two holes through the width of each ledge, and then forcing pins through them directly into the solid hull.

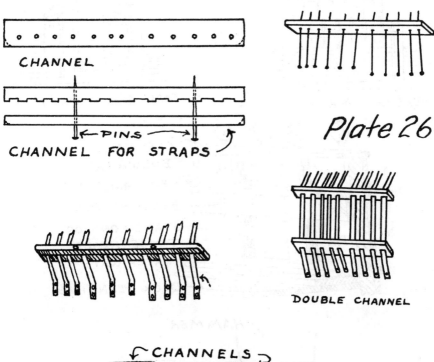

CHANNEL

CHANNEL FOR STRAPS

PINS

Plate 26

DOUBLE CHANNEL

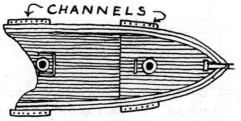

CHANNELS

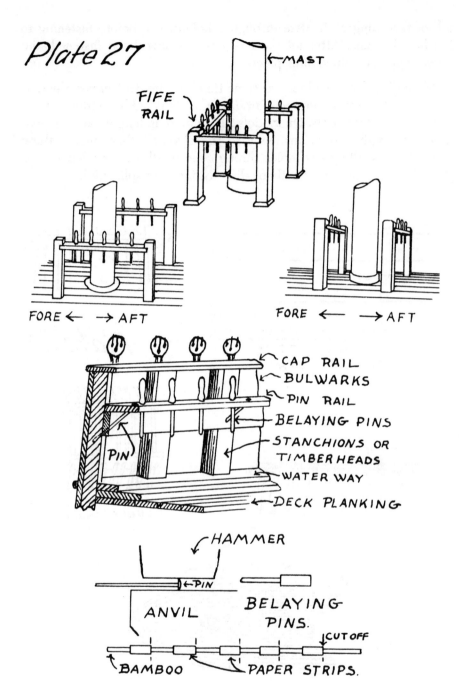

Plate 27

MAST

FIFE RAIL

FORE ← → AFT

FORE ← → AFT

CAP RAIL
BULWARKS
PIN RAIL
BELAYING PINS
STANCHIONS OR TIMBER HEADS
WATER WAY
DECK PLANKING

PIN

HAMMER

PIN

ANVIL

BELAYING PINS.

CUT OFF

BAMBOO

PAPER STRIPS.

54

Fife rails are placed about the bases of the masts. Standing approximately waist high, they are supported by firmly-based stanchions, and are pierced through by several drilled holes to accommodate removable pins, called belaying pins, to which ropes from running gear are made fast—or belayed.

Fife rails differ in size and placement, depending upon the rigging of their particular masts—a foremast, and a main mast, for instance, might be enclosed on three sides, while the mizzen mast may have only two short fife rails placed fore and aft of it—or be flanked by them on port and starboard. The fife rails on some ships were supported by turned stanchions; some stanchions had sheaves placed in their bases to accommodate the lines leading from heavy tackle.

Reproduced to scale in small models, the fife rail assembly would be quite tiny, so do not attempt anything too intricate. Use straight upright pieces for supports. Make the rails of bamboo—small pieces of this material are quite strong, even with holes drilled through them. (A pin vise can be used for this drilling.) Glue rails into shallow mortises cut into the uprights; then glue the uprights into their proper places on deck.

In larger models, the increased tension of rigging during certain weather conditions may pull the fife rails from the deck unless the supports are anchored solidly. If they are heavy enough, drill a hole at an angle through each, and run small pins through, driving firmly into the deck. Supports can also be anchored by tenons fitted into mortises cut in the deck. Allow enough extra length when cutting supports.

Some masts which have such simple rigging that fife rails are not necessary are encircled with pierced metal bands that look like circular shelves. They are called spider rings, and hold the necessary number of belaying pins.

Pin Rails. Some pin rails resemble channels somewhat in that they are flat ledges of wood set edgewise to the timber heads, inboard of the bulwarks. Holes are drilled through for the belaying pins, the same as for fife rails. They are placed at all shroud sections at the bulwarks. On some of the smaller boats, they are fastened directly to the shrouds. Additional short pin rails holding only three or four belaying pins are sometimes situated in the bows, fastened to the side of the cap rail.

On large models, it would be wise to drill a hole at each end of the pin rail (at an angle), through which pins can be driven into the timber heads. They look like braces, and add strength to the structure.

BELAYING PINS. Belaying pins can be made from common pins if these pins are correct in scale. Roll the head of the pin between a hammer and anvil. This will elongate it so that it will resemble the handle of a belaying pin quite successfully. Cut off the pin at the correct length and blunt the end slightly with a file.

For smaller pins, use bamboo splinters. Sandpaper lightly to remove any angularity, and contrive handles by wrapping very narrow strips of glued paper at regular intervals. When dry, cut off the individual pieces with a razor blade.

BARK

All ship's ladders, when completed, certainly look like complicated affairs, but the actual stages of construction are very simple in themselves. If your working drawings do not specify measurements for ladders, figure out the sizes suitable for your model.

DECK LADDERS OR COMPANIONWAYS. Begin construction for these ladders by cutting your long sides; or string pieces, as they are called, out of thin balsa wood or cardboard. The following instructions will be given, assuming that all of the ladders will be the same size and run at the same angle. (If there are variations they will be done in the same way, but individually.)

So, then (if possible) cut two side strips long enough for all you are going to use on your model, and construct them all at the same time, in order to save time and effort. The treads, or steps, are to be glued between these pieces. Regardless of the angle of the ladder, the treads must be set in so that they are parallel with the decks. To arrive at the correct angle for the treads draw a simple exact-size diagram representing your deck levels. Now set one of the string pieces on the drawing and adjust it until you get the ladder in just the position you want it in the model. Fasten down to the drawing board, and draw a series of lines across the piece for its entire length; these represent the treads. Have them evenly spaced and parallel with the deck line. Then draw corresponding lines on the opposite piece.

Cut a large number of treads from balsa wood or bamboo strips. The use of a jig for this operation will not only save time, but will also give you treads of uniform size.

Place the two long side pieces on edge, parallel with each other, and with the tread marks on the inside. Glue the center and the two end treads into place. These will hold the pieces up edgewise, and also serve as separators. Cut two long extra cardboard strips, and set up as protectors on the outside of each string piece; now place pinch cocks on the outside of these cardboard strips in such positions that they will interfere as little as possible during the rest of the work. Then glue the remaining treads into place. Set aside to dry completely.

Cut the bottoms of the string pieces to fit the deck—the treads will be parallel with the angle of the deck if your calculations were correct. A very slight difference is not serious. If the difference is too much,

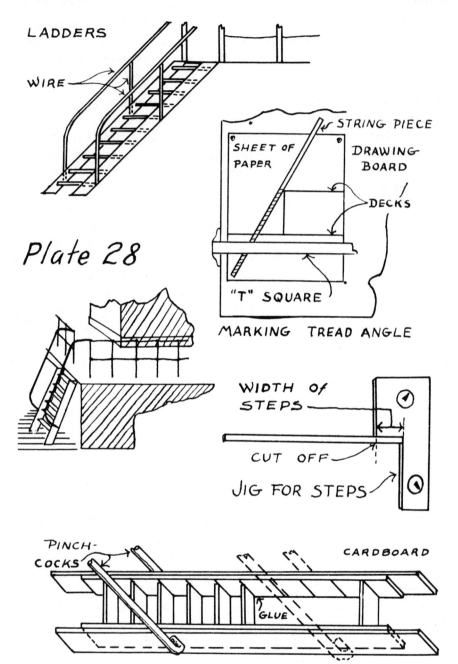

LADDERS

WIRE

STRING PIECE

SHEET OF PAPER

DRAWING BOARD

DECKS

Plate 28

"T" SQUARE

MARKING TREAD ANGLE

WIDTH OF STEPS

CUT OFF

JIG FOR STEPS

PINCH-COCKS

CARDBOARD

GLUE

change the slant or pitch of the entire ladder by moving it closer to—or farther away from—the bulkhead. Measure the length needed for each ladder, and cut it carefully from the full-length section. As you know, this cut should also be the same as the angle of the treads.

Handrails and supports can be made of bamboo slivers or of fine wire. Glue to the sides of the ladder as shown. Glue the upper ends to the rail supports of that deck.

PERPENDICULAR LADDERS. Perpendicular ladders, fastened to bulkheads or other perpendicular surfaces, are the simplest of all ships' ladders to make. For the side pieces use two long splinters of bamboo—long enough for all the ladders you need. On a sheet of paper draw two straight, parallel lines, spaced the width you want the ladders to be. In just three or four spots glue the bamboo strips lightly to these lines. Cut the short crosspieces—the rungs—out of bamboo slivers also; glue the ends, and place across, but not beyond, the long strips. Space them evenly, and keep them straight. When dry, remove from the sheet of paper by cutting around the temporary glue spots. These blobs of glue can easily be removed with a knife. The necessary lengths for various ladder positions can now be cut from the long ladder. Glue, and set against the bulkheads or walls.

SIDE LADDERS. These look much more complicated than the deck-to-deck ladders. To be sure, they do have a few additional pieces, but none are difficult to make. If two or more side ladders are needed, proceed as you did with the others: make one long length, and cut the individual ladders from it.

The ladder itself can be constructed much as the first one discussed. Some of the minor differences turn out to be advantages in this case: the tread angle is not too important, although all treads should be parallel with each other; the bottoms of the side, or string pieces, need not be cut on an angle—here, two tiny wheels will be glued into place—the tops of the string pieces will be glued to a square, cardboard platform.

One edge of this platform is glued to the deck, and further support is given by two or three braces (bamboo strips, glued into place) resting on a small block of wood, which is glued to the hull. The top of the platform may have a circle drawn on it with ink.

Two lines of chain connect the sides (near the foot of the ladder) to

59

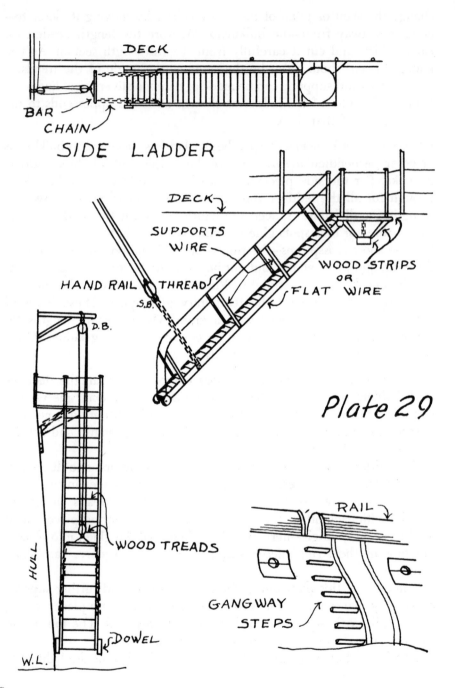

DECK

BAR
CHAIN

SIDE LADDER

DECK

SUPPORTS
WIRE

HAND RAIL THREAD
S.B.

D.B.

WOOD STRIPS
OR
FLAT WIRE

Plate 29

HULL

WOOD TREADS

DOWEL

W.L.

RAIL

GANGWAY
STEPS

a cross-bar raised high enough for ample head clearance. By means of a fine, twisted wire, which forms a loop, or hook, at the center of this cross-bar, the ladder is suspended by a hoisting tackle running down from an overhead swinging bar, or boom. Even if the side ladder of your particular model is to be stationary, and not workable, be sure that you place this boom in the proper position on the main deck (or wherever it is located), and at the correct angle to the ladder so that, if it were actually workable, it could function correctly to raise and lower the ladder.

The rail supports can be made from bamboo strips glued to the string pieces; tie and glue thread to these to represent rails. The platform rail supports can be glued directly to the platform, or, better yet—can penetrate it and be flush with the bottom.

Some side ladders may be shorter than the one pictured; some have landing stages, or platforms at the bottom. As shown in another illustration, in some early ships where the hull had extreme tumblehome contour—inward curvature of the bulwarks—triangular pieces of wood were bolted directly to the hull to form steps, on which the old tars clawed their way aboard.

GANGPLANKS. Cardboard can be used for the base of your gangplank—the size according to your scale. On this base, glue slivers of bamboo at regular intervals to represent stops. Drill small holes at each corner, and wherever else necessary, for rail supports to penetrate.

Supports, which can be of wood or bamboo strips, should be cemented in firmly, and trimmed so as to be flush with the bottom. Bamboo braces, which are optional, can be glued into place at the corner supports.

Next, handrails—the same length as the base of the gangplank—made of bamboo or cardboard, can be cemented to the supports. One or two slack-line rails should be run along the supports halfway between the rails and the base. They can be made of thread, tied, and lightly glued to each support. At the base of each corner support, fasten a heavy thread, which should be at least as long as a rail support. Tie a simple overhand knot in the end of each such thread.

JACOB'S LADDERS. This type—no doubt named after Jacob's dream—is the only flexible type of ship's ladder. It provides quick and easy access to and from the ship while at sea, and has shipboard uses as well. It is

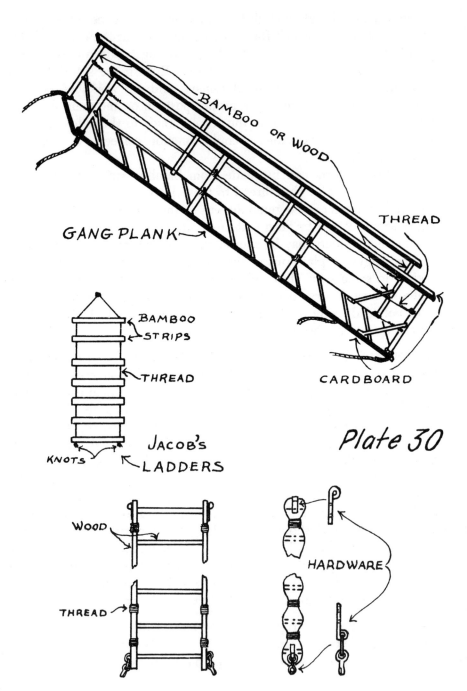

BAMBOO or WOOD

THREAD

GANG PLANK→

BAMBOO
STRIPS

THREAD

JACOB'S
KNOTS
LADDERS

CARDBOARD

Plate 30

WOOD

HARDWARE

THREAD

62

most usually a rope ladder with rigid wooden rungs fastened by bindings, but there are many variations too: sometimes the ladder is of wire, instead of rope; rungs themselves can be made of rope; rigid rungs have been made of iron; sometimes rigid rungs are passed through separate strands of the rope sides, and bound into place. Some Jacob's ladders are entirely rigid, generally short and for small boats; others are rolled or folded up and stowed away when not in use.

To make a simple miniature rope ladder for a model: stretch out two parallel lengths—6", or more—of thread on a sheet of cardboard. Anchor the ends to the cardboard with cement. Cut the number of rungs you need, space evenly, and glue into place across and over-lapping the threads. When dry, cut the thread ends loose, tie dangling ends of the lower threads into knots. Bring the top ends together to form a triangle and tie another knot. Trim off all excess thread.

Another Jacob's ladder shown in PLATE 30 is rigid. The ladder itself can be made from thin wood strips, which are cut into continuous wavy, or undulating, contour as viewed from the side. Glue the treads (also of thin wood or bamboo) between the wide portions. Encircle the narrow sections with thread "servings." The use of the hardware shown in the illustration is optional. If you do not care to use it, drill a hole through each side, just below the upper rung. Make an eye, or loop in one end of a short wire, pass the wire through the holes, bringing the eye up against the one side. Allowing enough wire for a second eye opposite, cut off the excess length. The ladder can then be hung from these eyes.

BRIG UNDER STORM SAIL.

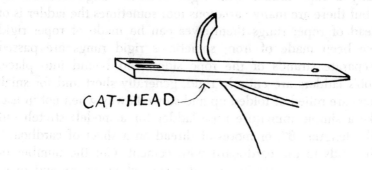

CAT-HEAD

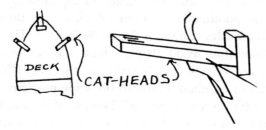

DECK

CAT-HEADS

Plate 31

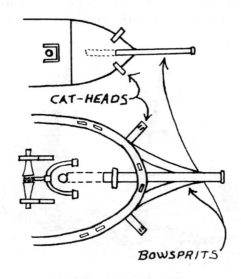

CAT-HEADS

BOWSPRITS

Cat-heads are projecting pieces of timber or iron in the bows of a vessel, and are used as supports for hoisting the anchor.

For models they can be made from thin strips of wood, one for each side, with two, or even three slits cut in the outboard ends. For large size models, these slits would be equipped with sheaves. The inboard end of the cat-head is sometimes fitted to the deck with a long angle cut, which gives it an upward and outward pitch; this type can be glued directly to the deck. To guarantee its remaining in place, drive a half-pin through it into the deck. Another way of attaching cat-heads is to fit the inboard ends into a mortise cut into a short upright timber, which, in turn, is securely fastened to the deck. A brace bracket is sometimes combined with either form of support for added strengthening. This brace can be made from a thin piece of wood fitted snugly between the cat-head and the exterior side of the hull.

DECK PUMPS. Many fishing vessels using sail today are still equipped with single-action deck, or hand pumps. A pump of this kind has one plunger, and is operated by a detachable lever. Some of the older pumps were double-plunger equipped, and had two large handles.

To make the head of a single-action pump, use a small block of wood or a dowel; drill a hole down through the center, and carve the rounded shape of the head. Set it by gluing to a circular cardboard base slightly larger than the dowel.

The exterior support for the handle, the handle itself, and the plunger can all be fashioned from a length of wire, varying in thickness according to the size of the model. This fashioning will be an all-pieces-in-one process, so have your wire long enough. From the center, fold the wire back upon itself, mark the length you want for the handle, and twist the wires together down to that point. Now branch out the two single strands at right angles to each other. One of these will represent the plunger and will extend from the base of the handle across the pump head, then run down through the center hole. Let it penetrate the cardboard base, and snip off excess wire flush with the base. The second single wire is the support. Pierce a hole in the base, run the wire through, and snip off as before. For a larger pump you can add realism by making a socket for the handle, and metal fittings for the support and plunger.

65

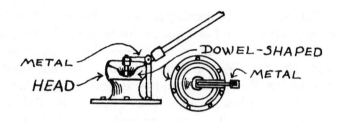

METAL
HEAD
DOWEL-SHAPED
METAL

Plate 32

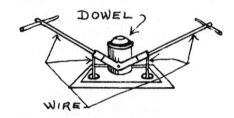

DOWEL

WIRE

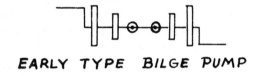

EARLY TYPE BILGE PUMP

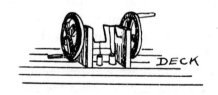

DECK

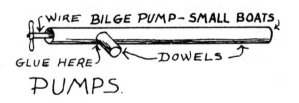

WIRE BILGE PUMP—SMALL BOATS

GLUE HERE   DOWELS

PUMPS.

To make a double-action pump, round the top of a small dowel piece —this will be the pump head—and glue it to a cardboard base (round or square); it will probably resemble a cut-off fire hydrant when you have finished. Mark the spots where the two plungers are to penetrate the base, and punch out two disks of cardboard with a paper punch. Glue them over the marks, using tweezers to set into place.

For handles, plungers, and supports, proceed much the same as for single-action pumps, using two lengths of wire instead of one, of course. Fold the middle of each wire over a small crosspiece of bamboo and proceed to twist the strands together for handles, as before. Spread out the single strands. Drill and pierce small holes through the double cardboard thickness for the plungers to penetrate. Adjust (temporarily) the pump handles at the proper angle; notice that if they were to continue, they would meet and form a flattened-out V-angle. Now, to simulate supports for these handles, cut out a piece of cardboard into this same V-shape. Glue to the side of the pump head, and pin for additional security. Set the handles into place again. Cement two of the wire ends into place behind the V, after snipping off any excess length; the remaining two strands extend vertically to penetrate the drilled holes in the double cardboard. Snip off flush with the bottom, as before.

CARGO SHIP.

CAPSTANS

Plate 33

A capstan is an upright drum or cylinder—a large hand winch—shaped somewhat like an hour glass, and revolves on a pivot. By means of long levers (capstan bars) inserted into holes around the top, it moves and raises heavy weights, or exerts power by traction upon rope or cable wound around it. Loops of these ropes are passed down over the top to give a good purchase or grip. I think we all remember scenes in the movies where tough-looking sailors walked 'round and 'round, pushing capstan bars and keeping step to some lusty sea chantey, while they pulled a dripping anchor out of the briny deep. At the base of the capstan are a number of pawls, or catches, which rotate with the drum but fall into notches so as to prevent it from going in the opposite direction.

To make a capstan, use a small block or dowel of soft wood, which is a little taller than you consider actually necessary for the finished product. In all carving—small pieces, especially—it is well to have some extra length that can be held in a vise; then, when the carving has been completed, excess material can be removed from the bottom. Mark the various carving stations, rough out the general contour, then carve, shape, and sandpaper to the finished form.

For very small capstans, use wood for only the central portions, and shape only slightly. Cut two or three small disks of cardboard in graduated sizes, and glue one after the other to the top of the drum to form a top which will seem to taper. Do not attempt to drill or cut holes for capstan bars, or place any of the trim; if you want to indicate or simulate such trim, wait until after the general painting is completed; then you can "paint on" narrow lines to get the effect you want.

Before attaching capstan to deck, cut a cardboard disk for the base and glue it down; do this for all sizes. To fix capstans firmly to the deck in addition to using glue, drill a small hole down through the center of the drum (if it is not too small). Place a short pin in the hole, and drive it into the deck. For the larger capstans, where a pin would be too short to give substantial support, use brads (small nails), or drill a hole into the capstan from the bottom and another into the deck; glue in a short length of wire to connect the two.

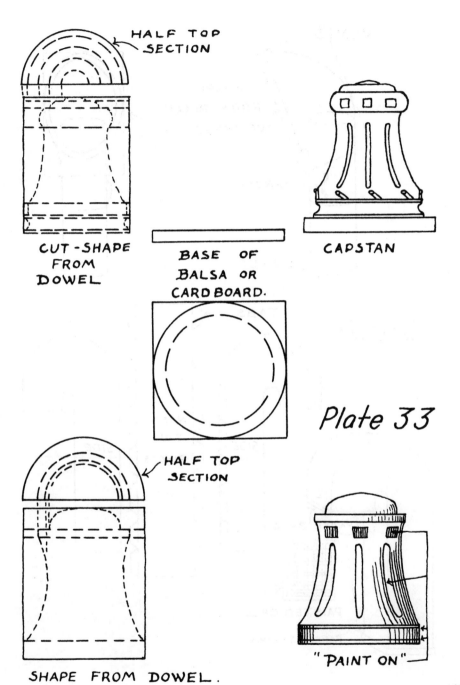

HALF TOP
SECTION

CUT - SHAPE
FROM
DOWEL

BASE OF
BALSA OR
CARD BOARD.

CAPSTAN

Plate 33

HALF TOP
SECTION

SHAPE FROM DOWEL.

"PAINT ON"

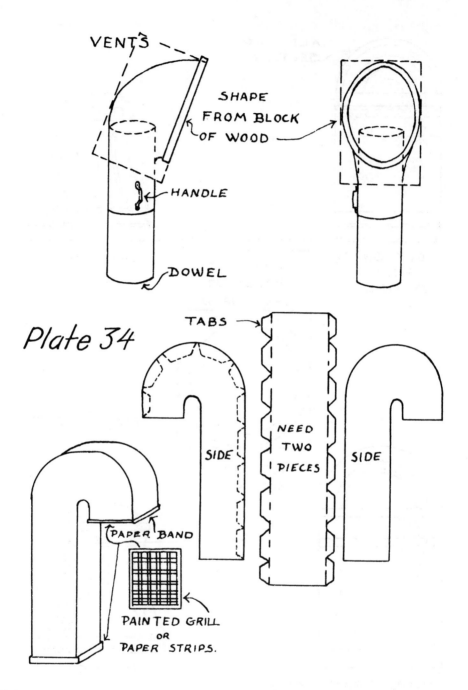

VENTS

SHAPE
FROM BLOCK
OF WOOD

HANDLE

DOWEL

Plate 34

TABS

NEED
TWO
PIECES

SIDE

SIDE

PAPER BAND

PAINTED GRILL
OR
PAPER STRIPS.

70

VENTILATORS

Any contrivance on board a ship which draws off stagnant air or admits fresh air is called a ventilator, or vent. Some are movable, and can be turned to take advantage of a breeze from any direction; some are stationary. They are built in many shapes and sizes, but the most familiar type is the funnel-shaped vent. In fact, their appearance on the deck of your model will arouse almost more pleasure and admiration than you feel you deserve. People who haven't had the chance to come within a thousand miles of a ship will recognize this characteristic feature, because they have seen them in the movies. Picture (and stage) directors seem to like to have them around as backgrounds for all kinds of action.

One method of making this type of vent is to shape it from a block of wood. Mark the contour of the curving funnel on the block and do the profile cutting; then carve and shape it. When this is done, hollow out the funnel mouth for a short distance. For a finish around the exterior rim of the hollow, wrap two or three turns of very narrow glued paper along the edge, and allow to dry. Now give it a light sanding and finish with a coat of shellac.

Another way to make the same vent requires less carving. Select a very small block of wood for the funnel head, and drill a hole in the bottom so that you can insert a dowel the size of the shaft you want. The only carving necessary is that of the funnel head. Proceed as before, merging the block into the dowel.

A second type of vent, resembling nothing so much as a stubby rectangular cane handle, can also be cut from a rectangular block of wood. Mark out the contour, and profile-cut with a coping saw or jig-saw. Sandpaper with coarse and fine paper. A grill should be applied over the mouth, and can be simulated by "painted-on" criss-cross lines, or by gluing down narrow strips of paper. Paper strips can also be used to build up a neat trim around the base of the vent, and another around the outlet.

This "cane" vent can also be made from thin cardboard. Make layout drawings on the cardboard—there will be two simple side pieces cut exactly alike, an inner and an outer strip, both with tab borders. Except around the curves, where they must be cut into small segments, these tabs can be long continuous strips. Crease neatly, and glue to the inner sides of the side pieces. If necessary, use pins to hold in place until

71

Plate 35

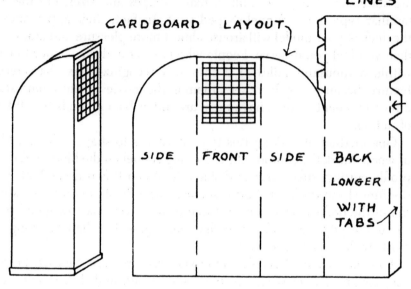

CARDBOARD LAYOUT

SIDE | FRONT | SIDE | BACK LONGER WITH TABS

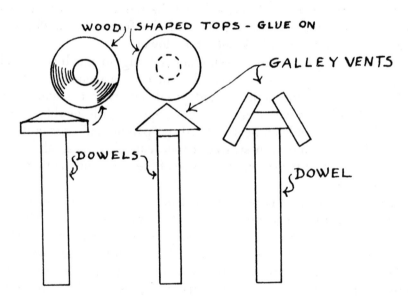

WOOD, SHAPED TOPS - GLUE ON

GALLEY VENTS

DOWELS

DOWEL

72

dry. The grill piece can be glued in separately—or it can be a continuation of the short inner strip, or longer outer strip—or a continuation of one of the side pieces; whichever seems easiest to you.

The straight upright vent is the simplest of all to construct. Select a rectangular block of wood of the right proportions, and with saw and rasp, curve the back slightly over the top to join the front panel. Sandpaper smooth. Attach a simulated grill, and frame it with a paper strip. As before, apply a paper trim around the base. When dry, shellac.

This one can also be made of cardboard, and all in one piece. Lay out as shown in the illustration and be sure that the back piece is sufficiently long to cover the curvature. The grill can be drawn directly on the cardboard and needs no trim, but the base should be finished off as before. Shellac.

There are also smaller vents used on board ships, which allow for the escape of smoke, fumes, cooking odors, etc. Three of these little "chimneys," or vents, are shown in the illustration; all are simple to construct. Use dowels for the shafts—for very small vents, matches will do. The tops, which vary in size and form, can be made from balsa or pine, and need very little shaping.

FOUR-MASTED SCHOONER.

If power is the heart of a ship, then the compass must be its mind. A pedestal case, or enclosure (usually standing about waist-high), which houses the compass and the lights for illuminating the compass card is called the binnacle. This housing used to be of very simple construction, but on most contemporary ships it has evolved into an elaborate and intricate affair.

Its location on board is established only after careful analysis of the ship's construction materials, most probable cargoes, and other peculiar characteristics of the ship. The binnacle has features that have a direct influence on the compass: two cast-iron spheres—one placed on each side of the housing—help to correct deviation; also, the binnacle is fitted to receive permanent magnets and soft-iron pieces to offset other inaccuracies.

The straight pedestal binnacle is the easiest to make—especially if very small. A small rectangular block of wood can be used for the body, with a slightly larger block glued to the top of it. Shape the larger piece into a truncated, or cut-off pyramid. On one of the slanted sides glue a round paper disk, or draw a circle with ink or paint. This represents the glass window. Glue the pedestal to a base of thin wood or cardboard which extends a little beyond the pedestal on all sides. The right angle formed by the joining of the two pieces can be left as it is, or can be filled in with plastic wood to form a gentle curve. Two small shaped brackets for the sides of the pedestal can be made from wood or cardboard, and glued into place. Glue a small bead on top of each—to represent the spheres described above. When everything is dry, shellac your binnacle.

Reproductions of elaborate pieces of mechanism should not be attempted if the scale of the model limits you to a very small binnacle; even for large models, some of the dowels are made from parts of matchsticks.

The body can be made by inserting a small dowel into the underside of a larger one, and then gradually tapering the upper piece down to meet it. For the head, or top, glue a thin circular block of wood on the body, so that it has a slight overhang all around. When dry, shape into the form wanted. Paste a paper "window" to the front of this piece. On each side of it glue two short dowels upright into place; these can be made from matchsticks with the ends rounded. The base—of thin wood

BINNACLES

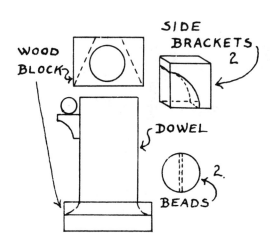

WOOD BLOCK

SIDE BRACKETS 2

DOWEL

2. BEADS

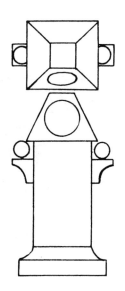

Plate 36

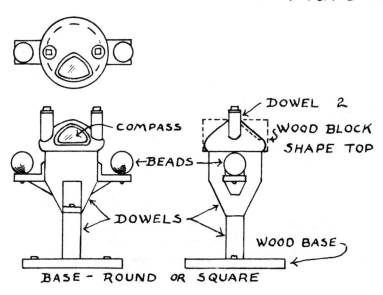

COMPASS

DOWEL 2

WOOD BLOCK SHAPE TOP

←BEADS→

DOWELS

WOOD BASE

BASE - ROUND OR SQUARE

BINNACLE

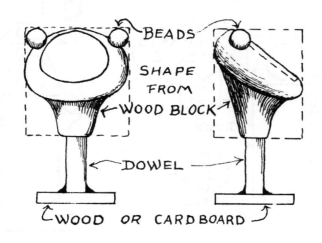

BEADS

SHAPE
FROM
WOOD BLOCK

DOWEL

WOOD OR CARDBOARD

TOWING BITTS

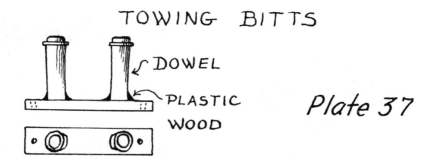

DOWEL

PLASTIC
WOOD

Plate 37

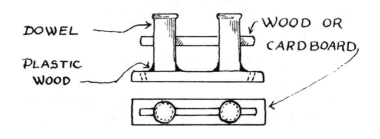

DOWEL

WOOD OR
CARDBOARD

PLASTIC
WOOD

or cardboard—may be square or circular. Cement the dowel to it, and drive a short pin through from the bottom for additional reinforcement. Brackets of wood or cardboard are attached to both sides of the body. Here, as before, beads can be glued to each bracket to complete the binnacle. When dry, shellac the whole.

The construction of a third type of binnacle begins as the second one did; a dowel is inserted into the lower end of a small block of wood which is then carved to shape. Then the compass window is pasted on. This body, which consists largely of curves, could also be shaped from plastic wood impaled on a dowel. The base may be square or round.

TOWING BITTS. Towing bitts are fixed vertical posts of timber or iron, set—usually in pairs—in a heavy metal base. Sometimes the two pillars are joined by a metal bar or rail. Hawsers, cables and other lines are made fast to these heavy-duty deck fixtures.

If they are in keeping with the scale, use half-pins, brads, short brass nails—the kind used for curtain fixtures—or other nails not provided with broadened heads. Cut cardboard bases to size, and drill small holes into them, drive the pins or nails through into the hull, allowing them to project the necessary height above the deck.

For larger bitts, use small dowels—matchstick size, or larger. Construct the base of thin wood or cardboard, and cut or drill two holes to admit the dowels. Glue dowels in, and cut off flush with the bottom; cement base to the deck. For large bitts with wooden bases, reinforce cementing job with pins. If you want a rail, drill through each dowel at the correct height, and run a wire through to project slightly on both sides. Plastic wood can be used for rounding out the angle at the base of each bitt.

CHINESE JUNK.

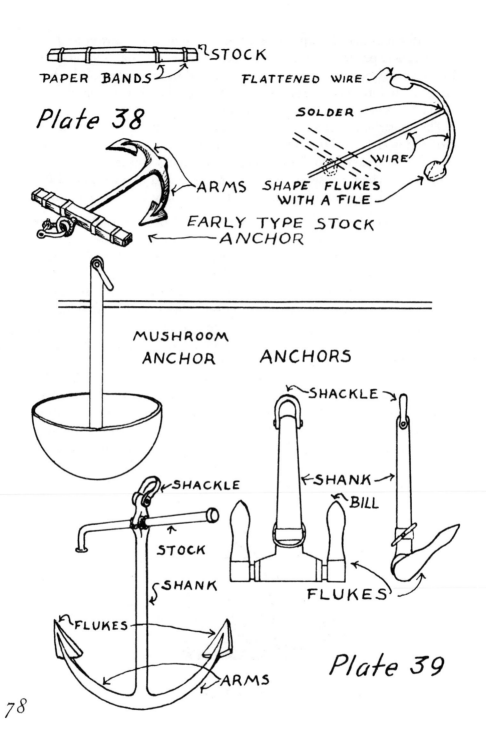

PAPER BANDS

STOCK

FLATTENED WIRE

Plate 38

SOLDER

WIRE

ARMS

SHAPE FLUKES
WITH A FILE

EARLY TYPE STOCK
ANCHOR

MUSHROOM
ANCHOR

ANCHORS

SHACKLE

SHANK

BILL

SHACKLE

STOCK

SHANK

FLUKES

FLUKES

ARMS

Plate 39

There are two general classifications of anchors: those with stocks; and those without. Early anchors had cumbersome stationary stocks of timber, often reinforced with heavy metal bands. The arms terminated in flattened triangular pieces of metal, called "flukes," which did the actual holding of the ship to the ocean floor.

To make an anchor of this kind for a model, use a matchstick for the stock, and shape it slightly. The bands can be made of narrow paper strips glued into place. The shank and arms can be made of thin wire soldered together. Allow the top of the shank to trans-pierce the stock through a drilled hole. The flukes can be formed by flattening the ends of the arms and shaping with a file.

For larger anchors the shank and arms can be cut from thin wood in one piece, and shaped slightly with a knife. Remember to have the arms at right angles to the stock, which can be made as above, though heavier. Form an eyebolt of thin wire, pierce or drill a small hole for it into the end of the shank, and glue into place. The flukes can be made of thin cardboard cut to shape and glued to the arms.

Another kind of stock anchor permits "unstocking" for convenient stowing; the metal stock slides through a hole in the shank to be lashed flat against the shank—the upper end being bent at right angles, and provided with a round-headed end, so it will not slip out of the shank. If your model calls for this kind, use a piece of wire passed through the shank. Add a ring or shackle fitting.

You may never have occasion to construct a mushroom anchor, but in case you do, you can begin by raiding the matchbox again. Use part of a matchstick for the shank, topped with a ring, or shackle fitting. The mushroom can be made from a number of things: half a wooden bead—small button mold—hollow earring setting, etc.

Most modern anchors are stockless, and have also eliminated the curved arms; the movable flukes, or bills, are much larger than in the old ones, and are connected by a shaft which allows them to move as much as 45° to either side of the shank.

Cut the shank and base from wood, and shape slightly. The flukes can be shaped from thin wood and glued directly to the sides of the base. If the anchor is to be stowed in the hawse hole of your model, the flukes must be fastened at an angle, so the shank can be fitted up into the hawse pipes, leaving just the flukes and base visible from the exterior. Omit the shackle, or ring fitting.

79

A ship's skylight imparts a warm, homey quality, suggesting comfort and cheer below decks. I think that is why the building of them is so much fun.

A very small skylight with a shallow gable roof can be carved directly out of a small oblong block of wood. The "lights" (skylights), or window-panes, can be painted on, or thin paper cut-outs can be glued over the top. Shellac when dry.

Larger skylights permit more realism. A low wood base, or platform, should be constructed first; if you want a neat, overhanging-edge effect. glue on a slightly larger rectangle of cardboard. Draw a continuous lay-out of the sides and gable-end pieces on thin cardboard, leaving a tab on one end. Lay out the roof separately—large enough to extend beyond, or form eaves over, the walls. Mark out the lights, or panes, in single or double rows on each side of the center ridge. Cut out the pane sections very carefully with a razor blade. Cement old film or gelatine sheets to the inside. Although nothing within can be seen through them, these simulated windows do somehow give an illusion of depth.

When the roof is completed, score a light cut along the ridge with a sharp knife—only deep enough to insure a straight edge when folding; be careful not to cut through the cardboard. Fold the wall pieces on the dotted lines, glue the tab into place and set up. Glue the roof in place, centering it so the overhang is equal all around. Shellac all areas before attaching it to the deck.

On real ships the two halves of a skylight roof are hinged at the peak so they can be opened for better ventilation. If you want to capture this extra touch of realism for your boat, you can do so without much difficulty; however, on cardboard structures, it will be best to confine this improvement to only one side. Glue the opposite half down to the walls with a little extra glue, making it firm and secure. Glue bamboo slivers to the inside corners of the walls to prop the skylight open.

Some skylights have outside metal rods placed lengthwise across them for glass protection. On a model this effect can be achieved by cementing wires into place over the panes.

Occasionally a model calls for two skylights close together on the same raised deck.

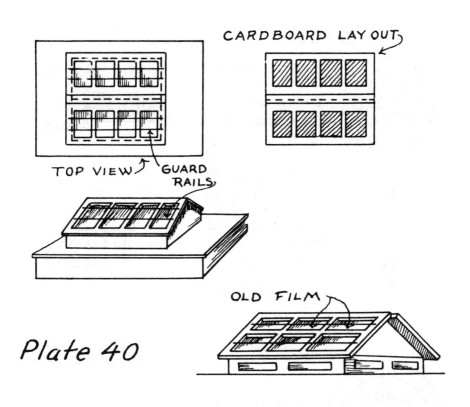

CARDBOARD LAY OUT

TOP VIEW GUARD RAILS

OLD FILM

Plate 40

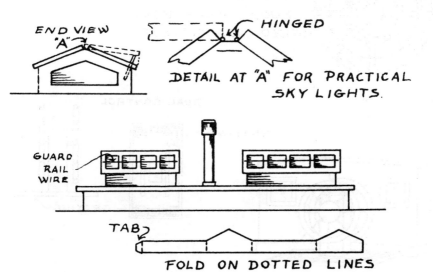

END VIEW "A"

HINGED

DETAIL AT "A" FOR PRACTICAL SKY LIGHTS.

GUARD RAIL WIRE

TAB

FOLD ON DOTTED LINES

STEERING WHEELS

CARVE FROM

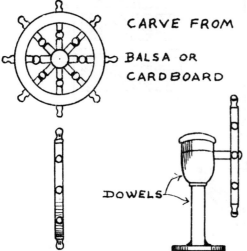

BALSA OR
CARDBOARD

WHEEL HOUSINGS

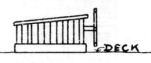

DECK

DOWELS

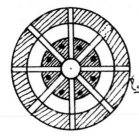

Plate 41

WHEEL IN
WOOD OR CARDBOARD
SHADED AREA CUT OUT

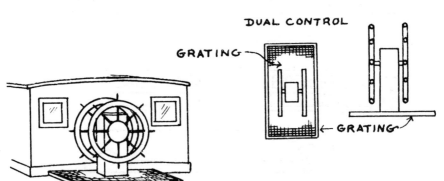

DUAL CONTROL

GRATING

GRATING

The construction of a steering wheel sometimes seems like a third-degree test of a model-builder's patience—as the carving becomes more and more involved, the fragile little piece seems to become less and less manageable. Some wheels are intricately carved; there are eight spokes in most, although wheels for small boats may have as few as four. Some large vessels have double wheels—dual control—which are operated as one; both are manned when weather conditions, currents, etc., become too much for the strength of one helmsman. Most wheels are set on a wooden grating to provide better footing for the steersman.

Lay out the drawing for your model wheel on thin wood or cardboard, and shade the areas to be cut out. Wheels ½″ or less in diameter are too small for cutting out—draw and shade in the details and cut the outside just enough to indicate spokes. For a larger cardboard wheel, cut out the shaded areas with a razor blade—try to have clean-cut corners. Shellac and set aside to dry; then remove any angularity by lightly sandpapering. Drill a small hole at center of the wheel.

If you are to work on a very small wheel of wood, glue both sides of a piece of paper and sandwich it in between the wood lay-out piece and another larger wood piece; this double wood thickness will provide extra strength during the cutting and also furnish support for holding. Drill a hole through all thicknesses at the center of each shaded segment. Insert a coping-saw blade and saw out each triangle; if the divisions are too small for this, use a razor blade. Cut the outer area carefully so as not to break off the spoke handles. When rough-cutting is done, remove the lower wood piece—it may be necessary to steam or heat it slightly to loosen the glue. Finish the shaping with a razor blade and fine sandpaper strips.

Steering wheels are attached to pedestals or to small wheel housings, which contain the mechanism for operating the rudder. A wheelhouse can be constructed of a small solid block of wood, with top or wheel side at a slight angle; the sides can be scored to simulate planking, if you wish. On the top, glue a piece of cardboard with a slight overhang all around. A pedestal can be a simple oblong block of wood set on end, or a shaped dowel, as illustrated. Double wheels are placed fore and aft of a simple block pedestal.

Use a pin to attach small wheels; then make a few turns of glued paper strips on the pin to represent the shaft. Drive it into the housing or pedestal up to the paper shaft.

83

STEERING
ARRANGEMENTS

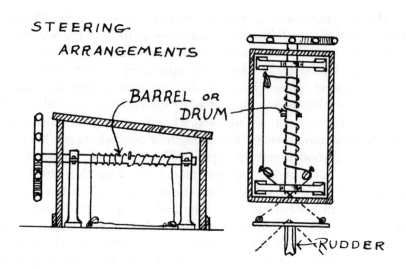

BARREL OR
DRUM

RUDDER

Plate 42

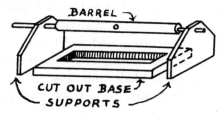

BARREL

CUT OUT BASE
SUPPORTS

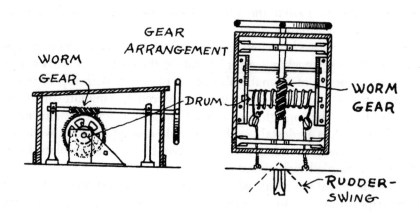

GEAR
ARRANGEMENT

WORM
GEAR

DRUM

WORM
GEAR

RUDDER-
SWING

Most workers are so enthusiastic by the time they have completed two or three models that they are ready to take on workable, or movable steering arrangements. To avoid frustration, this ambition had better be confined to ships with steering layouts enclosed in housings as shown on PLATE 9, page 18. It would be rather impractical for models with gear and gear shafting confined within the limited space of pedestal mounts, PLATE 41. Such work is for jewelers' fingers.

There are two processes of transmitting action from steering wheel to rudder: direct and indirect. By the direct method the wheel shaft (which is also a gear) is connected by two movable arms to the rudder post (PLATE 43). By the indirect-coupling method—the one most often employed—the steering wheel controls and relays action through two lines or chains, wound on a drum, or barrel. As described in the section on rudders, page 19, they lead through pulleys to the tiller bar, where they are fastened—one to the port end, and one to the starboard end, of the bar. Each time the wheel is moved, a corresponding action takes place at the rudder. All the various parts for such a set-up can be built of wood; metal can be used, however, for any or all parts.

The actual steering mechanism—barrel, shafts, and supports—will be confined within the wheel housing; the pulleys should already be attached and in working order on a platform below decks.

Draw a rectangle, marking the inside measurements of the wheel-house on the deck. Cut out two upright supports—somewhat triangular in shape, with lopped-off corners. Drill holes near the top center of each for the shaft to penetrate. Set them up temporarily in their places near the end walls; mark lines on the deck along the inside of the supports, and cut a rectangular base of thin wood to fit between the supports. Cut out the center area, reducing base to a sort of horizontal frame; mark and cut out corresponding area in the deck.

Next cut a dowel (for the barrel and shaft ends) long enough to extend well beyond the supports; mark it where it contacts the inside of each support. From these marks whittle the dowel down to make shafts that fit and penetrate the support holes—a very short end for the rear, but long enough forward to connect with the steering wheel. Drill a hole large enough for a heavy linen thread through the exact center of the barrel. Your various pieces are now ready to be assembled.

Insert shaft ends into support holes and attach supports permanently to the ends of the cut-out base. Glue the set-up into place around the

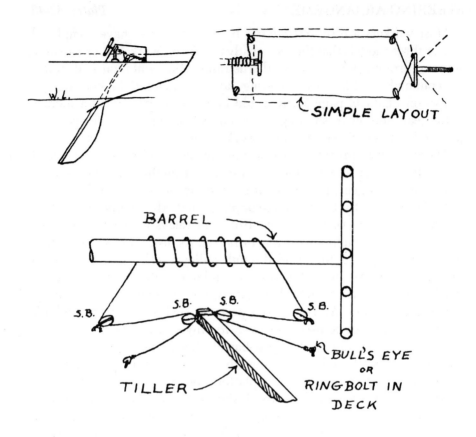

W.L.

SIMPLE LAYOUT

BARREL

S.B. S.B. S.B. S.B.

BULL'S EYE
OR
RINGBOLT IN
DECK

TILLER

Plate 43

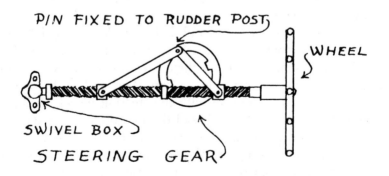

PIN FIXED TO RUDDER POST

WHEEL

SWIVEL BOX

STEERING GEAR

deck opening, after fishing up the two coils of thread which have been set aside, ready for use, since the preparation of the tiller, etc.

Set rudder at dead center during the threading of the barrel. Take the coil from the port pulleys; wind it clockwise five turns around the forward part of the barrel—quite tightly, and toward the center. Pick up the other coil rising from the starboard pulley, and give it five turns counterclockwise on the after part. When completed, pass the thread through the center hole of the barrel; tie threads together into a temporary knot. Do not cut off excess thread until you have given the mechanism a try-out as follows:

Try swinging the rudder gently from side to side; if it works easily give it hard right rudder; that is, move to starboard as far as the rudder will go without forcing; watch the thread as you do this. Don't expect more than a 45° swing from the center line. The forward part of the barrel winds up the thread, pulling the tiller bar forward on the right-hand side; the after part unwinds the thread, allowing slack and enabling the left half of the tiller bar to move or swing aft.

If all the turns of thread leave the after part of the barrel on this full right rudder swing, you will need an additional turn or two.

For example: If the after five unwound before full rudder was acquired, untie the temporary knot and add two more turns both fore and aft—making fourteen turns in all; pass the thread through the hole again and test once more. When satisfactory, place rudder at dead center; force a splinter into the hole of the barrel; cut off, leaving a little of it projecting at one end for easy removal if necessary.

Build the cardboard wheel housing around the steering mechanism, as described in the previous section, allowing the shaft to protrude through a hole in the forward end. Have your steering wheel ready, with a square hole cut in the center. Hold the wheel at right angles to the shaft; viewing it from the side, place a mark on the shaft at a point where the wheel has sufficient clearance from the housing; from this mark forward cut the shaft square to fit the steering wheel. Cement the wheel in place, and when dry, trim off the shaft flush with the front of the wheel.

If you have an assortment of gears, try a gear arrangement as pictured in PLATE 42; the basic principles are the same. The barrel may run fore and aft, or athwartship. The tiller may be attached differently and may also be equipped with eyebolts, to which the rope or chain is fastened.

The tremendous cargoes stowed away in the holds of ships are loaded and unloaded with the aid of derricks and winches. These winches, which are power-driven, lower and raise the goods by means of ropes or cables wound up on horizontal drums. Some winches are "open"— having the working mechanism exposed—and others are housed; that is, most of the mechanism is enclosed within a wooden shelter.

The simplest type of housed winch can be made from a small oblong block of wood. Slant the top slightly if you wish. Cut two pieces of cardboard slightly larger than the block; these will serve as base and deck (roof), for the housing. Shape two wide and open sheaves from small dowels—from a matchstick, if the scale is correct—and glue them directly to the sides of the housing. For larger sheaves, where the scale permits shafting to show, drill small holes through the sheaves and drive pins through them. Wrap narrow strips of glued paper to the pins to represent shafting.

An interesting type of housed winch begins with a wooden cube for the main piece, or body. Glue a smaller block of wood, oblong in shape, to the top of it. Shape two sheaves as described above, and drill holes through them for thin wire or pins to penetrate—these are to represent shafts. Resting these shafts on the cube, drive them carefully into the ends of the top block until the sheaves almost come into contact with the lower one. On one side of the cube—near the base, and parallel to it —glue a thin strip of wood to form a ledge. To the outside ends of this strip glue two bamboo slivers (levers) in an upright position, but tipping very slightly forward.

Drill two holes into the large block, halfway between the top and the wood ledge, as illustrated. Insert glued slivers of bamboo and glue the other ends to the levers. Finally, glue the whole set-up to a base.

Where the scale permits open winches, they can be made of wood or cardboard; but metal can be used altogether or for parts. Drill holes in two supports for the drum shaft to penetrate. The drum can be made from a short dowel, with cardboard disks glued to the ends to serve as collars, or flanges. Shape sheaves as for housed winches and drill a hole through all of the pieces for a wire shaft; arrange the pieces in correct order and glue into place. Glue the supports firmly to a wood or cardboard base.

WINCHES

HOUSED WINCH

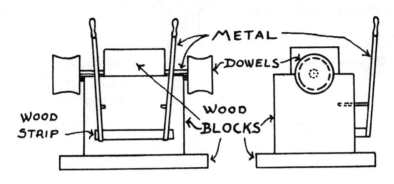

METAL

DOWELS

WOOD BLOCKS

WOOD STRIP

Plate 44

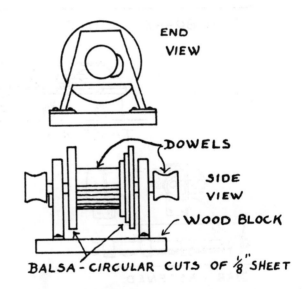

END VIEW

DOWELS

SIDE VIEW

WOOD BLOCK

BALSA–CIRCULAR CUTS OF $\frac{1}{8}$" SHEET

OPEN WINCH

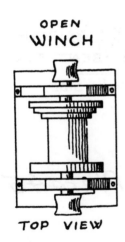

TOP VIEW

WINCH HOUSINGS

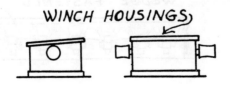

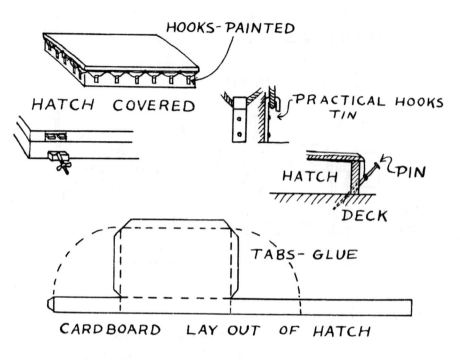

HOOKS-PAINTED

HATCH COVERED

PRACTICAL HOOKS
TIN

HATCH PIN

DECK

TABS- GLUE

CARDBOARD LAY OUT OF HATCH

RING

BENT PIN.

THREE RINGS ON EACH SIDE.

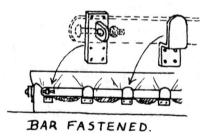

BAR FASTENED.

Plate 45

WEDGE FASTENED

CANVAS
COVER

90

The large openings that appear in the decks of vessels for the admittance of cargo are called hatches. They are bordered by perpendicular wood or metal frames, varying in height, which support hinged or wholly removable covers. During rough weather heavy tarpaulins are battened down over the hatches to keep out the rain and salt water.

For solid hull models, hatches should only be simulated. Use thin squares or oblongs of wood; complete the effect by gluing on a slightly projecting lid of cardboard. Glue directly to the deck in the proper place, and shellac. If you wish to paint on some trimming or fastenings, wait until after the general painting is finished. Although the simulation of tarpaulins and fastenings is not uncommon in small models, it is best, as a general rule, to keep the hatches as simple as possible. Actual hardware should be used only for the larger hatches.

If the hatch is two or three inches square or larger, it can be constructed from a one-piece cardboard layout. Use thin cardboard with tabs for gluing parts into place. Score and fold exactly on the corner lines and then assemble. If the cardboard is white it will need no painting—only a coat of shellac. A cloth cover can be added if you like, and fastened down by pins driven through the hatch sides into the deck. Thread lashings will give the appearance of a tarpaulin battened down.

Practical hatches should be built in models having hollow hulls. Cut your hatch opening, and then glue wood, balsa or heavy cardboard strips into a vertical frame around it, flush with the bottom. See that the corners are well glued. Cardboard, if used, can be cut in a continuous strip, which is scored and bent at the corners and glued together by a tab. A very narrow strip of wood should next be glued to form a ledge around the inner side of the frame—at a depth equal to half the thickness of the cover.

This cover can be made of thin wood sheets. Cut a piece so that it fits exactly within the frame, resting on the narrow ledge; then cut another piece which extends a little beyond the outside of the hatch. Glue the two pieces together to form a two-ply removable cover. Simple fastenings for hatches can be fashioned from short pins, and rings fastened by pins bent into the shape of small staples. Small rings (for lifting) should be stapled to the four corners of the hatch cover.

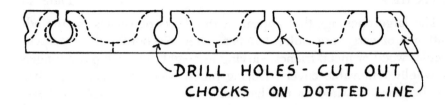

DRILL HOLES - CUT OUT
CHOCKS ON DOTTED LINE

CLEATS

PIN
WIRE

WOOD - SHAPED

Plate 46

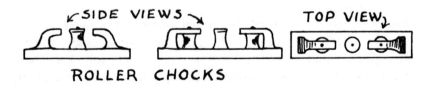

SIDE VIEWS

TOP VIEW

ROLLER CHOCKS

Chocks are heavy blocks or castings made of wood or metal, which have two horn-shaped arms curving inward toward each other from a solid base. Ropes or cables are run between these arms for mooring, towing, etc.

To make very small chocks, use a strip of bamboo; for larger ones, thin wood. On your strip draw a series of them end-to-end—enough to furnish the entire model. In the center of the oval areas enclosed by the curving arms, drill holes as large as possible; then finish inside and outside, cutting and shaping with a razor-blade point. Sandpaper all angular edges lightly and cut apart the individual chocks. Cement in place to deck.

Some chocks are equipped with from one to three rollers to allow rope to run through with less friction; on this type of chock the tips of the arms are farther apart; they are longer and more angular, and flattened down over the rollers like clamps. Draw the series of chocks on a strip of wood or bamboo; drill, cut out and shape as for simple chocks. Glue a small cylinder—flush with the top of the arms—in the center for your roller; and smaller ones, if used, under the arms. If the rollers are not too small, drive pins down through them into the deck.

CLEATS. Cleats are generally of metal, but can also be made of wood. Comparatively few cleats are necessary for a model, which is a good thing, because they are so tiny when reduced to scale. A cleat is a small device with two arms, used for securing a rope or the like. They can be drawn on bamboo and cut out as chocks were. To make small wire cleats, flatten the center of a short wire; drill a small hole through, and bend the wire into a cleat, cutting off the excess wire.

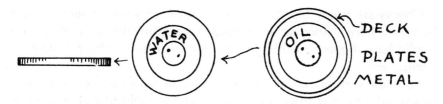

Plate 46a

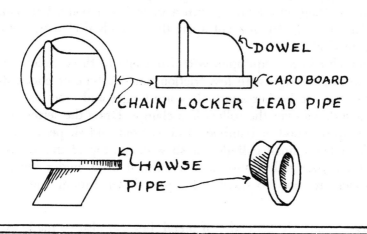

DOWEL

CARDBOARD

CHAIN LOCKER LEAD PIPE

HAWSE PIPE

GLOUCESTER FISHERMAN

Actual hawse pipes—the fittings for hawse holes—are not necessary for small models. Simply drill a hole; drill half the hole from the deck, the other half from the exterior, at the point for the hawse hole opening. You are cutting this hole at an angle, so be careful not to splinter the hull, or mar it. Punch out two cardboard disks with a paper punch, pierce a hole through the center of each, and glue one over the deck opening, the other over the exterior hole; these will serve satisfactorily as a trim, or finish. Shoe eyelets or small metal grommets—reshaped slightly—can also be used.

For large models the hawse pipes (two halves) can actually be metal tubes with proper deck and hawse-hole fittings.

Half-sections of the elbow-shaped locker-lead pipes (chain leads) can be shaped from blocks of wood fitted together and glued to a cardboard base. Anchor chains lead from these pipes.

Deck plates, leading to water and fuel tanks, can be disks of brass sunk into and flush with the deck.

Native-made model of a dhow from Mombasa, East Africa. (In the collection of The Mariners' Museum, Newport News, Va.)

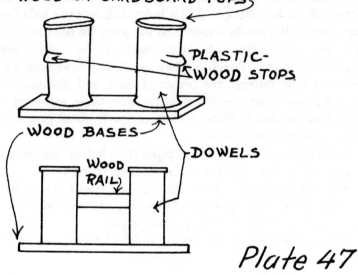

WOOD OR CARDBOARD TOPS

PLASTIC-WOOD STOPS

WOOD BASES

DOWELS

WOOD RAIL

Plate 47

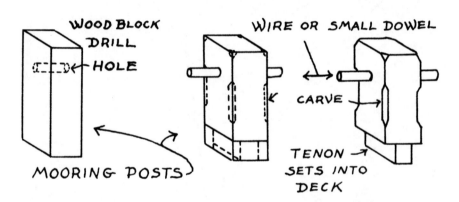

WOOD BLOCK
DRILL
HOLE

WIRE OR SMALL DOWEL

CARVE

MOORING POSTS

TENON
SETS INTO
DECK

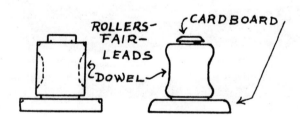

ROLLERS-FAIR-LEADS

CARDBOARD

DOWEL

A mooring post is a sturdy piece of timber set solidly into the deck, and is used for securing heavy rope, chain or cable. It is meant for heavy-duty work and looks the part.

To build one, use a rectangular or square block or peg of wood having the dimensions—including tenon—you want for the finished product. Mark out on it the length of the post, position of the tenon and the carving stations indicated in the drawing; for this last detail use a try square, if you have one, to encircle the block with accuracy. Drill a hole through the block at a point a little above the center point; cement a wire or a heavy pin into the hole so that it projects equally on both sides. Cut off excess, and blunt tips with a file. Hold in a vise while shaping edges and corners and cutting away superfluous wood around the tenon. Cut a mortise in the deck to admit the tenon and glue post into place.

BOLLARDS. Bollards are vertical wood or iron posts, set on ships or wharves for mooring purposes; they resemble bitts so much that, when reduced in scale to ship-model size, the directions for making the bitts can be followed successfully. Bollards are often used singly as well as in pairs; some of them (as well as bitts) are provided with bulges, or stops, on opposite sides, which hold ropes and cables fast, preventing them from slipping upward when tidal conditions make deck and wharf levels vary in height. These bulges can be shaped as required out of plastic wood, smoothing and leveling the edges out toward the front and back of the post.

ROLLERS OR FAIR-LEADS *Plate 47*

These large metal fixtures, which resemble spools, are attached to heavy bases by sturdy pivots; they are part of the equipment of heavy ships with tremendous anchor chains—especially ocean liners and Navy vessels. The chains are run around one or more of these rollers during the heaving in and running out of the cable.

Use slightly shaped dowels for miniature fair-leads and cement them to circular bases of wood or cardboard. If large enough to be workable, use pins as pivots.

All vessels are governed by certain international regulations for preventing collisions at sea, for sending signals of distress, etc. A ship's
lights communicate definite information to seamen and others who can
read their messages; whether that particular ship is under way, anchored, grounded, out of control, towing or being towed, or in distress.
These regulations are interesting and worth looking up for those who
love ships. They can be found in naval and marine handbooks, and in
encyclopedias, under "Rules of the Road at Sea."

SIDE LIGHTS. The side lights—red for port and green for starboard—
which glow so picturesquely from "ships that pass in the night," are
placed in the neighborhood of the foremast—sometimes attached
directly to the foremast shrouds; frequently perched on the roofs of
deckhouses. The lamps themselves are set in corners of half-boxes.

These boxes can be made from thin wood or cardboard; for the
former, cut base, side and end pieces from balsa, if available, and glue
together to form the half-boxes. The end pieces are attached to the
after part of the base, the long pieces to the inboard sides, so that
the lights are visible abeam and from out over the bow. Use beads—
if possible, one red and one green—to represent glass window enclosures. They can be glued to small squares of cardboard, which in
turn can be cemented into the box corners after it has been painted.
Round-headed pins can be driven down through the beads, cardboard
and wood bases, and snipped off flush with the bottom; these hold the
beads down firmly and help convey the impression of lanterns. Beads
with lateral cuts and markings seem even more realistic, but they are
rather difficult to obtain.

A cardboard half-box is easily constructed from one piece: lay out the
bottom, side and end pieces—with or without a tab—drawing dotted
lines along the folding edges. Cut out, fold, and glue together. Proceed
with beads as above.

If large enough, the lamps themselves can be made from cardboard.
Cut a small rectangle of cardboard for each, with wide flaps at the
sides. Cut an opening in the rectangle for the window and glue a
colored gelatine plate inside. Glue flaps so that the window front
presents a curved surface across the corner, hold with pinch cocks. A
cone-shaped top with slight overhang can be cut and glued over each
lamp.

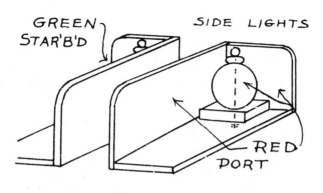

GREEN
STAR'B'D

SIDE LIGHTS

RED
PORT

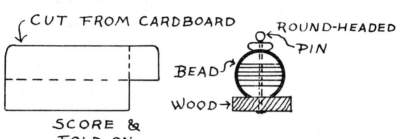

CUT FROM CARDBOARD

ROUND-HEADED
PIN

BEAD

WOOD

SCORE &
FOLD ON
DOTTED LINES - GLUE

Plate 48

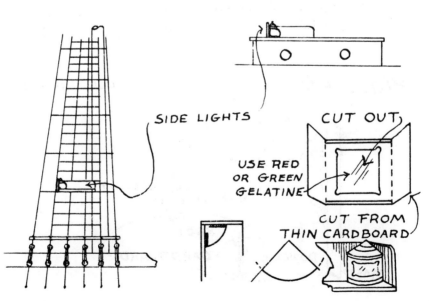

SIDE LIGHTS

CUT OUT

USE RED
OR GREEN
GELATINE

CUT FROM
THIN CARDBOARD

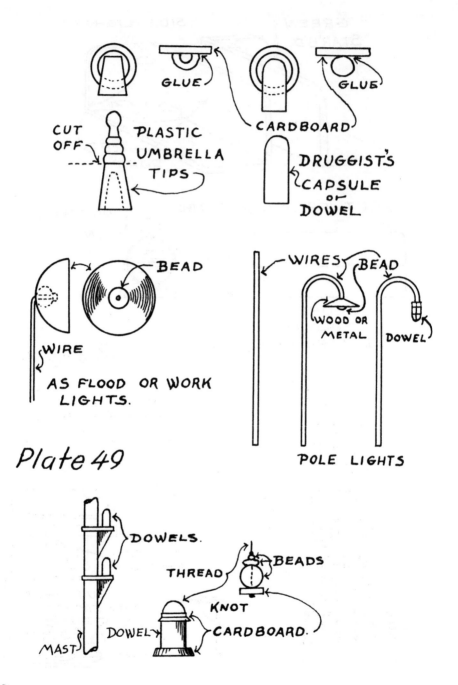

GLUE

GLUE

CUT OFF

PLASTIC UMBRELLA TIPS

CARDBOARD

DRUGGIST'S CAPSULE or DOWEL

BEAD

WIRE

AS FLOOD OR WORK LIGHTS.

WIRES

BEAD

WOOD OR METAL

DOWEL

Plate 49

POLE LIGHTS

DOWELS.

THREAD

BEADS

KNOT

CARDBOARD.

DOWEL

MAST

Deck Lights—Working Lights. Regular deck lights are simple shaded bracket lamps, and can be made from various odds and ends. A few ideas will be suggested here, with the expectation that the reader's ingenuity will probably surpass them.

For the wall plaques, or plates, cut cardboard disks and glue to the walls at the proper places. Matchstick dowels can be shaped to resemble shaded lights. The tips of umbrella ribs, usually ornamental plastic castings, have many uses: the lower part can be cut off and used for shades and the tips used for some other purpose. (By this time you probably wouldn't think of throwing anything away anyway.) Glue lights to the cardboard plates as illustrated. Druggists' capsules—cut down to size, if necessary—are so adaptable to this purpose that they look made to order. Beads of this general elongated shape can be used also.

Work lights, or flood lamps, are as easily constructed. Wire can be used for the supporting pipes, and the shade-reflectors can be made from any small hollowed-out half-spheres; the empty settings from earrings would be good. Solder or glue each reflector to the wire; then glue a tiny bead to the center of it to represent an electric bulb—an imitation pearl is perfect for this.

Riding Lights. A vessel at anchor must carry a white light forward which is clearly visible for a mile around. Sailing ships have lanterns suspended in the rigging; modern vessels have either fixed lights (for all purposes) or are equipped with lanterns that are hoisted by halyards for that purpose.

An effective riding light can be made from two beads, a cardboard disk and a piece of thread. Knot the thread below the cardboard base, and sew through base, middle bead, and finally, a much smaller bead; pull thread taut and tie another knot on top, crowding all parts together. Another hanging lantern can be made from a tiny dowel with flat cardboard disks glued to top and bottom; use a short thread for a handle. A white or transparent capsule, with the curved end cut off, could be used instead of a dowel.

For mast lights of modern vessels use transparent capsules, small dowels, or matchsticks, depending on the scale. Glue each to a small bracket base.

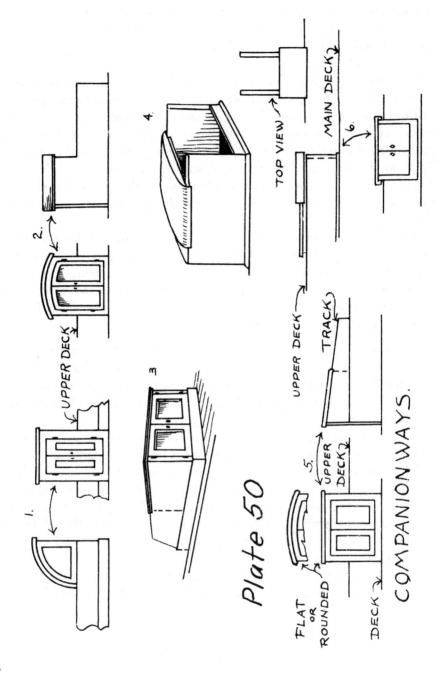

Plate 50

COMPANION WAYS.

Although most dictionary definitions restrict a companionway to "a set of steps leading from the deck to a cabin or saloon below; also the space occupied by these steps," seamen in general are apt to refer to almost any shipboard ladder or stair, short of a Jacob's ladder, as a companionway or companion.

This chapter is concerned only with the housings of companionway entrances and their construction. The illustrations show two general types; one is squat and flat, with sliding deck (roof)—in reality a half-deck—which may have a removable front as in Drawing 4, PLATE 50, or two small doors (3, 5 & 6). To allow sufficient transit room, these low half-roofs are made to slide back on tracks from the entrances. The second type of entrance is high enough to make a sliding deck unnecessary, and is topped with either a flat or rounded roof. This kind usually has two fairly large doors, as in Drawings 1 and 2.

Unless your model happens to be quite large, or you want your companionways actually workable, construct them as simply as possible, yet with a mind to creating an effective illusion. The housings shown in the illustrations can be built of thin wood, cardboard, or a combination of the two; or shaped from a block of wood. After the block is shaped as required, draw an exact-size outline of the front on a piece of paper; then draw on the doors, hinges, trim, etc., in ink. Cut out and glue to the block. Shellac for finish.

Use thin wood or cardboard for simulated sliding half-decks. The simplest roof (No. 4) slides back entirely on the housing structure itself. No. 3 has false side extensions which serve as the track. These can be made of strips of thin wood glued on edge, in a vertical position. No. 5 has extensions; these continue back from the roof to form tracks with a gradual slope. No. 6 has miniature grooved tracks, which can be made from slivers of bamboo.

OIL TANKER.

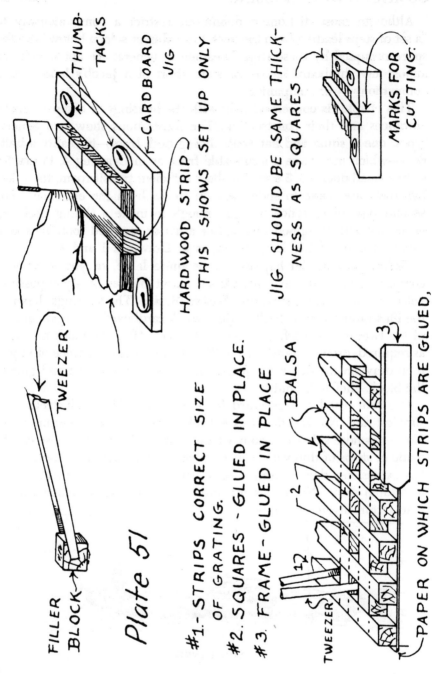

THUMB-TACKS

CARDBOARD JIG

HARDWOOD STRIP

THIS SHOWS SET UP ONLY

JIG SHOULD BE SAME THICKNESS AS SQUARES

MARKS FOR CUTTING.

TWEEZER

FILLER BLOCK

Plate 51

#1.- STRIPS CORRECT SIZE OF GRATING.

#2. SQUARES - GLUED IN PLACE.

#3. FRAME - GLUED IN PLACE

BALSA

TWEEZER

1 2 2 3

PAPER ON WHICH STRIPS ARE GLUED,

On sailing vessels where the helmsman stood out in the open, the decking under his feet and all around the wheel was covered with a wooden grating. It gave him firmer and drier footing in rough, slippery weather. Gratings are used extensively throughout modern ships; most of them are open and of metal. Open-work gratings form platforms, walks, landings and floor panels between decks, and fair-weather covers over hatches.

Very small gratings for small ship models should be merely simulated; this can be done satisfactorily by painting or drawing narrow lattice lines on thin wood or cardboard foundations. Actual gratings must be constructed with painstaking and conscientious accuracy to look effective; here is one time when indifferent work could cause a lot of wasted time and effort.

If the grating is to have a solid base, cut the size base wanted from wood or cardboard; if open-work, mark the outside measurements of the grill panel on a sheet of paper—keep this temporary base on a cardboard foundation during work. From here on, procedure is the same for both kinds.

Have on hand enough thin rectangular pieces of balsa or bamboo to supply the entire grating. From these cut several individual strips, or bars, the length of the panel; reserve one to act as spacer.

Glue the first bar to the base, leaving enough space for the border-frame to be added later; lay spacer snugly against bar and glue the second bar into place on the other side of it. Remove spacer and continue across the panel until all the lengthwise pieces have been laid.

Set up a jig—either a simple right-angled affair or a three-sided jig—of cardboard or wood the exact thickness of the grating bars. Glue down firmly to a cardboard base and reinforce with thumbtacks. Set the spacer along the stopper edge and mark the jig on the other side of the spacer. Place a ruler on the jig marks, and cut through on these lines.

Next, arrange a row of bars side by side within the jig, set the ruler on the jig cuts and slice through the bars. Repeat until you have all the filler cubes you need. Guided by the indispensable spacer again, mark faint lines across all the lengthwise bars; then glue two sides of each cube, and set into place with tweezers. Glue the frame around and let the whole grate dry.

To remove the temporary paper base, set on a paper-covered flat plate which has been slightly heated. When dry, shellac the grating. *105*

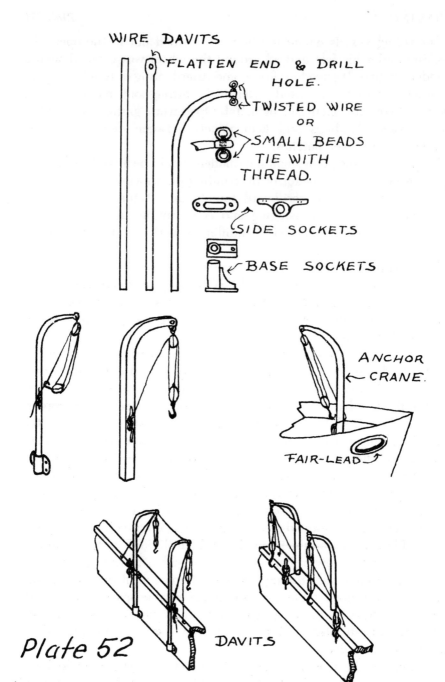

WIRE DAVITS

FLATTEN END & DRILL HOLE.

TWISTED WIRE OR

SMALL BEADS TIE WITH THREAD.

SIDE SOCKETS

BASE SOCKETS

ANCHOR CRANE.

FAIR-LEAD

Plate 52

DAVITS

Many whaling vessels of the Moby Dick period were equipped with sturdy wooden davits—generally three timbers for each, shaped and bolted together. They were stationary fixtures with the arc turned seaward; shackles or other fittings were bolted through the tips of the curving ends. The sketches show some of the familiar types of metal davits in general service today; they have a certain beauty because of their practical and efficient simplicity. Passenger liners are especially well equipped with modern power-driven davits, and although they may not have quite the romantic picturesque appeal of the old ones, they are highly efficient. Basically, davits are much alike, but there are minor variations in construction. Out of ten ships, for instance, one might find as many as seven with slightly different launching devices. They are set up in pairs at each lifeboat station. Any of them are quite simple to reproduce for ship models.

Use wire in scale with the ship; cut off the necessary length and bend the upper end into an arc. Flatten the tip of the bent end on your anvil and drill a small hole through it. Trim the flattened area with a file. With very fine wire or thread, fasten two small beads into place— one at the top, and the other at the bottom of the hole. The bottom bead can serve as the upper block of the launching tackle, if you like.

Mark the places on the deck or rail where the davits are to be attached; drill holes just large enough and only deep enough to hold them upright—not over ½″ deep, unless the model is quite large. To keep the davits from swinging back and forth, run a thread across from one upper bead to the other; tie securely to both and continue lines down and fasten to deck or some other anchorage.

Pivotal sockets which allow the davits to swing inboard or outboard can be used for some of the larger models. These may be fastened to the deck or to the timberheads. Side supports are needed for these workable davits to give them additional anchorage.

ANCHOR CRANES. On some small modern boats not equipped with winches or the old-style cat-heads, anchor cranes are necessary. A crane can also be made from a not-too-flexible wire, bent at its upper quarter to form an arc large enough to allow the anchor to clear the hull. Drill a small hole ½″ deep in the deck at the forepeak. Set the wire hoist in this hole; it will not be necessary to glue it in place—the hole will serve as a socket and pivot. Attach anchor tackle to the upper tip of the hoist. *107*

Ship model working charts may call for anywhere from one to thirty lifeboats. Reduced to scale, these boats—and all boats to be stowed aboard—would be very small; lifeboats for passenger ship models are really too tiny for anything but suggestion of contour. Any of these small boats can be shaped from blocks of soft wood. Do not attempt to hollow out the interiors of small covered lifeboats; paint a cover for each one, with overhanging or scalloped edge effect to indicate that the cover is lashed down. (*See* PLATE *61, page 122.*)

For boats large enough for shaped interiors, hollow out as much as necessary; cut thin narrow strips of balsa or cardboard for the thwarts, or seats, and glue into place. If the boat is large enough to show rib and interior construction details, use bamboo splinters for the work, because they have the necessary pliability.

Some of the small boats are equipped with centerboard, sail, demountable rudder, oars, and steering oar. A centerboard is a keel, pivoted at the forward lower corner of its case or housing, which can be lowered vertically through the bottom of the boat to prevent leeway, or raised into a watertight casing amidships. A steering, or sculling oar is also shown in an illustration. If scale permits, add oarlocks.

Fishermen usually become quite sentimentally attached to the dories they stow on their vessels; and really, they are fine little boats—deep, flat-bottomed, with high, flaring sides tapering to sharp prow and stunted stern, and they take to the surf like seagulls. If your fishing vessel model calls for a dory, add a steering oar; cut a groove for it at the flat stern end.

CASKS. On models, casks or barrels are used primarily for decoration, and, believe me, they never fail to add a jolly "Yo-ho-ho" touch. Begin with a very small dowel; mark out the lengths of several casks and indicate also where slight shaping is to be done; do this shaping with a fine rasp or a knife. Sandpaper slightly, and wrap thin, glued paper bands or paint lines around each cask to simulate hoops. When dry, cut off the individual casks and dip each in shellac.

BALSA BOAT WITH BALSA SAIL.

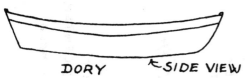
DORY   ←SIDE VIEW

SMALL BOAT

←HALF PLAN

MAST→

PORTABLE RUDDER→   SMALL SAIL BOAT

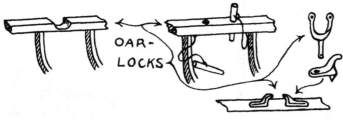
OAR-
LOCKS←

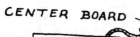
CENTER BOARD

SCULL→

Plate 53

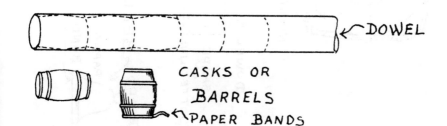
←DOWEL

CASKS OR
BARRELS
←PAPER BANDS

109

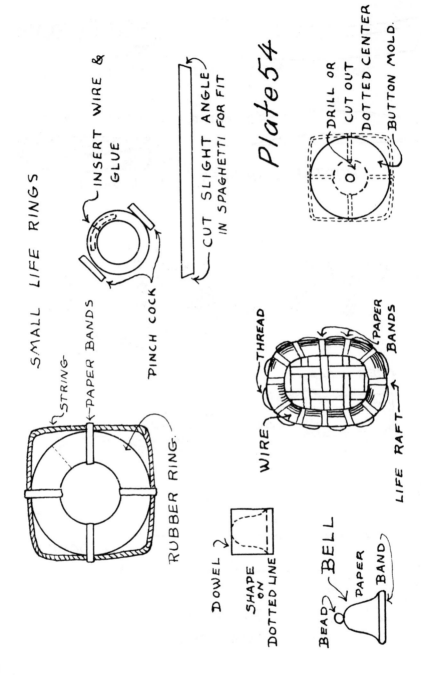

SMALL LIFE RINGS

INSERT WIRE & GLUE

STRING
PAPER BANDS
PINCH COCK
RUBBER RING.

CUT SLIGHT ANGLE
IN SPAGHETTI FOR FIT

Plate 54

DRILL OR CUT OUT DOTTED CENTER
BUTTON MOLD.

THREAD
WIRE
PAPER BANDS
LIFE RAFT

DOWEL
SHAPE ON DOTTED LINE

BEAD
BELL
PAPER BAND

Rafts are prosaic looking structures, but stories about them have been thrilling the human race ever since Ulysses sat in the midst of his reeling boards and said, "Woe is me!" And the radio, newsreel and press of our own day have contributed such moving accounts to these time-honoured stories that I think almost every model builder feels a spark of emotion as he fashions these ungraceful, unadorned little adjuncts to his ship.

There are two general types of life rafts: the semi-solid, crate-like structure of timber and the modern inflated rubber raft. The former is of such simple construction that it presents no problem for the model builder; one can be made from a small block of thin wood, with the reinforcement braces, etc., painted on. The rubber raft can be made from rubber-insulated wire, radio "spaghetti" (hollow, flexible plastic tubing), or heavy wire, bent to shape, and ends soldered together. Use thread for the hand lines; hold it in place with thin paper bands wrapped around the raft body. The flooring can be of a solid piece of cardboard or of interwoven paper strips glued to the raft body.

LIFE PRESERVERS. Life preservers can be made from a variety of odds and ends: rubber-covered wire, spaghetti tubing, button molds, etc. If tubing is used, cut a piece the length of the preserver and insert a curved, glued piece of wire into the ends; press ends together and hold with pinch cocks until dry. Cut a piece of thread or string long enough to form a square around the preserver. Glue paper strips around preserver and string on four sides, capturing string ends under one of them, for neatness. If button molds are used, simply cut or drill out enough of the centers to leave narrow circles. Finish with rope and bands as described above.

SHIPS' BELLS   *Plate 54*

A ship's bell is easily carved from a very small block of wood or the end of a small dowel. Shape and sandpaper; then cut from the dowel. Paint or glue a thin band around the base of the bell. A bead can be glued to the top, with the bead hole running horizontally so that the bell can be hung by a thread run through it; if the bell is too small for a bead, drill a hole a short distance into the top and insert a thin glued wire. When dry, form a small eye and cut off excess wire.

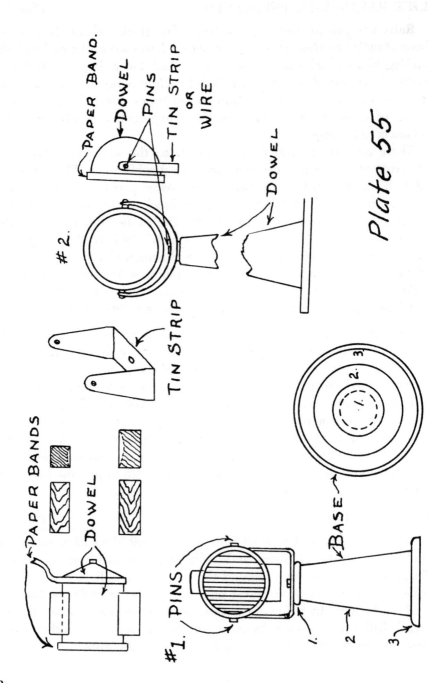

PAPER BAND.
DOWEL
PINS
TIN STRIP
OR
WIRE

#2.

DOWEL

Plate 55

TIN STRIP

BASE

PAPER BANDS

DOWEL

#1. PINS

1
2
3

A very small searchlight can be made by gluing a couple of shaped pieces of wood together to form a stationary fixture. Larger lights should have workable pivots and swivels, which call for small pieces of metal in addition to the wood.

SEARCHLIGHT No. 1. Use dowels for the pedestal and light, or head. Shape the head with its back tapering to form a shallow conical surface. Drill pin holes into the side centers of the head. Paint parallel perpendicular lines on the lens surface or paste on a paper face which has the lines drawn on; then glue narrow paper bands around the lens and also around the base of the cone—this gives an effective trim, or finish. A short pin can be driven into the peak of the cone for an effective bolt effect. Cut two tiny wood blocks to serve as accessory fittings, and curve the inside of each slightly to fit the head—one on the top and the other on the bottom; glue into place.

For the pedestal use a slightly tapering dowel. Glue a thin, circular cardboard or wooden disk to the top; cut it so that it projects slightly all around. Next, drill a hole down into the center of the pedestal.

Cut a simple metal bracket from a piece of tin (cigarette tin is good) and bend it to shape, so that the length of its base is the same as the width of the head. The tapering arms must be long enough to support the head and give it sufficient clearance above the base. Drill three holes into the bracket as illustrated; then drive a short pin through the base into the pedestal, quite firmly, but allowing the bracket to move laterally. Drive pins through the bracket arms into the head to serve as swivels. Glue the pedestal to a wider cardboard or wood disk base, which in turn is glued to the deck.

SEARCHLIGHT No. 2. The head can be made from a dowel with a rounded end, or from half of a large wooden bead. Trim lens edge with paper bands, drill holes into side centers near the edge, and construct pedestal the same as for searchlight No. 1. The bracket for this one should be of wire, strong enough to support the head without bending or kinking. Flatten the center and ends of the wire on an anvil, drill holes through these points and file smooth. Attach base and head with short pins.

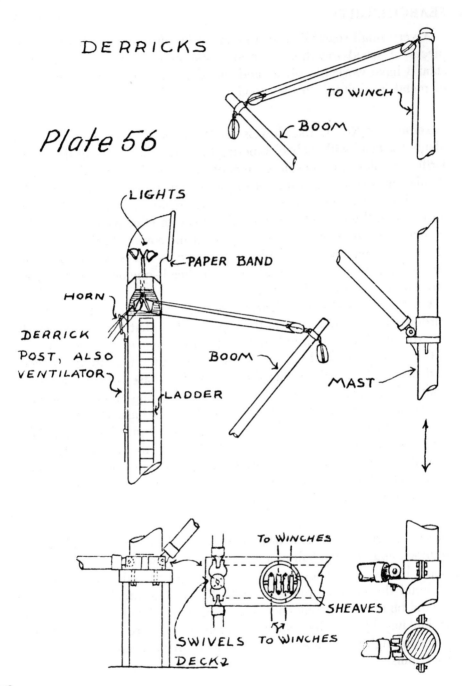

DERRICKS

Plate 56

TO WINCH

BOOM

LIGHTS

PAPER BAND

HORN

DERRICK POST, ALSO VENTILATOR

LADDER

BOOM

MAST

TO WINCHES

SHEAVES

SWIVELS

TO WINCHES

DECK

As stated under Winches, page 88, ships carrying cargo are equipped with winches and derricks for loading and unloading. That section told how to make winches for models; this one will deal with derricks, the hoisting mechanism which the winches operate. Derricks, by the way, got their name from a 17th century Tyburn hangman. These pieces of hoisting apparatus are powerful and versatile, being capable of handling practically anything, from a sling load of food cases to a complete locomotive. Some ships have multiple derricks, which make possible the manipulating of cargo from both port and starboard sides of the vessel at the same time. Although derricks are basically the same, there are variations in style and rigging.

A derrick unit consists of a central mast, or post (these vary in size), which has a heavy crossarm set near the base for the purpose of supporting one or more booms; and another near the top, which contains sheaves for the operation of the various booms. When stowed, these booms are rendered immobile by stays leading from the head blocks to the sides of the vessel.

There is also a simpler type of derrick, which has a single boom and post; the post has a simple collar fitting, with a swivel-bolt for a boom rest and a post band near the top for holding a double-sheave block.

To make derricks, use dowels for the posts and the booms, tapering them slightly. The crossarms can be shaped from small blocks of wood with holes drilled through the centers so they can encircle the posts. Cement them to the posts in their proper positions; if braces are necessary to support the lower crossarm, make some of thin triangular pieces of wood, and cement to post and under-side of the block. The boom fittings in this lower crossarm are simply swivel bolts; the boom ends are fitted with bands holding two double blocks each. Lines or cables lead from the various tackles to the winches.

On some ships the derrick posts serve as ventilators, and are made of tubular metal terminating in funnel vents. Ladders, mounting to the crossarms, are generally attached to such posts. The frequent addition of ships' horns, or whistles, and ships' floodlights turn them into veritable pillars of service, and show how well space is utilized on a boat. The lights are placed in the most advantageous spot—usually on the upper crossarm—for illuminating the hatches and surrounding area during night loading and unloading. Generally, there is at least one

115

light for each boom. (Of course, work lights are also placed at other convenient and advantageous spots on the ship.)

To make this type of derrick post, use a straight dowel for the section up to the crossarm; the vent opening above this can be shaped from a small block of wood and cemented to the top of the crossarm. The mouth, or opening, of the vent can be hollowed out slightly to give a realistic appearance, and a narrow strip of paper glued around for trim. The lower crossarm can be furnished with swivel fittings for the booms, as described above.

HOISTS. A hoist such as the one pictured can be carved out from one block of wood or made from small shaped pieces glued together. It should be angular in shape, with the sharp edges sandpapered down. A wire, bent to shape, forms a good crank handle.

To simulate a block, or sheave, at the tip, drill a small hole vertically through the hoist tip. With a small file or piece of folded sandpaper, shape a shallow groove around the end. The tackle can consist of a single-sheave block with a hook attached. The cable begins at the top of the block, leads up over the end of the hoist, then down through the vertical hole, back to and through the block. Continue up over the hoist tip and through the hole once more. Tie a knot at this point, large enough so that it can't slip through; cut off excess thread or wire.

Dutch 17th Century yacht. In spite of their somewhat clumsy appearance, these vessels were very good sailors. (Crabtree Collection, The Mariners' Museum, Newport News, Va.)

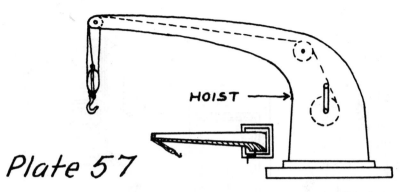

HOIST

Plate 57

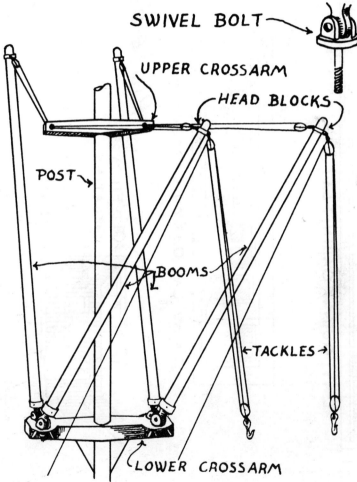

SWIVEL BOLT

UPPER CROSSARM

HEAD BLOCKS

POST

BOOMS

TACKLES

LOWER CROSSARM

117

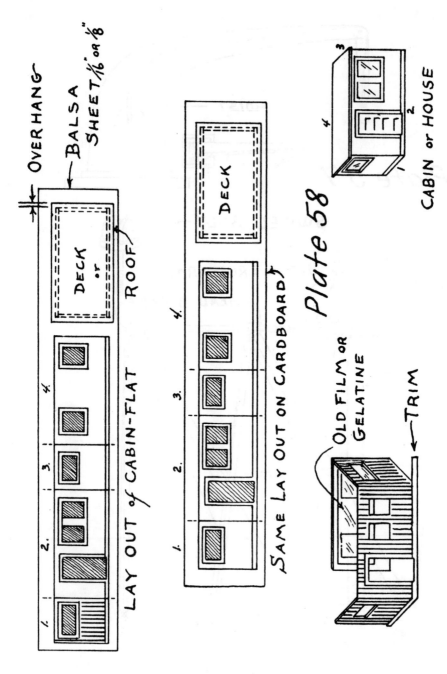

OVERHANG

BALSA SHEET 1/16" OR 1/8"

DECK or

ROOF

4.   3.   2.   1.

LAY OUT of CABIN-FLAT

DECK

4.   3.   2.   1.

SAME LAY OUT ON CARDBOARD

Plate 58

OLD FILM OR GELATINE

TRIM

CABIN or HOUSE

Any structural part of a ship above the main deck is known as super-structure; this includes deckhouses, cabins, bridges, etc.

In kit models, as you know, the superstructure pieces are already laid out on thin balsa or fiber composition sheets; the doors, windows, etc., marked for cutting out. The guide lines printed on these prefabricated models are sometimes rather heavy; to avoid possible inaccuracies, it is a good idea to assemble the component parts of your cabin or deck-house on a temporary substitute deck. This could be of cardboard, curved slightly to conform to your particular deck surface. Check layout to your satisfaction, then cement to the permanent deck in the proper places.

If you are working on an original design and must plan your own cabins, etc., lay out the walls in one continuous piece on a sheet of balsa or cardboard. Draw in all the architectural details and cut out doors and windows. Clear pieces of camera film make fine window-panes. Use tiny strips of tape for door hinges. If your cabin is to show planking, draw or gouge the plank lines before adding trim around the doors and windows—make this trim of very narrow strips of thin cardboard. Leave the base trim until after the cabin is assembled. All this trim, by the way, helps surprisingly to give a professional finish to your work. Balsa cannot be creased, so cut the wall divisions apart, and then glue together. The roof, or deck, can be of wood or cardboard cut large enough for a narrow overhang all around. Superstructure portholes can be treated the same as rectangular windows—cut them out, back with film, and use circular trim.

Proceed with cardboard layouts almost exactly as for balsa or fiber. Mark corners with dotted lines; score and fold on these lines and be sure you have allowed a tab for gluing. If the cardboard structure is unusually large, or if some weight is to rest on the decking, reinforce the structure with one or more inner partitions, or bulkheads. These bulkheads are best made of heavy cardboard pieces the same height as the walls and with generous tabs at each end. Set the cabin or deck-house upside down and glue the flaps to the walls. The roof should then be strong enough to support railings, lifeboats, etc., over a long period of years.

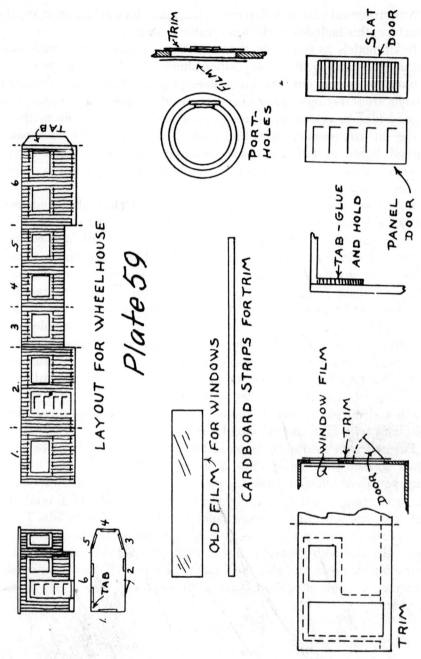

LAYOUT FOR WHEELHOUSE

Plate 59

TAB

TRIM

FILM

PORT-HOLES

SLAT DOOR

TAB - GLUE AND HOLD

PANEL DOOR

OLD FILM FOR WINDOWS

CARDBOARD STRIPS FOR TRIM

WINDOW FILM

TRIM

DOOR

TRIM

TAB

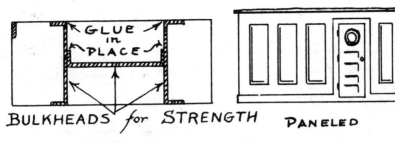

BULKHEADS *for* STRENGTH

PANELED

DECK HOUSE

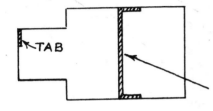

TAB

Plate 60

DECK HOUSE – RAILS – DORY LASHED DOWN

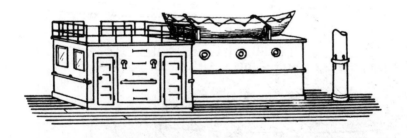

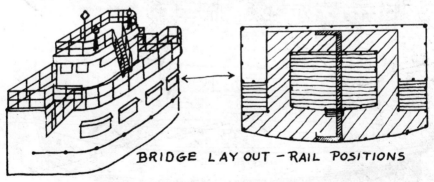

BRIDGE LAY OUT – RAIL POSITIONS

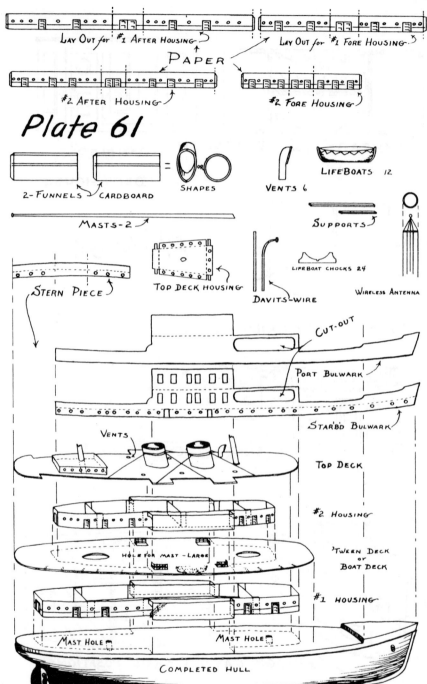

Lay Out for #1 After Housing

Lay Out for #1 Fore Housing

PAPER

#2 After Housing

#2 Fore Housing

Plate 61

2-Funnels Cardboard = Shapes

Vents 6

LifeBoats 12

Masts-2

Supports

Stern Piece

Top Deck Housing

Davits-wire

LifeBoat Chocks 24

Wireless Antenna

Cut-out

Port Bulwark

Starb'd Bulwark

Vents

Top Deck

#2 Housing

'Twern Deck or Boat Deck

Hole for Mast - Large

#1 Housing

Mast Hole

Mast Hole

Completed Hull

122

This plate shows the general procedure for constructing and setting into place multiple decks and their respective housings.

Complete the hull and set in position the necessary small deck fixtures of the main and fore decks. Anchors and anchor chains should show.

The next step is to lay out the bulwarks in three pieces; use cardboard, and make sure all measurements are correct. Cut out the windows, and place film behind them if you wish. These bulwarks can be cemented into place now, or left until all other pieces are assembled.

The housings between decks can be made from solid pieces of wood for small models, or from cardboard strips set on edge (use white or light cardboard). Lay out the housings in long strips as for smaller cabins or deckhouses, with end tabs for gluing. Draw the doors, windows, and any other details necessary. Score and fold corners; glue and assemble the housing in the proper place. Lay out the deck for this housing so that it extends slightly fore and aft, and glue into place. For additional housings and decks, proceed as above.

The masts are not "stepped" until the final deck is in place. Glue the mast bases and insert carefully down through the successive openings into the hull. Funnels and vents are mounted on the final deck. The funnels are easily made from thin cardboard glued into shape with tabs. Masts, and sometimes vents, should be given footings of paper bands for trim.

After all these pieces have been assembled, the lifeboats and their cradles, or chocks (not the same chocks we have described previously), can be set into place. Install davits next. Final touches are the stays for funnels and masts, the wireless antenna, and the necessary painting. Keep in mind that all cardboard and wood pieces should be shellacked before painting.

OIL TANKER.

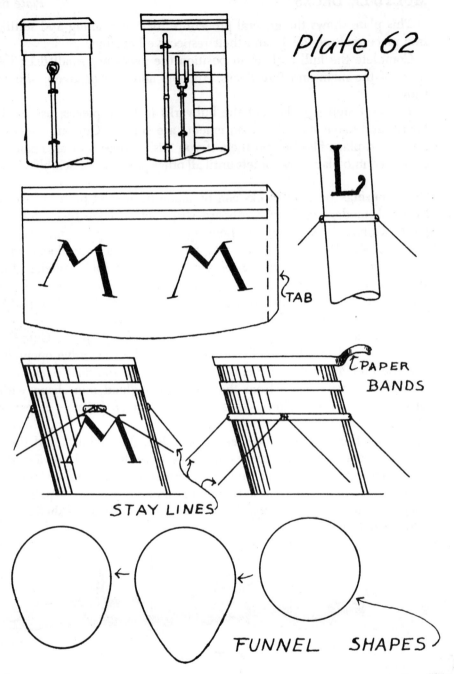

Plate 62

TAB

L

M M

PAPER BANDS

STAY LINES

FUNNEL SHAPES

124

Ships with multiple decks usually are equipped with two or more funnels having a slight rake aft.

Miniature reproductions are very easy to make. Use pliable cardboard and make a layout of the funnel with a generous tab at one side. Draw on the necessary insignia or emblem and trim called for in the plans; the coloring can be left until later. Roll the cardboard into a cylinder, glue tab, and hold in place with pinch cocks. When dry, press into egg or pear shape if the ship design calls for such. Use paper bands for trim. Pierce or drill small holes for stays; these stays can be of thread or wire, knotted on the inside of the funnel. These funnels can also be formed from ready-made cardboard cylinders if you can find any small enough—druggists' tubes, etc.

Some funnels have exterior fixtures and fittings attached; such as whistles, horns, perpendicular ladders, steam outlets, loudspeakers, etc. These can be cemented directly to the funnel. Some funnels, particularly on Navy vessels, have grills spread across the top.

Detail—U.S.S. *Missouri*. Battleship, 45,000 class. Starboard side, looking to port. (Courtesy Gibbs & Cox Inc. of New York.)

125

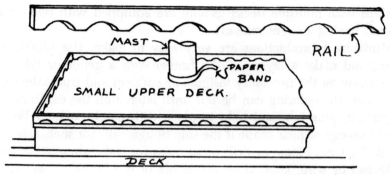

MAST

RAIL

PAPER BAND

SMALL UPPER DECK.

DECK

Plate 63

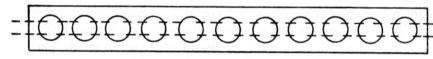

CUT ON BROKEN LINES – SMALL RAILS.

ANOTHER SMALL RAIL

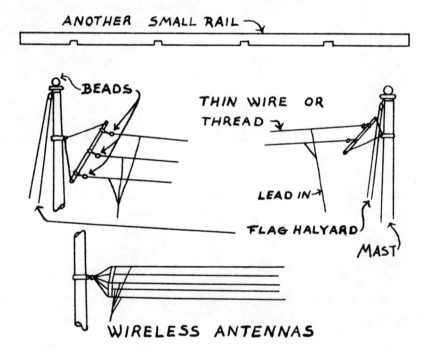

BEADS

THIN WIRE OR THREAD

LEAD IN

FLAG HALYARD

MAST

WIRELESS ANTENNAS

SMALL DECK RAILINGS *Plate 63*

Small upper-deck railings can be made from thin cardboard strips. Punch equally-spaced holes along a center line of each strip, then set a ruler on the holes so that the holes show only small arcs along the top; cut through the cardboard divisions. Repeat on the opposite side, so that you have two rail strips. Glue into place along an upper deck— the shallow arcs will simulate drainage outlets (for rain and spray). One can also use solid cardboard rails with small rectangular drainage openings.

WIRELESS ANTENNAS *Plate 63*

Wireless antennas vary only slightly in pattern. These, too, are easy to make for models. An antenna may have only one wire with an insulator at each end; or two to four wires whose insulators are attached to small horizontal crosspieces which in turn are secured to the masts. There is also a circular type of antenna whose several wires pass over vertical hoops to terminate in common insulators fastened to the masts. Every antenna has a lead-in wire—a single wire attached to a cabin, or the bridge, and leading up to the antenna, where it branches into a lead for each wire. Thread can be used for all of these wires, or very fine copper wire. Beads make convincing insulators; bamboo splinters are good for crossbars, and the end hoops can be made of cardboard or any such light material.

HARBOR TUGBOAT.

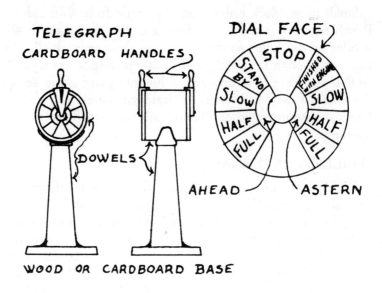

TELEGRAPH

CARDBOARD HANDLES

DIAL FACE

STOP

STAND BY

FINISHED WITH ENGINE

SLOW

SLOW

HALF

HALF

FULL

FULL

DOWELS

AHEAD

ASTERN

WOOD OR CARDBOARD BASE

Plate 64

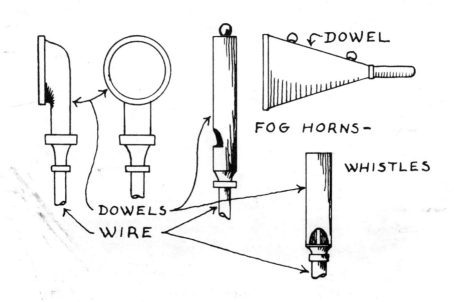

DOWEL

FOG HORNS-

WHISTLES

DOWELS

WIRE

BRIDGE TELEGRAPHS *Plate 64*

Very small telegraphs can be simulated by combining a slightly shaped dowel, such as a matchstick, with two bamboo splinters to represent handles. For larger fixtures, proceed much the same as for searchlights, using small dowels for both head and pedestal. The head, in this case, is double-faced; each face, or dial, topped with a control handle, which on the actual instrument slides around to communicate directions or signals from the captain or the pilot to the engine room. This mechanism need not be movable for models. Cut two very narrow V's of cardboard and glue to the top of each face; top with handles—these can be paper-covered bamboo strips. If the face, or dial, is large enough in scale to permit detail, the illustration can be consulted for correct divisions; ink in on white cardboard. If small, glue white disk in place and mark only division lines. The pedestal should stand on a circular base, which can be of wood or cardboard.

FOG HORNS AND WHISTLES *Plate 64*

All ships are equipped with horns or other sound devices for signaling. In foggy weather especially, these give vigorous service. "Rules of the Road at Sea" in marine handbooks, etc., has been mentioned as an interesting source of information about ships' lights; the rules concerning ships' sound signals are interesting too, and well worth looking up.

Horns and whistles are easily simulated for ship models; they are mounted on pipes attached to the funnels, vertical walls, or some other part of the superstructure. Wire can be used to represent pipes. Some horns look like miniature funnel ventilators; they can be shaped from matchstick dowels unless scale permits larger ones, in which case larger dowels, small blocks of wood, or plastic wood can be used.

Whistles are easily made from matchstick dowels. Cut the length required, shape the base slightly, and cut out a small arched niche near the base. Glue a very small bead to the top of the cylinder.

Small horns operated by lung power—they are like megaphones with a whistle at the end—should be omitted from models except for the good-sized ones of whaling boats, dories or other small boats which require this particular piece of equipment. One can be made from cardboard or shaped from a dowel. The small loops for hanging the horn can be made from thin wire, twisted once or twice, and cemented into pierced holes.

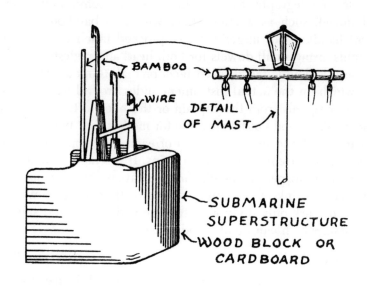

BAMBOO

WIRE

DETAIL OF MAST

SUBMARINE SUPERSTRUCTURE

WOOD BLOCK OR CARDBOARD

Plate 65

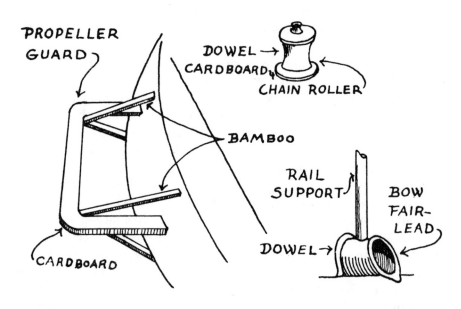

PROPELLER GUARD

DOWEL

CARDBOARD

CHAIN ROLLER

BAMBOO

RAIL SUPPORT

BOW FAIR-LEAD

DOWEL

CARDBOARD

The small amount of superstructure necessary for submarines is simple and easily constructed. Here you can almost go the limit in streamlining. Everywhere necessary, as around the superstructure, round off sharp edges slightly, and fill in angular intersections with plastic wood to give a slight curve.

A superstructure for a small model can be made in one piece from a small block of wood, shaped slightly and ¾ of its top area hollowed out. Larger edifices can be built out of cardboard. (No instructions are given—by now you probably can make cardboard layouts with your eyes shut.)

The mast and periscopes (there are generally two) can be made from small dowels or pieces of bamboo. The periscopes are cemented into rather sturdy bases, which in turn are cemented within the hollowed-out area.

The mast, which is topped by a lantern-type light fixture, is also mounted within this area. The small crosspiece can be fitted with one or two blocks at each side, and very fine copper wire or thread run through them to serve as pennant halyards.

The searchlight, a small, shaped piece of wood with a paper-band edge (if large enough) can be mounted on a bent wire arm. Any other small fixtures necessary—hatches, gratings and miscellaneous small trim—can be inked or painted on. Submarine deck fixtures are few; your working drawings will probably give the necessary details for these.

Propeller guards can be constructed of cardboard, the braces of bamboo strips. Cement directly to the hull. The bow fair-lead can be made from a small dowel piece slanting at the forward end. Drill a hole horizontally, large enough for a light chain to pass through. Cement a rail support to the top center. This fair-lead can also be made of cardboard rolled into a short cylinder, with paper-band trimming run around the open ends. Chain rollers, described in detail on page 97, are made from small dowel pieces, shaped and mounted on cardboard bases.

Your sub may call for a deck gun or two—one forward, and one aft of the superstructure. (*For guns, see* PLATE *128, page 219.*)

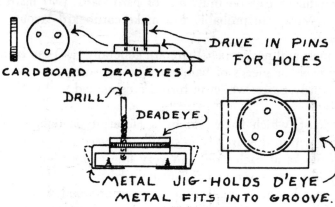

CARDBOARD DEADEYES

DRIVE IN PINS FOR HOLES

DRILL

DEADEYE

METAL JIG-HOLDS D'EYE
METAL FITS INTO GROOVE.

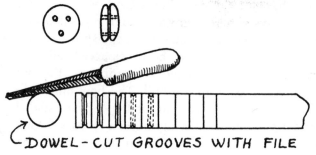

DOWEL—CUT GROOVES WITH FILE

CUT OFF

JIG FOR DEADEYES
MITER BOX-CUT WITH HACKSAW

Plate 66

For very small ship models, the deadeyes combined with the rigging would be so tiny reduced to scale that it would be almost impossible to make them in any detail. Small beads can be used satisfactorily in this case. Deadeyes for larger models can be made, as illustrated, of wood or cardboard, or shaped of plastic wood.

For cardboard deadeyes, use a paper punch which cuts out the size disk you want; punch out several extras, because some will be ruined in the process of piercing the holes for the ropes; use common pins to pierce these holes.

For wooden deadeyes, mark off individually on a dowel of the correct size and file a groove around each. There are two ways of drilling the holes; first, bore the three holes into the dowel as far as the drill will permit; then, using a small miter box jig, cut off separate deadeyes up to that point. Repeat process until all are finished. The second method is to cut all individual deadeyes from the dowel, hold in a jig, as pictured, and drill holes in each. Sandpaper the angular edges so the entire deadeye has a rounded appearance on both sides. The first method is the better one; but if the drill is not held absolutely straight, several 'eyes will be ruined in the process.

If you shape them from plastic wood, try to get them uniform in size. Roll a small amount of the paste between the fingers; then squeeze slightly to give flattish front and back surfaces. While still soft, penetrate with three pins and allow to dry. After round-shaping, remove pins, then file or sandpaper off any roughness around the holes. Hold between the fingers and file a groove around the edge of each deadeye.

To secure deadeyes to shrouds and stays, form a tight-fitting loop of a shroud or stay around each; then "seize" it—in nautical terms that means fasten the rope back upon itself with several lashings of cord.

To attach and fit chains, run a wire around the groove and twist tightly against deadeye; continue twisting to form a chain, or strap. It can be used this way; but better yet, solder the twisted piece and then flatten it into a strap on your anvil. Drill a couple of holes through it for bolting to the hull. Another method is to run a chain link, resembling a shackle, around the groove, then connect it to a narrow strap of tin which has the upper end turned over. Run a pin through the shackle eyes and the tin "over-turn," cut off excess pin and clinch, or drop a bit of solder on it. Chain can also be used.

133

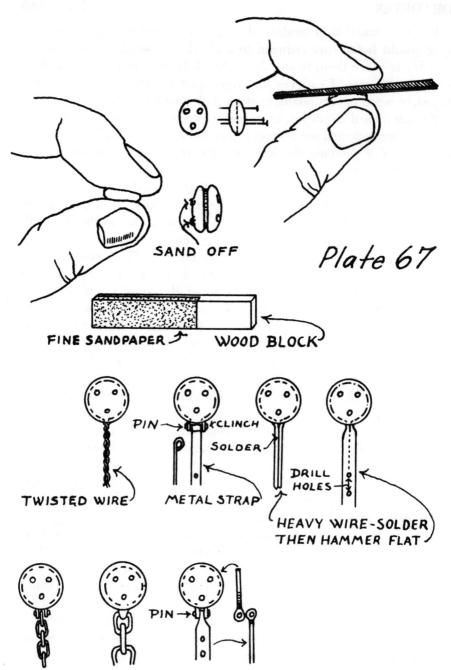

SAND OFF

Plate 67

FINE SANDPAPER → WOOD BLOCK

TWISTED WIRE

PIN → CLINCH
SOLDER
METAL STRAP

DRILL HOLES

HEAVY WIRE-SOLDER
THEN HAMMER FLAT

PIN →

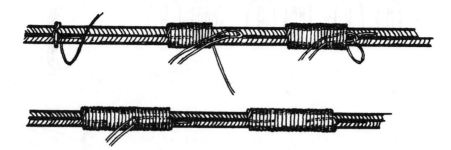

HOW TO SERVE OR SEIZE ROPES

LANYARDS BETWEEN DEADEYES

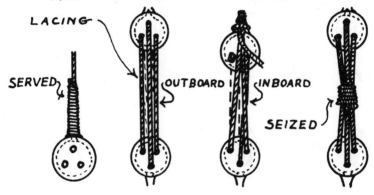

LACING

SERVED

OUTBOARD   INBOARD

SEIZED

Plate 68

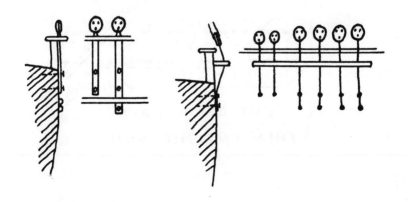

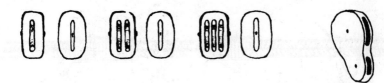

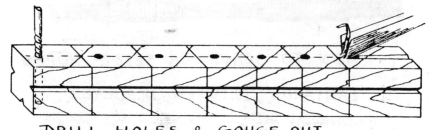

DRILL HOLES & GOUGE OUT

Plate 69

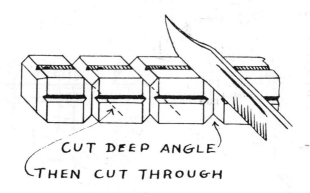

CUT DEEP ANGLE

THEN CUT THROUGH

Single and double blocks will be the ones most often used for your model fittings, although there may be occasional calls for triples. For extremely small blocks, resort to the use of beads, as for deadeyes; otherwise, any of them can be made from wood, metal, or plastic wood.

Several blocks can be cut from one long piece of wood which has the same thickness as that of the particular kind required—single and double blocks cannot be cut from the same piece. For single blocks, space, mark and drill holes directly on the center line as shown in the illustration; when all holes have been drilled, gouge shallow grooves *with the grain* lengthwise on the center lines of each side. Make sharp, clean angle-cuts at the block divisions, then cut through to separate the individual pieces. For double blocks, drill the holes close together, one on each side of the center line. For triples, drill a center hole and one on each side. Shape into blocks and finish by sandpapering until smooth.

Cigarette tin is good material from which to cut the sheave housings for metal blocks. A double block needs only a single housing, but two are necessary for triples. Drill holes in each housing plate to receive the pin, or axle, on which the sheaves are to revolve; additional holes can be drilled, if you wish, for brace rods or pins. The connecting link of the outer housing (*see illustration*) should be long enough to be neatly crimped and drilled through so the block can be fastened. An inner housing should be bent to shape and soldered at the top to the outer one, for triple blocks. The sheaves, or wheels, for these metal housings can be cut from a dowel having the right diameter. Mark the sheave divisions, file a slight groove around each individual wheel, and cut off. Drill center holes and mount within the housings. Snip off excess axle material outside of housing and clinch or solder.

To make simulated blocks from plastic wood, roll a sufficient amount of paste for each between the fingers—a little practice is necessary to judge the right amount. Squeeze slightly into flattened pellet shape; penetrate with two pins, one through the flat side near the top (for fastening); the other edgewise to make the sheave hole. Double blocks, of course, need *two* edgewise pins, and so on. If you wish to file a groove for the block strap on each flat side, eliminate the side pin-hole. Set aside to dry.

Fine twisted wire can be used to rig the blocks with straps and eyes, either at top or bottom. Make a small loop or eye by folding the wire on itself and giving it a full-turn twist. Solder wire when finished.   *137*

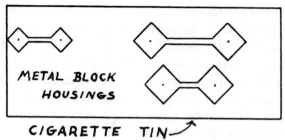

METAL BLOCK
HOUSINGS

CIGARETTE TIN

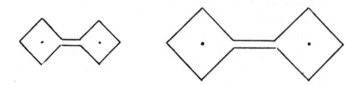

METAL BLOCKS — USE TIN

Plate 70

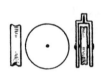

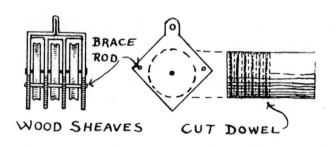

BRACE
ROD

WOOD SHEAVES   CUT DOWEL

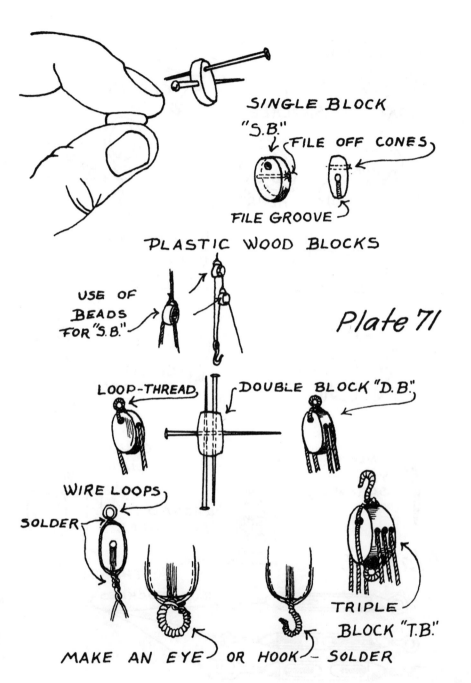

SINGLE BLOCK
"S.B."

FILE OFF CONES

FILE GROOVE

PLASTIC WOOD BLOCKS

USE OF BEADS FOR "S.B."

LOOP-THREAD

DOUBLE BLOCK "D.B."

WIRE LOOPS

SOLDER

Plate 71

TRIPLE BLOCK "T.B."

MAKE AN EYE OR HOOK — SOLDER

139

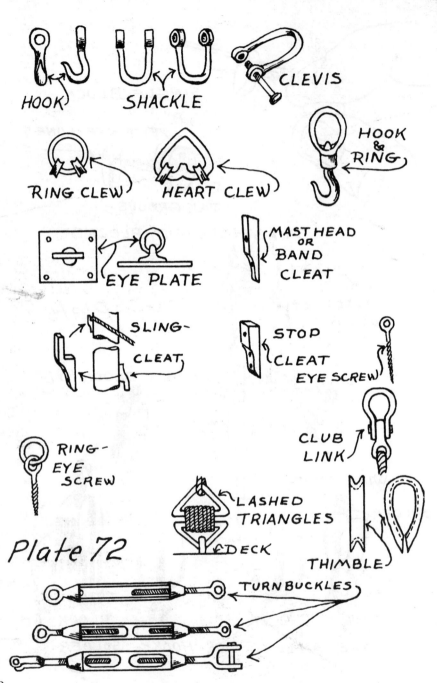

HOOK SHACKLE CLEVIS

RING CLEW HEART CLEW HOOK & RING

EYE PLATE MAST HEAD OR BAND CLEAT

SLING CLEAT STOP CLEAT EYE SCREW

RING EYE SCREW CLUB LINK

LASHED TRIANGLES DECK THIMBLE

Plate 72

TURNBUCKLES

140

Shackles are so necessary for ship fittings and fastenings that for these purposes they probably come next in importance after deadeyes and blocks. The dime-store jewelry counter is a bonanza for such fittings. Look for pieces that have the right kind of links for your purpose; very likely you will need two or three sizes. Disengage the separate links and press back into shape.

Good *hooks* can be made from half shackles or links, or from loops snipped off and shaped with the hook parts filed slightly to form points.

A *clevis* can be formed from a long-shanked shackle.

Ring clews and *heart clews* can also be tracked down to the jewelry counter, or can be formed from pieces of wire, soldered at the joints. The thimbles combined with these will have to be left out on small models.

A *hook-and-ring*—a swivel fitting—will have to be simulated. Fold a piece of fine wire and twist to form an eye, or loop, and a hook. Then solder.

Stop cleats and *sling cleats* can be shaped from wood and then glued into place.

To make *eye screws,* or eye screws with rings, use twisted wire to form a loop for eyes. Use a chain-link ring for the eye-screw ring, run a wire through it and twist the ends together tightly. Cut off excess wire after reaching the required screw length; solder the twisted wire. To fasten, drill or pierce a hole and cement the twisted wire into place.

An *eye plate* can be made from a small square or rectangle of tin. Pierce corner holes for fastening to deck; also pierce a center hole to admit a ring-eye screw. Solder underneath the plate.

Triangles can be formed from reshaped ring links.

For a *club link*, combine a link shackle with another link which has been twisted into two loops—at right angles to each other. A clinched or soldered pin will hold the two together.

Thimbles will have to be omitted from very small models. For large models with heavy and workable gear they can be shaped from tin.

Small, practical *turnbuckles* can be purchased for use on larger models, but dummy turnbuckles will have to be used for the smaller ships. To make them use wire correct in scale; cut the length wanted, allowing enough for an eye at each end. Apply enough solder to the middle portion to give a turnbuckle appearance.

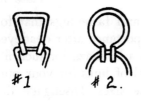

#1   # 2.

DEVIL'S CLAW

CHAINS & LINKS

Plate 73

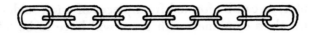

Any and all kinds of chain of any and all lengths hold promising possibilities for the model builder. At this point I seem to hear the model builder's family interrupt cynically, "What doesn't?" But the artist (or something) in him sends him serenely along on his mission of salvaging treasures from the junk heap.

To get back to the subject of chains: extremely fine ones, having about 32 links to the inch, are perfect for the rigging of small models. Heavier pieces can be used for any of the bowsprit stays—especially bob-stays—where chain is called for instead of cable or rope. Of all model rigging the anchor chain makes use of the heaviest pieces.

Ladder chains are just right for shackles and other similar fittings. These may have round or angular links, as shown in PLATE 73, #1 & #2. Pry the loops open to disengage the individual links; shape the links to the form you desire, then close the loops; they will become the eyes of that particular fitting.

A devil's claw can be formed from a ring link combined with part of another link which has been shaped into a hook. The claws used on models need not have two prongs; one is sufficient. They are used to hold chains, especially the anchor chain, fast.

MISCELLANEOUS ODDS AND ENDS. Dressmakers' hooks and eyes, when in scale, also make useful fittings; the eyes can be used for shackles and other fittings. The hooks are virtually indispensable to the builders of practicable model sailboats; sewn to the sail, they make it easier to "bend" them to the various stays. They can be used also for trusses, straps, futtock shrouds, etc. But the worker will certainly discover ingenious uses himself for this commonplace metal fitting.

Salvage old shoe eyes; they are potential portholes, hawse openings, deck openings, small life preservers, etc. Either cut off the riveted ends or straighten them out on the anvil, using a metal rod to penetrate the eye.

Eyebolts have many uses: as deck fittings; as ring bolts (when attached to rings); penetrated by jack stays they are used on the yards; they may also be attached to shackles or clevises. To make an eyebolt take a piece of wire and, with a pair of pliers, bend it around a pointed metal fid. Cut off excess pin or wire on an angle.

143

USES FOR HOOKS-EYES

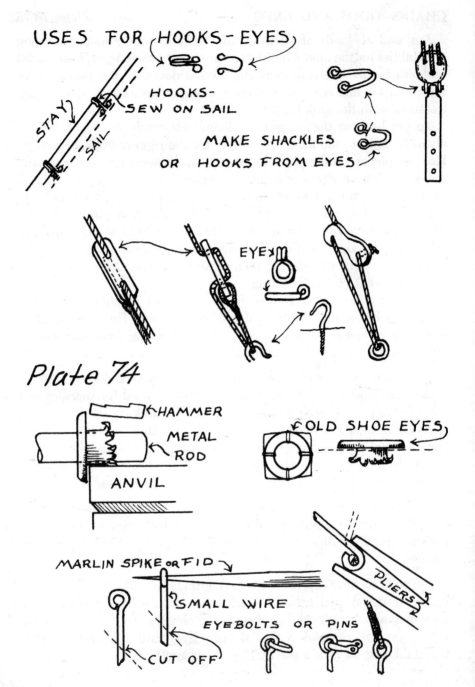

HOOKS—
SEW ON SAIL

STAY

SAIL

MAKE SHACKLES
OR HOOKS FROM EYES

EYE

Plate 74

HAMMER

METAL
ROD

ANVIL

OLD SHOE EYES

MARLIN SPIKE or FID

SMALL WIRE
EYEBOLTS OR PINS

PLIERS

CUT OFF

The interesting gear and fittings for early period ships should present no unreasonable difficulties. *Hearts* (heart-shaped blocks without sheaves) were used a great deal. Lanyards were reeved through them to extend the stays. *Bullet blocks* were small, ovoid pieces of wood with slits cut in the center for the passage of a rope. *Long blocks* and *sister blocks* were simple double-sheaved blocks, built in tandem-style, one above the other. They are still used, although only in rare instances. The *crow's foot* is probably the most intriguing piece of the lot. It is a long narrow, self-adjusting block which contains no sheaves, but has several holes drilled through it through which ropes are passed to be fastened to spars. All of these fittings are made of wood; the general instructions for constructing blocks can be observed here.

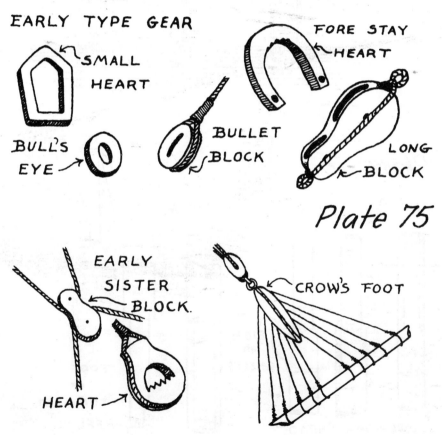

EARLY TYPE GEAR

SMALL HEART

BULL'S EYE

BULLET BLOCK

FORE STAY HEART

LONG BLOCK

Plate 75

EARLY SISTER BLOCK.

HEART

CROW'S FOOT

145

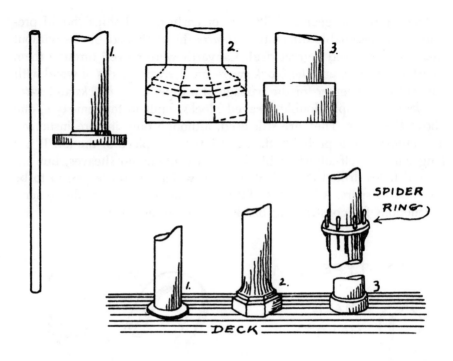

SPIDER RING

DECK

Plate 76

BALL
TRUCK
POLE

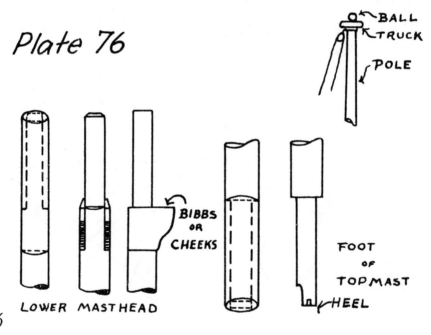

BIBBS
OR
CHEEKS

FOOT
OF
TOPMAST

HEEL

LOWER MASTHEAD

When anyone refers to the "rake" of a ship's masts (or funnels) he is speaking of their relative slope or inclination from the perpendicular position. There was a time when ships' masts were heavy and clumsy, and stood bolt upright; but gradual changes and improvements in ship design called for corresponding changes in masts and rigging as well. The trim of the masts, that is, the angle of the rake, contributes strongly to a ship's characteristics.

On ships with one or more masts, the masts usually have a slight rake aft. A conspicuous exception to this rule is the Arab dhow, which for centuries has been scurrying around on the Indian Ocean with its one extreme forward-raked mast, lateen sail, high poop deck, open waist and long over-hung bow.

Long narrow hulls and high, heavily aft-raked masts are characteristic of the swift Clipper sailing vessels. Due to the clever and sound design of ship and rigging, many of these ships set world's records for speed during the early China tea trade.

LOWER MAST. Masts are stepped, or fitted, into the solid block hull very easily. Drill a hole about 1″ deep into the hull at the angle you want the mast to have. For a hollow-hulled model a small block of wood, drilled to admit the mast, should be cemented into place before the deck is laid, and an opening cut into the deck for it. Cut a dowel for the lower mast and step it into its base *but do not glue*, until all masts are completed. Wrap the pieces, as they are completed, into separate pieces of tissue paper: foremast, mainmast, and mizzenmast parcels.

Run a footing around the base of the mast at the deck line. On some ships this base is extremely simple, and for models can be made with a couple of turns of glued paper strips, or from a plain metal washer. On others (historic ships of lavish eras) the bases are almost as ornate and elaborate as though footing temple or cathedral pillars. Carved decorative segments can be wedged together to encircle the mast base of such a model.

Taper the mast slightly toward the top. Measure and mark the correct length of it from the deck to the top of the lower cap. From this point downward to the top of the bibbs, the lower mast in most cases has to be cut square; from here to the bottom of the bibbs, continue the flat surfaces on two sides only. These bibbs—or cheeks, as they are also

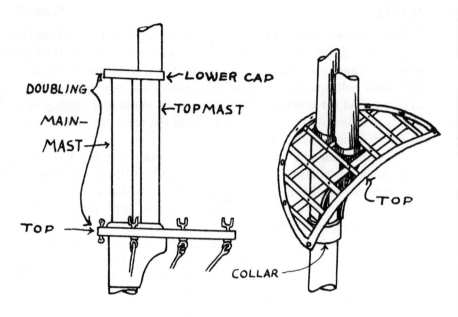

DOUBLING

MAIN-MAST

TOP

LOWER CAP

TOPMAST

TOP

COLLAR

Plate 77

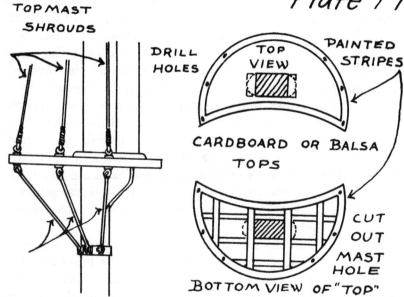

TOPMAST SHROUDS

DRILL HOLES

LOWER FUTTOCK SHROUDS

TOP VIEW

PAINTED STRIPES

CARDBOARD OR BALSA TOPS

CUT OUT MAST HOLE

BOTTOM VIEW OF "TOP"

called—are side pieces of timber which are bolted to the mast to support trestletrees. Make them of two thin pieces of wood (two bibbs for each lower mast); then fit and cement to the flat surfaces provided for them. Shape when dry.

The trestletrees are pieces of wood fixed horizontally fore and aft to the lower and topmasts. They can be fitted next to the mast on the bibbs, or without the bibbs. (The bibbs are omitted on some ships.)

Tops and Caps. Tops are small platforms, usually semicircular, surrounding the upper ends, or the heads, of the lower masts. On some models, the squared top of the lower masthead will penetrate a solid top; on others the top is built around the mast. Some of them are made

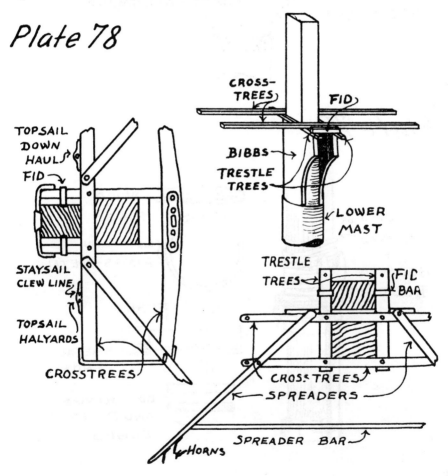

Plate 78

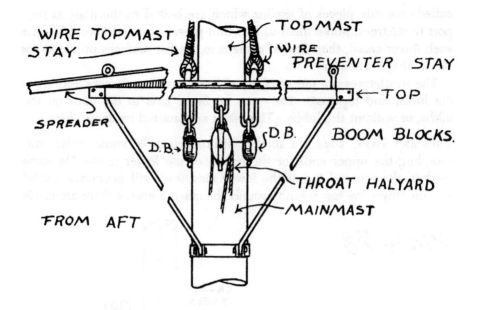

WIRE TOPMAST STAY

TOPMAST

WIRE PREVENTER STAY

SPREADER

TOP

BOOM BLOCKS.

D.B.

D.B.

THROAT HALYARD

MAINMAST

FROM AFT

Plate 79

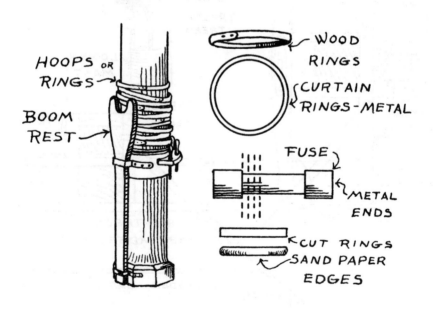

HOOPS or RINGS

BOOM REST

WOOD RINGS

CURTAIN RINGS-METAL

FUSE

METAL ENDS

CUT RINGS

SAND PAPER EDGES

of frame and latticework of metal or wood. As already explained, the bibbs and trestletrees form the base for the top. Two or more other pieces of wood or metal are fastened to the trestletrees at right angles; these are called crosstrees and they help to give greater spread to the upper rigging.

Tops have the important function of forming a base or footing for the topmast; they also give the upper rigging (shrouds) wider spread. These shrouds are sometimes fastened to eyebolts penetrating the top, or to deadeyes; the lower deadeyes lead through or over the top and are part of the lower futtock shrouds that form the anchorages for the topmast rigging. In very early ships, the tops were used as look-out stations; they were round platforms with rather high sides which resembled huge baskets, and must have been the origin for the term "crow's nest."

For the average model, attach the bibbs, glue thin strips of wood or cardboard in place to represent crosstrees and framework, and use a solid platform piece for the top, with a rectangular hole cut for the penetration of the lower mast. This hole should fit the mast snugly fore and aft, and leave openings at port and starboard wide enough for the upper ends of the lower rigging. Bolsters can be added to models large enough to permit them. They are quarter-round strips of soft wood placed on the trestletrees, or top, against the mast, and are put there for the shrouds to rest on and thus prevent chafing.

At the extreme top of the masthead, another horizontal piece of wood, called a cap (in this case, the lower cap) is fitted. This piece has two holes cut in it, one to fit the top of the lower mast, the other for the topmast to penetrate. The cap should fit the masthead snugly; if the masthead is square, cut both holes square. Do not glue either top or cap into place yet.

In many small ships and most fishing vessels, the crosstrees resting on the trestletrees take the place of tops. The crosstrees are long enough to allow for greater spread of the topmast rigging. Fastened to the crosstrees and running aft and outward are two strips of wood or metal, called spreaders. These "arms" give spread to the backstays and manage to hold them apart.

TOPMASTS. The topmast is the second mast from the deck—the one directly above the lower mast. The foot of it penetrates the lower cap, and rests on the top, with the cut and shaped heel fitting into a square

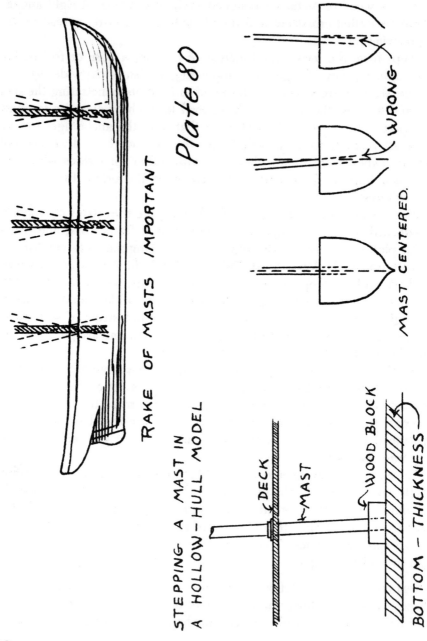

RAKE OF MASTS IMPORTANT

Plate 80

WRONG

WRONG

MAST CENTERED.

STEPPING A MAST IN
A HOLLOW-HULL MODEL

DECK

MAST

WOOD BLOCK

BOTTOM-THICKNESS

bar of wood or metal, called a fid. This section between cap and platform, where the lower mast and topmast overlap, is called the lower doubling. Some doublings have rigging gear between the two points so that weight and strain are received mainly by the lower mast.

The head of the topmast, in order that the topmast cap, trestletrees and crosstrees should fit properly, will have to be squared as was the lower mast. Proceed with all these fittings as before; also attach spreaders to crosstrees. Do not glue this mast into place until lower rigging has been placed.

TopgallanT Masts. Situated above the topmast is the topgallant mast. The foot of it penetrates the topmast cap and the heel is fitted into a fid, or the mast may have a hole drilled through the heel and be bolted to the trestletrees. The topgallant mast is a single pole subdivided into topgallant, royal and skysail masts, terminating in a mushroom-shaped cap at the summit, called the truck. This piece can be topped with a ball. The section between topgallant and royal masts is equipped with projections called "hounds" to support shrouds and backstay rigging. (See Plate 85, page 162.)

You may have noticed that some of the illustrations picture the head of the lower mast and the foot of the topmast as round, instead of square, at the doublings; in some cases one is square—generally the lower—and the other round. This is true especially of fishermen's ships. and other vessels of schooner rig.

Final Step. The final stage is to set the lower masts permanently; this must be done before any rigging is attached. Be sure that they are centered and that the angle of rake is correct. Cement into place and check quickly and critically before it dries.

If your model is a schooner, or a ship with fore-and-aft rigging on one or more masts, the lower masts will have to be encircled with several hoops for the sails; these must be passed down in place over the boom fastening before any of the upper rigging is made fast. Small metal curtain rings, or bamboo splinters with the overlapped ends whipped together, make good hoops. The fiber body from an electrical cartridge fuse is also excellent for hoop material, if the size is correct. These fuses come in several different sizes. Cut off the metal ends and save them for some other purpose. Mark and saw off as many rings as possible from the fuse, sandpapering the angular edges. These fuses should be cut in a small mitre jig, because the rings should be quite thin.

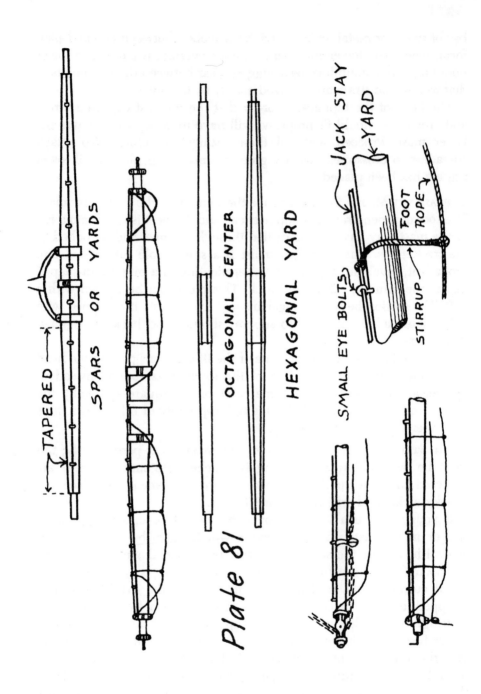

TAPERED

SPARS OR YARDS

OCTAGONAL CENTER

HEXAGONAL YARD

JACK STAY

YARD

FOOT ROPE

SMALL EYE BOLTS

STIRRUP

Plate 81

The slender spars slung crosswise from a mast for the purpose of supporting sails are called yards. To make them, use wooden dowels as near the actual thickness of the yards as possible; cut each a trifle longer than the exact finished length is to be. When thickness is correct, mark off a center section to be fitted with sling and truss bands. From here taper the yards evenly towards the ends, at first with small plane or knife, working with the grain; finish shaping by sandpapering. Then cut each the exact length required, including the end projections (the yardarms) if your model is large enough to permit this detail work.

Although most yards are cylindrical throughout, some have hexagonal- or octagonal-shaped center sections; on some rare occasions, a model calls for yards that are octagonal or hexagonal the entire length. These should be shaped with a small plane—the center section first—then tapering to the yardarms.

Yards support a good deal of running rigging and consequently need plenty of fittings. A row of eyebolts is fastened to the top of each yard, and a rod, strong rope, or wire run through and fastened to ferrules at each yardarm. This is called a jackstay; the head of the sail is fastened to it. Several stirrups—about three or four to each side of the center bands—are secured to the jackstay or to the jackstay eyebolts. These have thimbles in the lower loops to support foot ropes upon which the sailors can stand while reefing or furling sails. Inboard, these foot ropes are generally fastened to jackstay eyebolts on the inner side of the truss band, the outer end to ferrules bordering the yardarm, or by a loop fitted over the yardarm. Near the outboard end of some of the yards (this is in full-rigged ships only), a boom iron, or quarter iron, is fitted for the boom of the studding sail.

Each yardarm is equipped with another ferrule near the outer tip, and also with a sheet block, which fits between the two ferrules. These three fittings are sometimes combined into a single fitting. The very end of the yardarm is fitted with a pacific iron (a fitting through which the boom of the studding sail passes). Frequently these fittings are driven into the ends of the yardarms. (*See* PLATE *104, page 186, on Studding Sails, also* PLATE *184, on Square Sails.*)

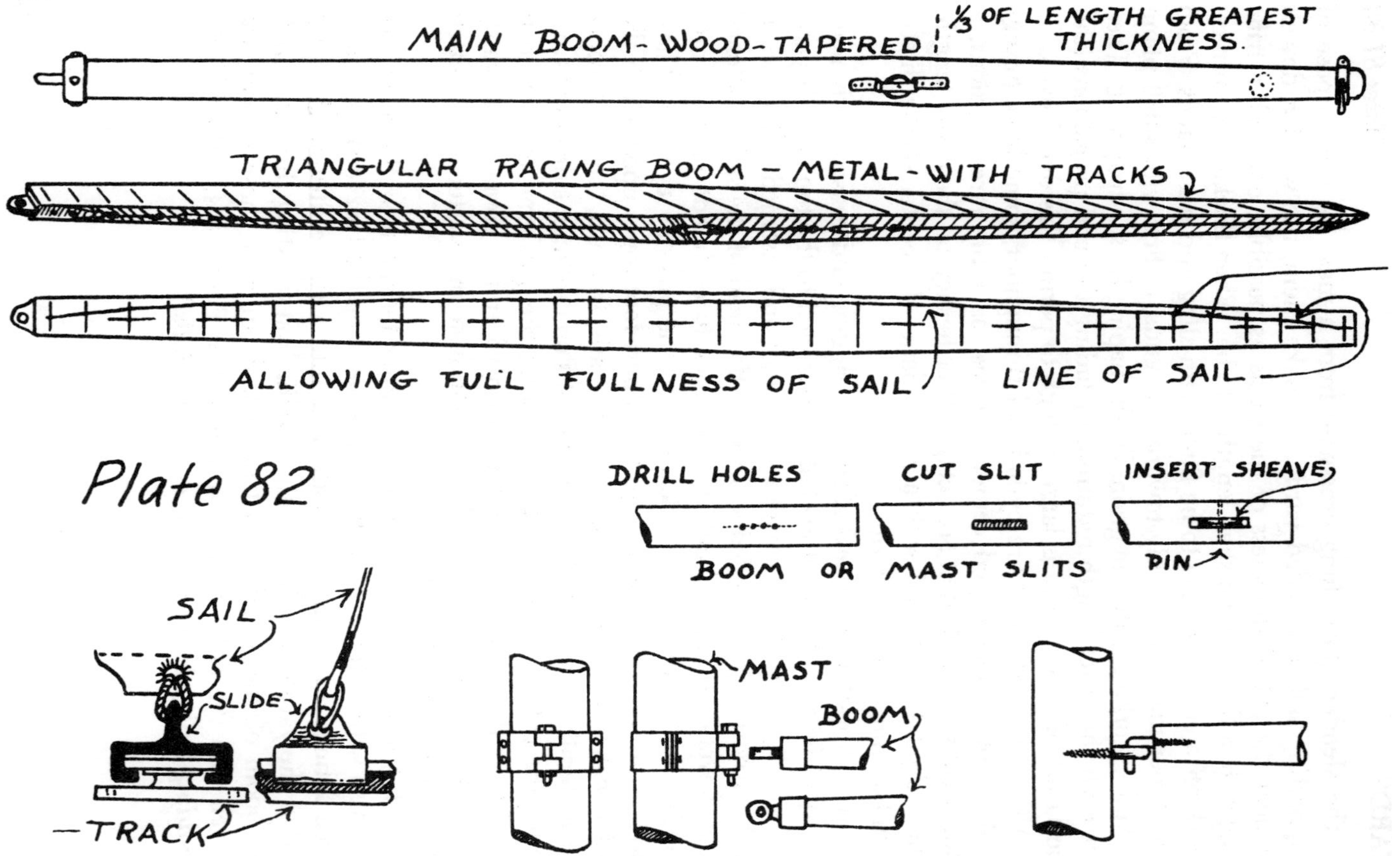

MAIN BOOM ~ WOOD ~ TAPERED. ⅓ OF LENGTH GREATEST THICKNESS.

TRIANGULAR RACING BOOM ~ METAL ~ WITH TRACKS.

ALLOWING FULL FULLNESS OF SAIL. LINE OF SAIL.

INSERT SHEAVE.

PIN.

CUT SLIT.

DRILL HOLES.

BOOM OR MAST SLITS.

MAST.

BOOM.

Plate 82

SAIL.

SLIDE.

TRACK.

156

Booms and Gaffs. A boom is a spar or pole which secures and extends the foot, or base, of a sail. Small booms are so easy to make you should have no trouble with them. The larger booms for fore-and-aft sails are fastened to the masts by swivel fittings, and vary in elevation from near the deck to head clearance level. Like yards, they are usually cylindrical; but generally they are much longer than yards. They taper gradually towards the ends from the heaviest portion—which is about ⅓ the length from the outer tip. Most often they are made from timbers, but many modern racing vessels are equipped with hollow, triangular booms of metal. One kind has slides running on a track down the length of the boom; another type has a series of short tracks and slides crossing the width of the boom, allowing greater fullness to the sail.

Select a dowel of the correct thickness for your boom and taper as required. If the model plan calls for a workable sheave in the outer end, drill a few small holes; then cut through them until you have a space to encompass the sheave. Drill a small lateral hole for the sheave pin, or pivot.

A gaff is a spar branching out from the mast which supports and extends the upper edge, or head, of a trysail, or fore-and-aft sail. It tapers considerably towards the peak, or outer end. The inboard end of the gaff tapers sufficiently to conform to two prong-like arms called jaws, which are bolted to it; they also partially encircle the mast—the side-view illustrations show how this part is shaped at a slight angle to the gaff-spar. They are joined around the mast by a sliding collar fitting called a parrel, which allows the gaff to be hoisted or lowered easily.

Parrels are made from a wide range of materials: heavy wire fixed to eyebolts in the jaws; chain, covered with canvas or rubber; wood, lead, or metal rollers strung on a wire; or double or triple thicknesses of rope served into one large, even roll. A small wedge-shaped piece of wood, called the saddle, is bolted and pivoted between the jaws to make the raising and lowering of the gaff easier. This piece will be omitted from the average model. In fact, most of the details described will be simulated, and not workable. Small beads, for instance, will be best to represent parrels. Shape the jaws from pieces of wood. The outboard end of the gaff is encircled by two, three, or four bands, to which blocks are fastened. Use your own best judgment about the degree of detail in the execution. For further fittings of gaffs and booms, see rigging Plates following.

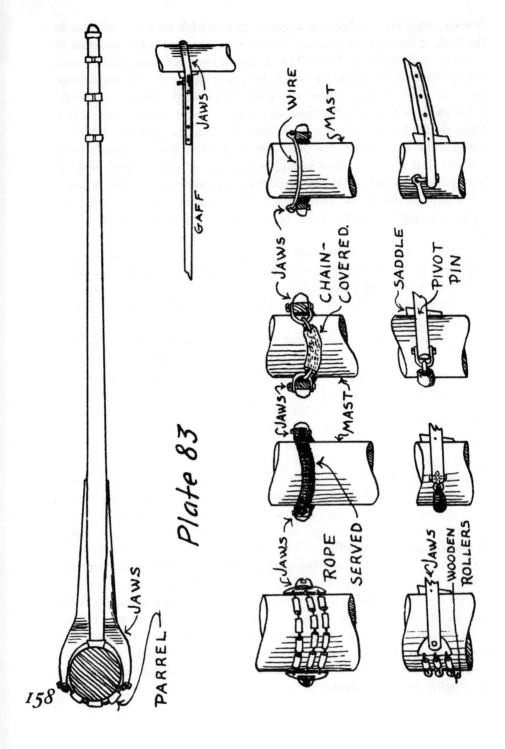

158

PARREL

JAWS

GAFF

JAWS

WIRE

MAST

JAWS

CHAIN-
COVERED.

SADDLE

PIVOT
PIN

JAWS

MAST

JAWS

ROPE
SERVED

JAWS

WOODEN
ROLLERS

JAWS

Plate 83

The U.S. brig *Lexington* was converted into a war vessel in 1775 with several other merchant ships of the same class. They were faster than or equal to anything afloat at the time. (Crabtree Collection, The Mariners' Museum, Newport News, Va.)

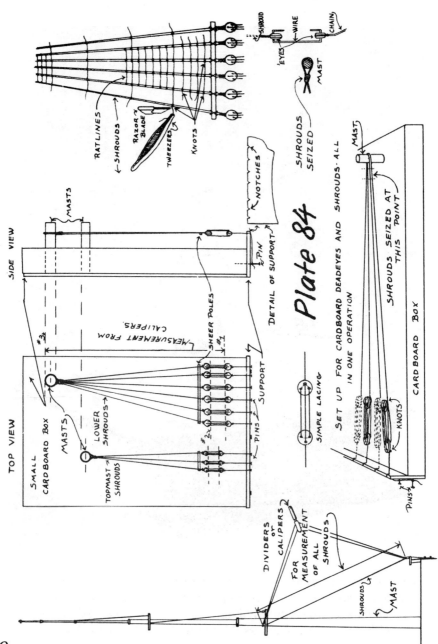

RATLINES
SHROUDS
RAZOR BLADE
TWEEZERS
KNOTS
SHROUD
EYES
WIRE
CHAIN
MAST
SHROUDS SEIZED
NOTCHES
DETAIL OF SUPPORT

MASTS
SIDE VIEW

TOP VIEW
SMALL CARD BOARD BOX
MASTS
LOWER SHROUDS
TOPMAST SHROUDS
MEASUREMENT FROM CALIPERS.
SHEER POLES
PINS
SUPPORT
#1
#2
PIN

Plate 84

SET UP FOR CARDBOARD DEADEYES AND SHROUDS · ALL IN ONE OPERATION

SIMPLE LACING

MAST
SHROUDS SEIZED AT THIS POINT
CARD BOARD BOX
KNOTS
PINS

DIVIDERS or CALIPERS
FOR MEASUREMENT OF ALL SHROUDS
SHROUDS
MAST

The preceding chapters have harped rather monotonously on the subject of scale, but in rigging, that theme is more important than ever. The thread and wire for the rigging should be selected with critical judgment.

Standing rigging, though adjustable, is permanent rigging, that is. not movable or workable in the operation of the ship. It has to stand up under excessive stress and strain. The thread, wire and chain for it should be slightly heavier than that used for running rigging. For the shrouds of average models, black or brown (preferably brown) cotton thread #8 or #10 is suitable; if the model is unusually large, use button or carpet thread. If wire is used instead of thread, use #20, #22, or #24 for medium-sized ships.

SHROUDS. Shrouds for small ships should not be assembled on the model, but separately, on a jig. A small cardboard box, laid horizontally, forms a good foundation. Cement and nail a vertical strip of heavy cardboard or thin wood along one end so that it extends above the box level to form a wall, or support. Draw a line across the box top about 1–1½" in from the support and parallel with it; this is Line #1 shown in PLATE 84, and it marks the upper limit of the chain deadeyes—the lower row. From the working drawings obtain the lacing distance between deadeyes; then draw Line #2, parallel with the first one. This line marks the lower limit of the shroud deadeyes.

With calipers or dividers measure the length of the shrouds from the opposite (port or starboard) side of the mast above the top, down to the cap rail of the bulwarks. Transfer this measurement to the box top, placing the lower caliper point to Line #1; mark the upper point, and draw the third parallel line. Below this line, and about 1" in from the side edge, cut a small hole in the box and insert a dummy mast which corresponds in shape and size to the one on the model.

Range the specified number of deadeyes on Lines #1 and 2; space them correctly and evenly. (The deadeyes for these small ships are, of course, just simulated.) The next step is to cut small notches into the support directly opposite the deadeyes; these are to guide and regulate the shroud lines. Drive corresponding pins into the support to which the shrouds can be tied.

Thread a needle with enough line for two or more pairs (a pair of shrouds consists of a double length of line which runs from the chain

161

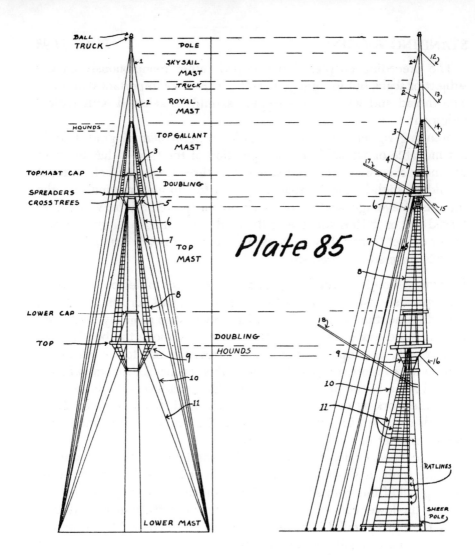

Plate 85

1- SKYSAIL BACKSTAY

2- ROYAL BACKSTAY

3- TOPGALLANT SHROUDS OR
     RIGGING

4- TOPGALLANT BACKSTAY
5- TOPGALLANT FUTTOCK SHROUDS
6- TOPMAST CAPSTAY

7- TOPMAST BACKSTAYS.
8- TOPMAST RIGGING OR SHROUDS.
9- LOWER FUTTOCK SHROUDS.

10- LOWER CAPSTAY
11- LOWER RIGGING OR SHROUDS.

12- SKYSAIL STAY
13- ROYAL STAY
        HOUNDS

14- TOPGALLANT STAY
15- TOPMAST STAYS
16- FORE - MAIN OR MIZZEN STAY
17- MIZZEN MONKEY GAFF
18- GAFF - NAMED FOR THE MAST

162

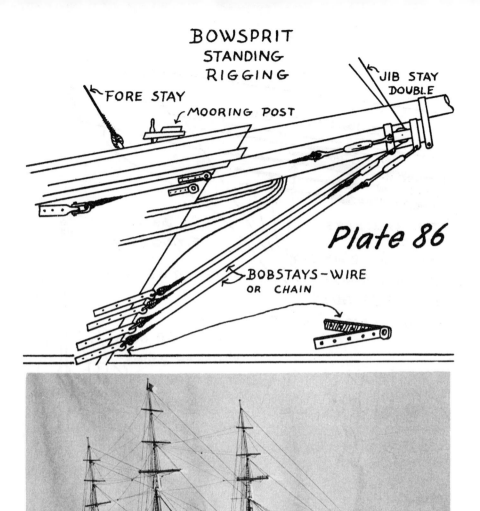

BOWSPRIT
STANDING
RIGGING

FORE STAY

MOORING POST

JIB STAY
DOUBLE

Plate 86

BOBSTAYS – WIRE
OR CHAIN

American clipper ship *Sovereign of the Seas*. Built by Donald McKay in 1852 at East Boston, Mass. Lost in the Straits of Malacca in 1859. (In the collection of The Mariners' Museum, Newport News, Va.)

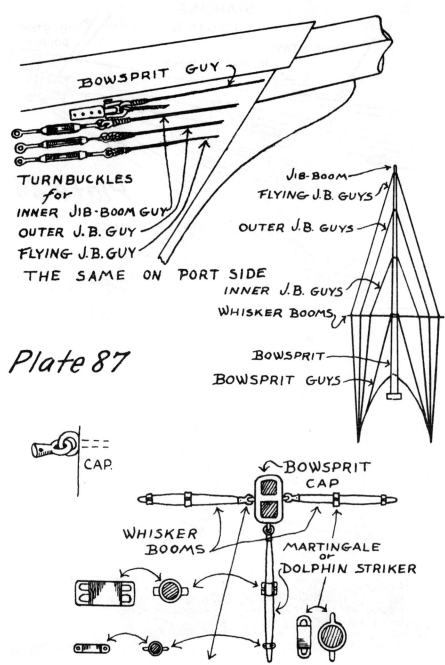

BOWSPRIT GUY

TURNBUCKLES
for
INNER JIB-BOOM GUY
OUTER J.B. GUY
FLYING J.B.GUY
THE SAME ON PORT SIDE

JIB-BOOM
FLYING J.B. GUYS
OUTER J.B. GUYS
INNER J.B. GUYS
WHISKER BOOMS
BOWSPRIT
BOWSPRIT GUYS

Plate 87

CAP.

BOWSPRIT
CAP

WHISKER
BOOMS

MARTINGALE
or
DOLPHIN STRIKER

deadeyes, up around the masthead, and back again.) Tie the end securely to the first pin, and sew the first pair of deadeyes to the shrouds. Bring the line around the mast, string another pair of deadeyes and secure to pin. Repeat the process for each pair. When the shroud assembly is completed, make a sheer pole of a strip of bamboo and tie to each shroud just above the upper row of deadeyes. Seize all shrouds against the mast with a few turns of thread; reinforce the seizing with a drop of cement.

Next, tie and cement the ratlines to the shrouds. The thread for these transverse ropes may be of lighter weight cotton: #40 or #50. When dry, remove the assembly from the jig and attach to the model.

To do this, pass the loop, or eye, over the masthead, or—if your model has a solid top—up through the shroud hole and then over the masthead. Force it down into position, resting on the top or bolsters. The chain ends are fitted into the split channels and tied to short pins, which serve as bolts. (*See Channels, page 52.*) Do not allow any slack in the shroud lines, but be very careful not to pull them too tight.

Repeat the process until all the shrouds have been completed. This method is not as complicated and tedious as it may sound; the work is generally a lot of fun, and after the first one is mastered, the rest progress rapidly.

For larger models, the shrouds are assembled directly on the ship. Taking the lower masts first, rig port and starboard pairs alternately. Pass each shroud line around the masthead and seize; then force into position. As described in the section on channels, page 52, the chain deadeyes are already in position, bolted to the hull. Connect the chain and shroud deadeyes temporarily with wire, spacing correctly. Pass the shroud line around the deadeye, and finish with a serving. (*See* PLATE 68, *page 135.*) When shrouds are completed, remove the temporary wire; thread a needle with the lanyard and lace deadeyes together. Tie the sheer pole in place. Attach the ratlines, either by overhand knots or by clove hitches, keeping the spacings uniform.

After the lower shrouds have been completed, cement the topmasts in place and proceed with the topmast shrouds in the same manner. In this case, the lower deadeyes are attached to the futtock shrouds. When this section has been completed, fasten the topgallant masts in place and complete the shrouds.

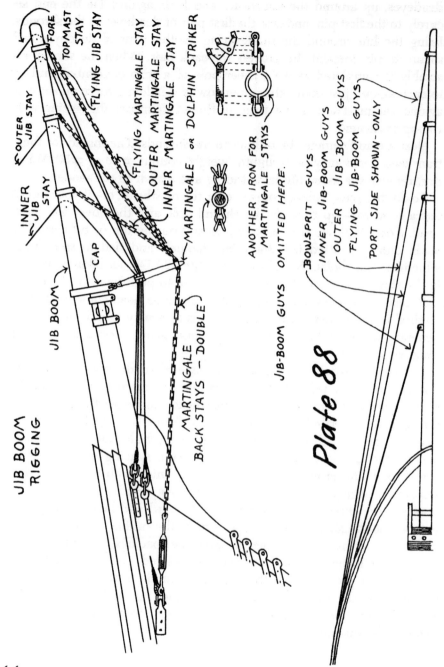

JIB BOOM RIGGING

FORE

OUTER JIB STAY

INNER JIB STAY

CAP

JIB BOOM

TOPMAST STAY

FLYING JIB STAY

FLYING MARTINGALE STAY

OUTER MARTINGALE STAY

INNER MARTINGALE STAY

MARTINGALE or DOLPHIN STRIKER

ANOTHER IRON FOR MARTINGALE STAYS

MARTINGALE BACK STAYS – DOUBLE

JIB-BOOM GUYS OMITTED HERE.

BOWSPRIT GUYS

INNER JIB-BOOM GUYS

OUTER JIB-BOOM GUYS

FLYING JIB-BOOM GUYS

PORT SIDE SHOWN – ONLY

Plate 88

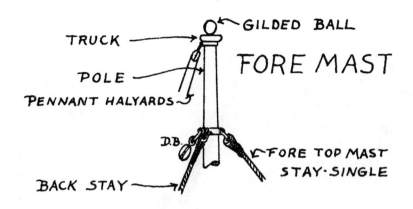

TRUCK

GILDED BALL

FORE MAST

POLE

PENNANT HALYARDS

D.B.

FORE TOP MAST
STAY · SINGLE

BACK STAY

Plate 89

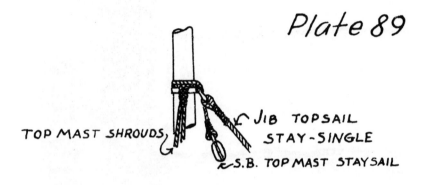

TOP MAST SHROUDS

JIB TOPSAIL
STAY - SINGLE

S.B. TOP MAST STAYSAIL

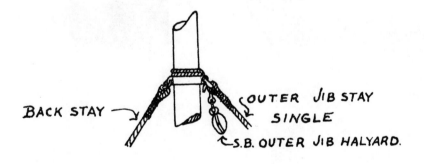

BACK STAY

OUTER JIB STAY
SINGLE

S.B. OUTER JIB HALYARD.

The *Progress*, American whaling vessel typical of the whaling barques, about 1840-1860. (In the collection of The Mariners' Museum, Newport News, Va.)

STAYS. The stays on all masts are much alike, differing, in some cases, at the anchorage points. Anyone not already familiar with their purpose and design should study the plates on rigging before beginning work on them.

The backstays for each mast should be placed after the shrouds have been completed. These are the supporting lines extending from the mastheads to the sides of the ship. Care must be taken not to pull the mast out of line when setting the skysail and royal backstays. Some ships have double backstays on each side, from topmast to skysail; some have triple topmast backstays and double royal and skysail stays. After placing these stays, check the mast; if out of line, make the necessary adjustments.

Before placing the fore-and-aft stays (the ones that run from mast to mast), complete the bowsprit and jib-boom rigging. Be sure that the bobstay, the martingale stays and the jib-boom guys are without slack. (*See* PLATES *86 & 88, pages 163 & 166.*) Do the mizzenmast fore-and-aft stays first; begin with the lower stay and work upward and forward. In some cases these stays are double at the tops and crosstrees. Schooners have heavy spring stays—stays running from cap to cap between masts. Proceeding forward, complete each mast in turn. Check previous rigging before fastening the main and foremast stays.

Finally, the yards can be attached, and the "lifts" (lines attached to the yards) fastened into place.

FOUR-MASTED SCHOONER.

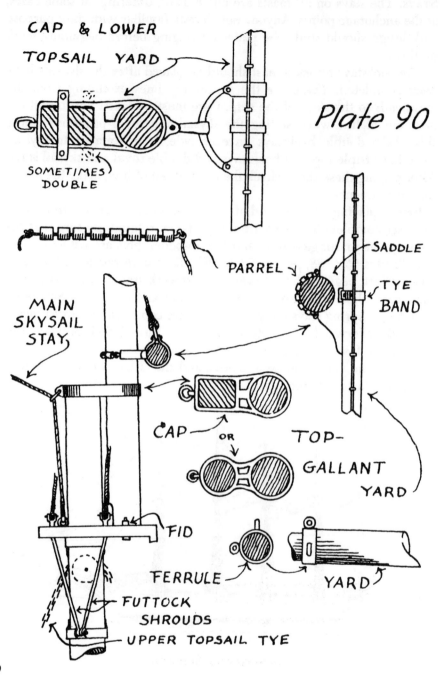

CAP & LOWER
TOPSAIL YARD

Plate 90

SOMETIMES
DOUBLE

PARREL

SADDLE

TYE
BAND

MAIN
SKYSAIL
STAY

CAP

OR

TOP-
GALLANT
YARD

FID

FERRULE

YARD

FUTTOCK
SHROUDS

UPPER TOPSAIL TYE

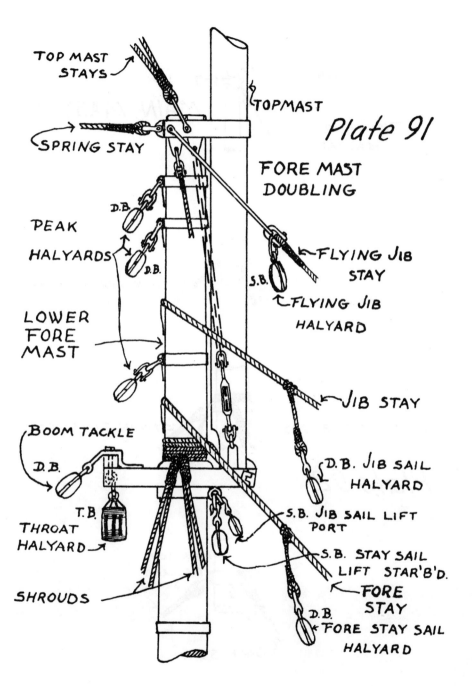

TOP MAST STAYS

SPRING STAY

TOPMAST

Plate 91

FORE MAST DOUBLING

D.B.

PEAK HALYARDS

D.B.

S.B.

FLYING JIB STAY

FLYING JIB HALYARD

LOWER FORE MAST

JIB STAY

BOOM TACKLE

D.B.

T.B.

THROAT HALYARD

SHROUDS

D.B. JIB SAIL HALYARD

S.B. JIB SAIL LIFT PORT

S.B. STAY SAIL LIFT STAR'B'D.

FORE STAY

D.B.

FORE STAY SAIL HALYARD

171

BALL → ← TRUCK

MAIN MAST

PENNANT
HALYARD →

BACK STAY → ←MAIN SKYSAIL STAY

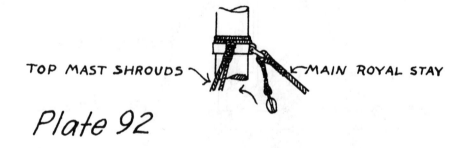

TOP MAST SHROUDS → ←MAIN ROYAL STAY

Plate 92

MAIN TOP-
GALLANT
STAY

←BACK STAY

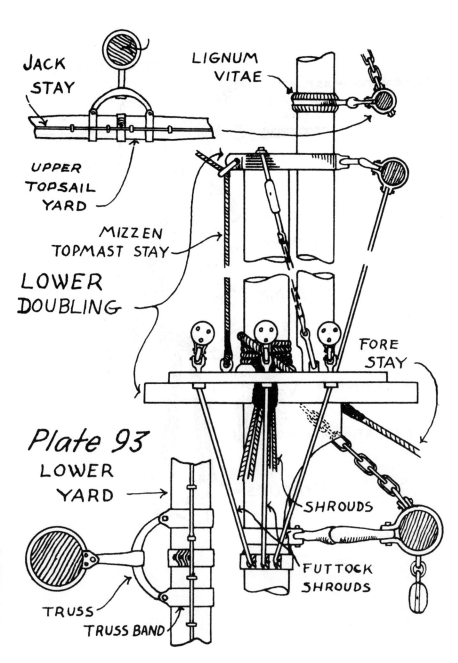

JACK STAY

LIGNUM VITAE

UPPER TOPSAIL YARD

MIZZEN TOPMAST STAY

LOWER DOUBLING

FORE STAY

Plate 93
LOWER YARD

SHROUDS

TRUSS

FUTTOCK SHROUDS

TRUSS BAND

173

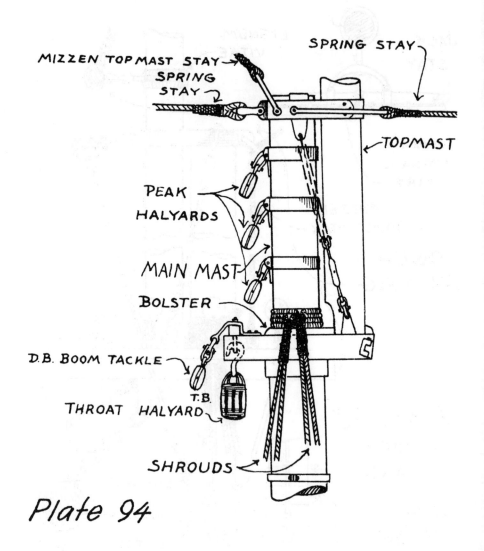

MIZZEN TOPMAST STAY
SPRING STAY

SPRING STAY

TOPMAST

PEAK HALYARDS

MAIN MAST

BOLSTER

D.B. BOOM TACKLE

T.B.

THROAT HALYARD

SHROUDS

Plate 94

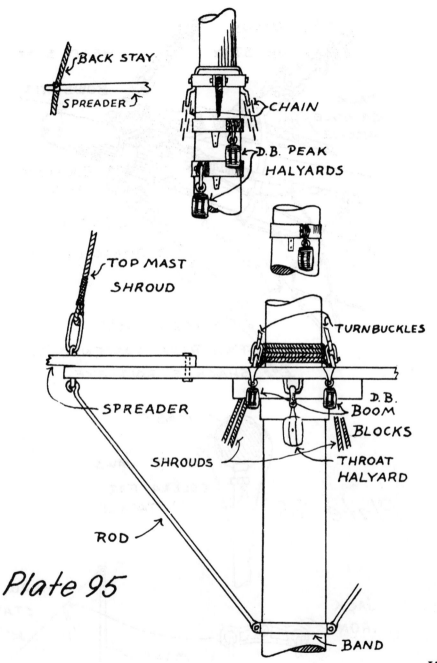

BACK STAY

SPREADER

CHAIN

D.B. PEAK
HALYARDS

TOP MAST
SHROUD

TURNBUCKLES

SPREADER

D.B.
BOOM
BLOCKS

SHROUDS

THROAT
HALYARD

ROD

Plate 95

BAND

175

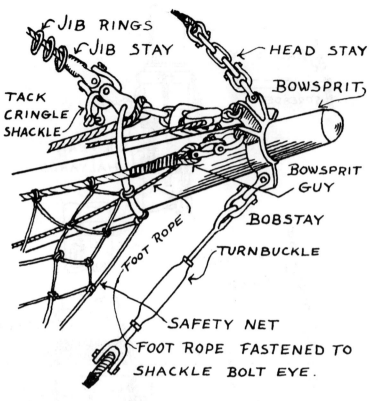

JIB RINGS

JIB STAY

HEAD STAY

BOWSPRIT

TACK
CRINGLE
SHACKLE

BOWSPRIT
GUY

BOBSTAY

FOOT ROPE

TURNBUCKLE

SAFETY NET

FOOT ROPE FASTENED TO
SHACKLE BOLT EYE.

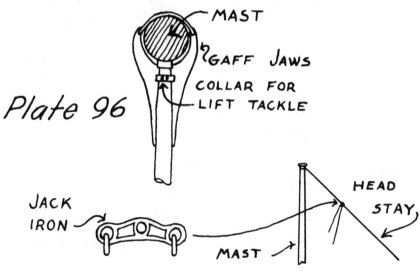

MAST

GAFF JAWS

COLLAR FOR
LIFT TACKLE

Plate 96

JACK
IRON

HEAD
STAY

MAST

176

TRUSSES

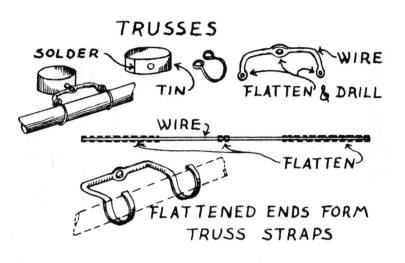

SOLDER

TIN

WIRE

FLATTEN & DRILL

WIRE

FLATTEN

FLATTENED ENDS FORM
TRUSS STRAPS

ROPE

WHIPPED END

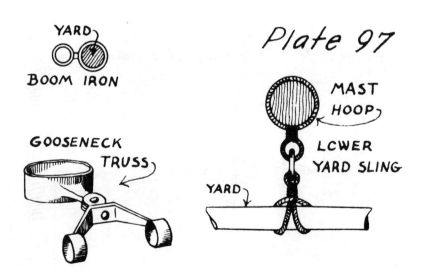

YARD

BOOM IRON

GOOSENECK
TRUSS

Plate 97

MAST
HOOP

LCWER
YARD SLING

YARD

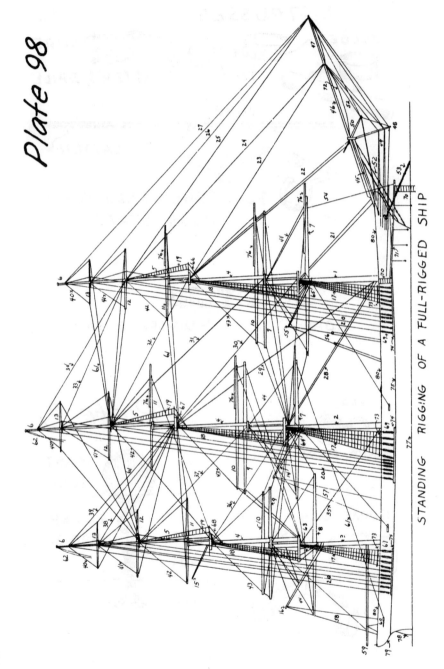

Plate 98

STANDING RIGGING OF A FULL-RIGGED SHIP

178

Standing and Some Running Rigging of a Full-Rigged Ship
(See Plate 98)

1—Foremast
2—Mainmast
3—Mizzenmast
° 4—Topmast
° 5—Topgallant mast
° 6—Royal and skysail masts
7—Fore and main yards
8—Crossjack yard
° 9—Lower topsail yards
°10—Upper topsail yards
°11—Topgallant yards
°12—Royal yards
°13—Skysail yards
14—Trysail gaff
15—Monkey gaff
16—Spanker gaff
°17—Lower shrouds
°18—Topmast shrouds
°19—Topgallant shrouds
°20—Backstays
21—Forestay
22—Fore-topmast stay
23—Jibstay
24—Outer jibstay
25—Fore-topgallant stay
26—Fore royal stay
27—Fore skysail stay
28—Mainstay
29—Main-topmast lower stay
30—Main-topmast upper stay
31—Main-topgallant lower stay
32—Main-topgallant upper stay
33—Main royal stay
34—Main skysail stay
35—Mizzen stay
36—Mizzen-topmast stay
37—Mizzen-topgallant stay
38—Mizzen-royal stay
39—Mizzen-skysail stay
40—Skysail lift
41—Royal lift
42—Topgallant lift

43—Upper topsail lift
44—Lift
45—Bowsprit
46—Jib boom
47—Flying jib boom
48—Martingale or dolphin striker
°°49—Martingale stays
50—Whisker boom
51—Whisker boom guys
52—Bobstays
53—Anchor chain
54—Boom halyard
55—Fore-gaff
56—Fore-gaff vangs
57—Trysail gaff vangs
58—Spanker gaff vangs
59—Spanker boom
60—Bumkin
°°61—Braces for adjusting yards
°°62—Pennant halyards
63—Mizzenmast lower futtock
   shrouds
64—Mainmast lower futtock shrouds
65—Foremast lower futtock shrouds
66—Fore-topgallant futtock shrouds
67—Main-topgallant futtock shrouds
68—Mizzen-topgallant futtock
   shrouds
69—Laniard (lanyard) binding between deadeyes, of rope or
   cord
70—Jacob's ladder
71—Boom
72—Foot ropes
73—Sheer poles
74—Channels
75—Strake
°°76—Studding sail booms
77—Water line
78—Rudder
79—Counter
80—Sheer line

° Indicates that the part named is numbered and shown on fore-, main-, and mizzenmasts.

°° Indicates the parts are named for the yards or masts to which they belong.

179

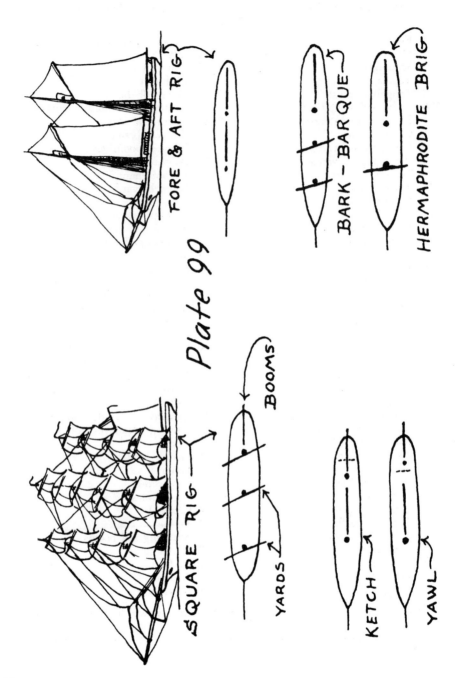

FORE & AFT RIG

BARK – BARQUE

HERMAPHRODITE BRIG

Plate 99

SQUARE RIG

BOOMS

YARDS

KETCH

YAWL

The number of masts on a vessel, and the shape, number, and arrangement of the sails in relation to them are the features that differentiate it from other types of ships.

Ordinarily, it is not necessary to equip your model with sails, but the time may come when you yearn for some new development of your craft. Some model plans do call for set sails, but the majority omit them entirely or have most of them furled so that the rigging and other details can be viewed unobstructed.

The three principal types of sails (square, fore-and-aft, and triangular) are shown in the accompanying illustrations. For the average model it is not necessary to include all of the sails' details.

The best material for sails is unbleached muslin. It should be cut generously to allow for narrow hems on all sides. Sew on reef bands, if you wish, and add reef points—short, dangling ropes used to reduce the size of the sail. With them, square sails are reefed at the head, fore-and-aft sails at the foot. To make them, use #30 or #40 cotton thread, preferably white or gray. Sew through the band, and cut off double lengths—a reef point for each side—plus a little extra for two knots tied tightly against the sail.

To make sails that appear set and billowing with wind, lay them out on newspaper and apply a coat of white shellac to front and back surfaces. Use pins to hold them outstretched until dry. Then shape them to the fullness desired and sew to their respective spars. Another method of achieving fullness is to sew wires into the hems. They can be inserted into the head and leeches of a square sail, the after-leech of a fore-and-aft sail, or into the foot and after-leech of a staysail. Any of the wires can then be bent to the shape desired.

The most complicated of sails, as far as rigging and fittings are concerned, is the square sail for the full-rigged ship. A detail drawing of the port side of two such sails shows them with most of the fittings and rigging necessary.

Following is a list of several other types of sails (some illustrated) which, though seldom used for models, are interesting:

Spritsail: A four-sided sail attached to yards and slung to the bowsprit. Another type of spritsail sometimes used on smaller boats is extended by a diagonal spar and footed with a light boom.

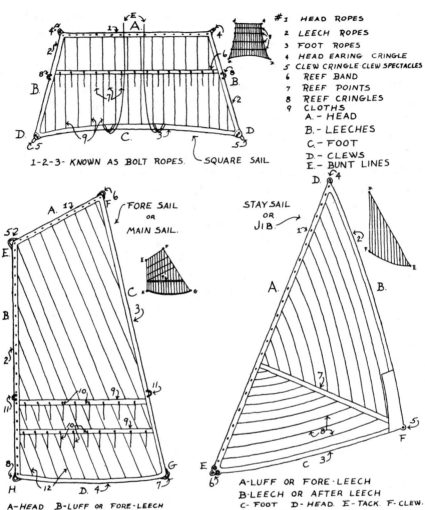

#1 HEAD ROPES
2 LEECH ROPES
3 FOOT ROPES
4 HEAD EARING CRINGLE
5 CLEW CRINGLE CLEW SPECTACLES
6 REEF BAND
7 REEF POINTS
8 REEF CRINGLES
9 CLOTHS
A.- HEAD
B.- LEECHES
C.- FOOT
D.- CLEWS
E.- BUNT LINES

1-2-3- KNOWN AS BOLT ROPES.   SQUARE SAIL

FORE SAIL
OR
MAIN SAIL.

STAY SAIL
OR
JIB.

A—HEAD B—LUFF OR FORE-LEECH
C—LEECH OR AFTER LEECH
D—FOOT E— THROAT F— PEAK
G— CLEW H— TACK
1—HEAD ROPE 2—LUFF ROPE OR FORE LEECH ROPE
3—LEECH ROPE OR AFTER LEECH ROPE
4—FOOT ROPE 5— THROAT CRINGLE
6—PEAK CRINGLE 7— CLEW CRINGLE
8—TACK CRINGLE 9— REEF BAND
10—REEF POINTS 11— REEF CRINGLE
12—CLOTHS 1-2-3-4— ALSO
   KNOWN AS BOLT ROPES.

A—LUFF OR FORE-LEECH
B—LEECH OR AFTER LEECH
C— FOOT D— HEAD. E— TACK. F— CLEW.
1—LUFF ROPE OR FORE-LEECH ROPE
2—LEECH ROPE OR AFTER LEECH ROPE
3—FOOT ROPE
4—HEAD CRINGLE 5—CLEW CRINGLE
6—TACK CRINGLE 7— GIRTH BAND.
8—CLOTHS   1-2-3- ALSO
KNOWN AS BOLT ROPES.

Plate 100

182

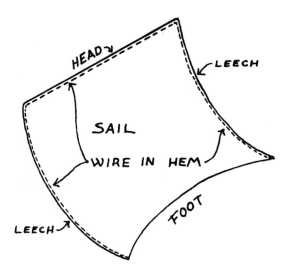

HEAD

LEECH

SAIL

WIRE IN HEM

LEECH

FOOT

Plate 101

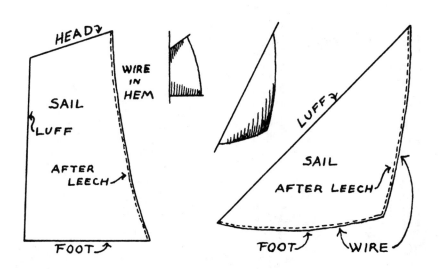

HEAD

SAIL

LUFF

WIRE
IN
HEM

AFTER
LEECH

FOOT

LUFF

SAIL

AFTER LEECH

FOOT

WIRE

183

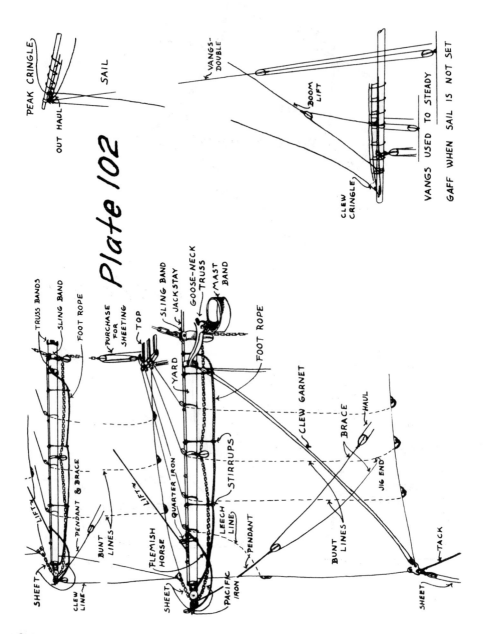

Plate 102

PEAK CRINGLE
OUT HAUL
SAIL

VANGS-DOUBLE
BOOM LIFT
CLEW CRINGLE

VANGS USED TO STEADY
GAFF WHEN SAIL IS NOT SET

TRUSS BANDS
SLING BAND
FOOT ROPE
PURCHASE FOR SHEETING
TOP
SLING BAND
JACKSTAY
GOOSE-NECK
TRUSS
MAST BAND
YARD
FOOT ROPE
CLEW GARNET
BRACE
HAUL
JIG END
LIFT
PENDANT & BRACE
BUNT LINES
FLEMISH HORSE
LIFT
QUARTER IRON
STIRRUPS
LEECH LINE
PENDANT
BUNT LINES
TACK
SHEET
CLEW LINE
SHEET
PACIFIC IRON
SHEET
SHEET

184

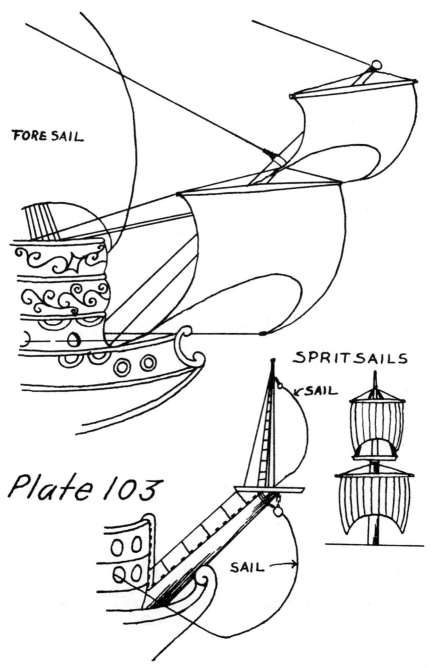

FORE SAIL

SPRIT SAILS

SAIL

Plate 103

SAIL →

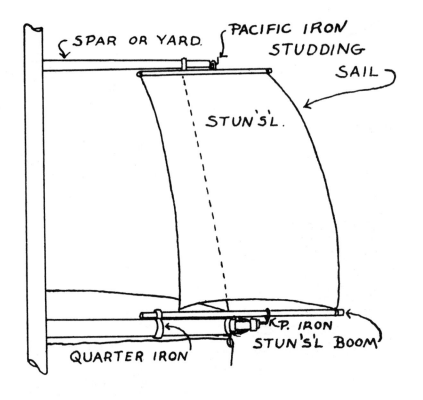

SPAR OR YARD.

PACIFIC IRON

STUDDING

SAIL

STUN'SL.

QUARTER IRON

P. IRON

STUN'S'L BOOM

Plate 104

LUGSAILS.

"LUGGER"

Spinnaker: A large, triangular sail extended from the mast by a spar (spinnaker boom). Used only when running before the wind.

Balloon jib: Large triangular sail used as a jib when running before the wind.

Lugsail: A four-sided sail bent to a yard that hangs obliquely from the mast, which is hoisted and lowered with the sail.

Lateen: A triangular sail rigged and handled much as a lugsail. If these interest you, make a model some time of the exotic little Arabian dhow. It will give your hobby shelf quite an Oriental atmosphere.

Studding sail (pronounced *stuns'l*): Used on clipper ships, they were extensions of the square sails. They were used to provide greater spread of canvas in good sailing weather.

RACING SLOOP—SPINNAKER BILLOWING.

DINGHY

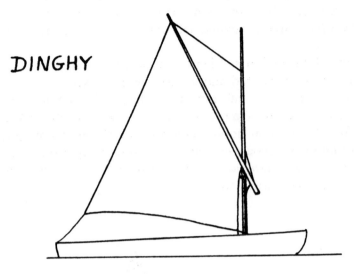

1. *Sailing dinghy,* with a lug type sail.

Plate 105

SLOOP

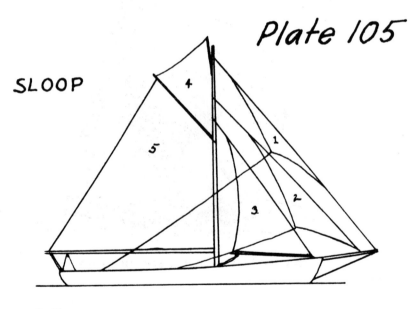

2. *Sloop*
    1—Flying jib
    2—Jib
    3—Foresail

    4—Main-gaff topsail
    5—Mainsail

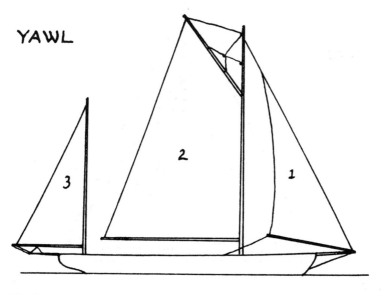

YAWL

3. *Yawl*
   1—Jib   2—Mainsail   3—Jib-headed spanker

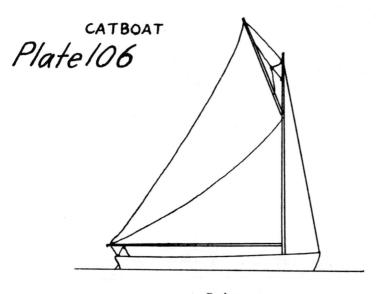

CATBOAT

Plate 106

4. *Catboat*
   Mainsail

189

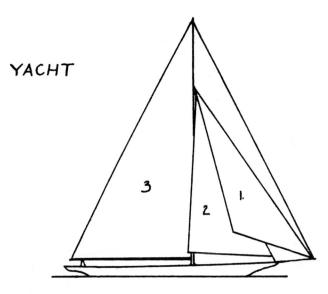

YACHT

5. *Yacht*
    1—Jib
    2—Foresail

3—Jib-headed mainsail, or Bermuda rig

Plate 107

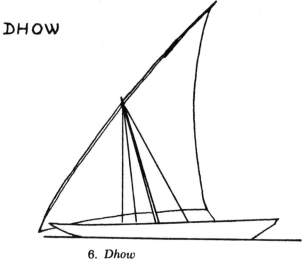

DHOW

6. *Dhow*
    1—Lateen sail

TOPSAIL SCHOONER

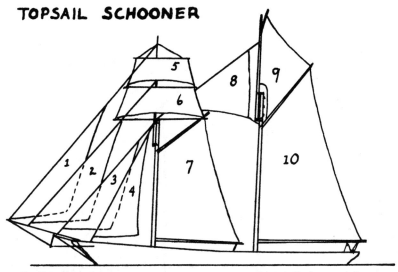

7. Topsail schooner

1–Flying jib
2–Fore-topmast staysail
3–Jib
4–Fore staysail
5–Fore upper topsail

6–Fore lower topsail
7–Foresail
8–Main-topmast staysail
9–Main-gaff topsail
10–**Mainsail**

Plate 108

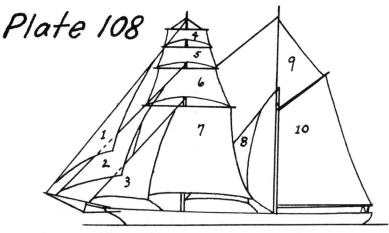

8. Brigantine (Hermaphrodite Brig)

1–Flying jib
2–Jib
3–Fore staysail
4–Fore topgallant sail
5–Fore upper topsail

6–Fore lower topsail
7–Foresail
8–Main staysail
9–Main-gaff topsail
10–Mainsail

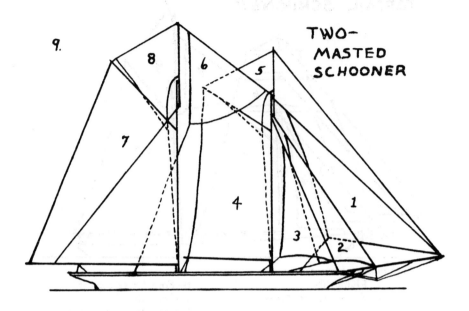

9.

8

7

6

5

4

3

2

1

TWO-
MASTED
SCHOONER

Plate 109

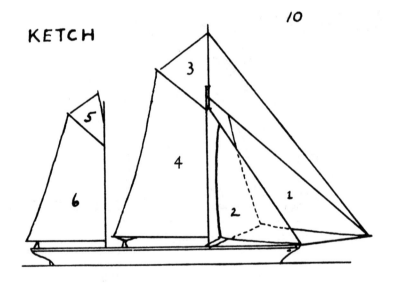

KETCH

10

5

3

6

4

2

1

STAYSAIL
SCHOONER

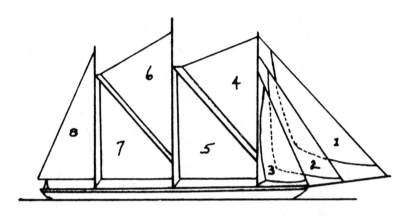

Plate 110

THREE-
MASTED
SCHOONER

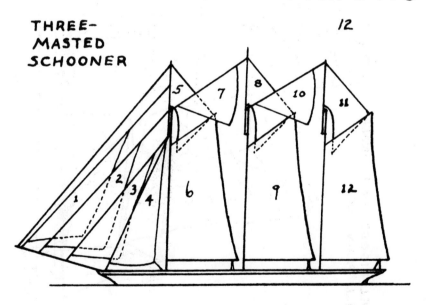

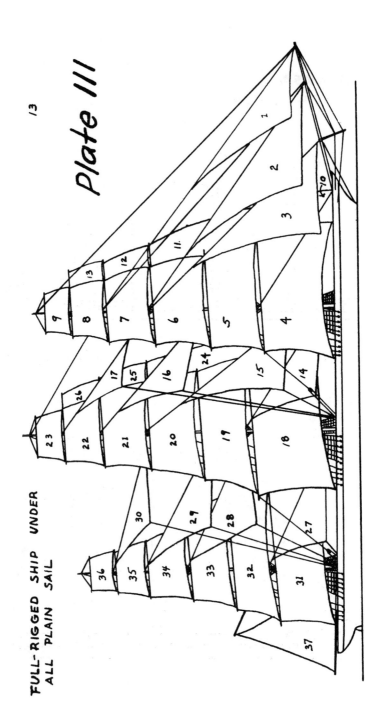

13

Plate III

FULL-RIGGED SHIP UNDER
ALL PLAIN SAIL

9. *Two-masted schooner*
   1—Flying jib
   2—Jib
   3—Fore staysail
   4—Foresail
   5—Fore-gaff topsail
   6—Main-topmast staysail
   7—Mainsail
   8—Main-gaff topsail

10. *Ketch*
   1—Jib
   2—Foresail
   3—Main-gaff topsail
   4—Mainsail
   5—Mizzen-gaff topsail
   6—Mizzen sail

11. *Staysail schooner*
   1—Flying jib
   2—Jib
   3—Fore staysail
   4—Fore trysail
   5—Main staysail
   6—Main trysail
   7—Mizzen staysail
   8—Jib-headed spanker

12. *Three-masted schooner*
   1—Flying jib
   2—Fore-topmast staysail
   3—Jib
   4—Fore staysail
   5—Fore-gaff topsail
   6—Foresail
   7—Main-topmast staysail
   8—Main-gaff topsail
   9—Mainsail
   10—Mizzen-topmast staysail
   11—Mizzen-gaff topsail
   12—Mizzen or spanker

13. *Full-rigged sailing ship**
   1—Flying jib
   2—Jib
   3—Fore-topmast staysail
   4—Foresail or fore course
   5—Fore-lower topsail
   6—Fore-upper topsail
   7—Fore-topgallant sail
   8—Fore-royal sail
   9—Fore skysail
   10—Fore-course studding sail
   11—Fore-topmast studding sail
   12—Fore-topgallant stuns'l
   13—Fore-royal studding sail
   14—Main staysail
   15—Main-topmast staysail
   16—Main-topgallant staysail
   17—Main-royal staysail
   18—Mainsail or main course
   19—Main lower topsail
   20—Main upper topsail
   21—Main topgallant sail
   22—Main royal sail
   23—Main skysail
   24—Main-topmast studding sail
   25—Main-topgallant studding sail
   26—Main-royal studding sail
   27—Mizzen staysail
   28—Mizzen-topmast staysail
   29—Mizzen-topgallant staysail
   30—Mizzen-royal staysail
   31—Crossjack
   32—Mizzen lower topsail
   33—Mizzen upper topsail
   34—Mizzen topgallant sail
   35—Mizzen royal sail
   36—Mizzen skysail
   37—Spanker

* This ship could also carry an outer jibsail and a fore staysail.

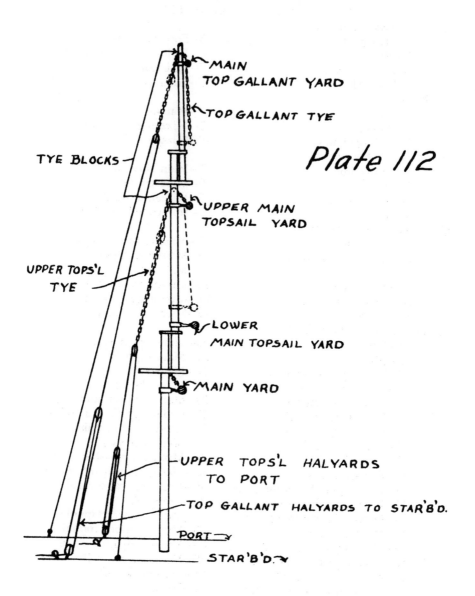

MAIN
TOP GALLANT YARD

TOP GALLANT TYE

Plate 112

TYE BLOCKS

UPPER MAIN
TOPSAIL YARD

UPPER TOPS'L
TYE

LOWER
MAIN TOPSAIL YARD

MAIN YARD

UPPER TOPS'L HALYARDS
TO PORT

TOP GALLANT HALYARDS TO STAR'B'D.

PORT

STAR'B'D.

The running rigging of all sailing vessels in general, and of square-riggers in particular, is quite intricate and complex. Running rigging is the gear that hoists and lowers sails, hauls or braces the yards to the wind, etc. Change in wind velocity means either to reduce sail or set more sail; alteration in course means alteration in position of sails. These changes mean hard work for the crew.

Running rigging is divided into two parts: the standing part, sometimes called "jig," and the "fall" or hauling part. The former is made fast to deck, mast, spars, or blocks. The haul is the free, or running, end of the rope manned by the crew.

Tackle is the combination of ropes and pulleys which gives increased power to the lifting end when the crew hauls on the free end; there are several kinds. All purchases are forms of tackle. A purchase is any tackle appliance capable of exerting greater power in moving or lifting a heavy load. An interesting piece of tackle much used on boats is the Burton tackle, of which there are several varieties, most of which consist of one single and one double block. In the Top Burton, this double block is a long, or fiddle block. A pendant is a short length of rope or chain which is suspended from a spar or yardarm, and has a block or spliced thimble at its free end to which tackle is attached.

For "working sail," that is, either setting or taking in sail, the running rigging is divided into the following two groups: (1) lifts, jeer and halyards, which control the hoisting and lowering of all spars, and the spreading or taking in of all sails; and (2) tacks and sheets, which hold down the corners of the sails.

In fore-and-aft rigged ships, the peak halyards, throat lifts and the boom sheeting comprise the main running rigging, plus the various halyards for the jibs.

In all square-rigged ships, the sail buntlines are attached as follows: (1) royal and upper topgallant buntlines to mast bands, (2) royals at the band above the tye block in the mast, (3) topgallant to band above the tye block in the mast, (4) upper topsail buntlines to band above tye block in the mast, (5) lower topsail buntlines to shrouds, (6) course buntlines to tops, and (7) clew garnet blocks fastened to trusses at the slings.

The accompanying illustrations, as well as several given under Standing Rigging, show in detail how and where most of the running lines described are attached.

If #8 or #10 cotton thread is in scale for the standing rigging, #30 or #40 would be suitable for the running rigging; if button or carpet thread is used for the former, use #20 for these lines, in brown or black, as specified before. Cotton thread numbers range from 8 to 100; the higher the number, the finer and lighter the thread.

Like small boys playing back-yard Commando, most model builders seem to get a big thrill out of going to work on warships or armed ships. Certainly they have variety to choose from: privateers, galleons, frigates, British ships of the line; today's multiform Navy vessels. Each is equipped with its own special armament. These pieces of artillery are not difficult to make, but require somewhat minute attention to detail—even when the details are only simulated. The all-over and trim painting contributes much toward an effect of realism.

GLOUCESTER FISHERMAN.

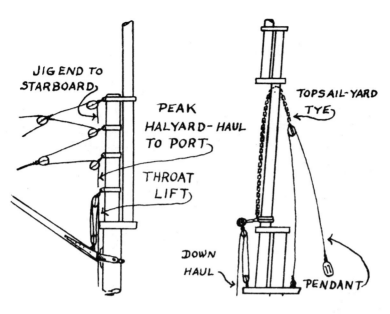

JIG END TO STARBOARD

PEAK HALYARD—HAUL TO PORT

THROAT LIFT

TOPSAIL-YARD TYE

DOWN HAUL

PENDANT

Plate 113

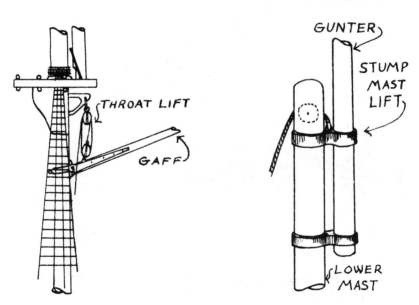

THROAT LIFT

GAFF

GUNTER

STUMP MAST LIFT

LOWER MAST

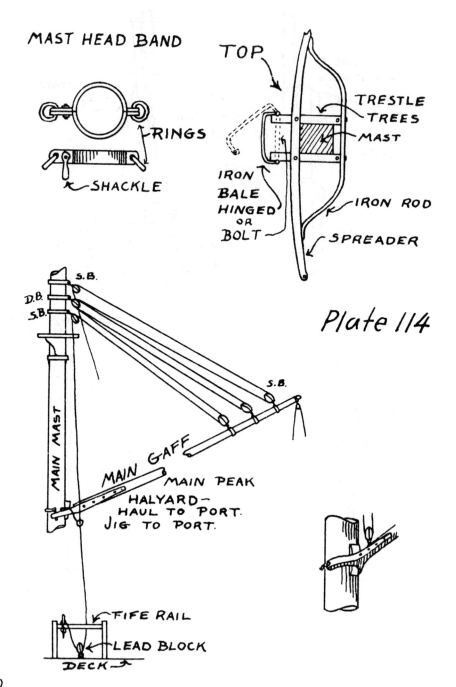

MAST HEAD BAND

RINGS

SHACKLE

TOP

TRESTLE
TREES

MAST

IRON
BALE
HINGED
OR
BOLT

IRON ROD

SPREADER

Plate 114

S.B.

D.B.

S.B.

S.B.

MAIN MAST

MAIN GAFF

MAIN PEAK

MAIN

HALYARD —
HAUL TO PORT.
JIG TO PORT.

FIFE RAIL

LEAD BLOCK

DECK

200

TYPES OF FISHERMAN RIGGING.

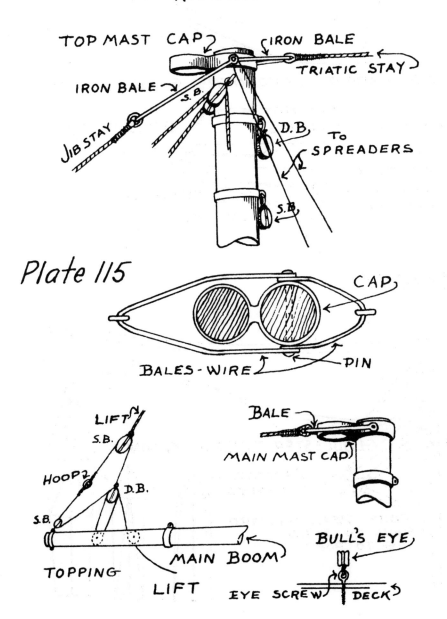

TOP MAST CAP

IRON BALE

TRIATIC STAY

IRON BALE

S.B.

D.B.

TO SPREADERS

JIB STAY

S.B.

Plate 115

CAP

BALES-WIRE

PIN

LIFT

S.B.

HOOP

D.B.

S.B.

TOPPING

MAIN BOOM

LIFT

BALE

MAIN MAST CAP

BULL'S EYE

EYE SCREW

DECK

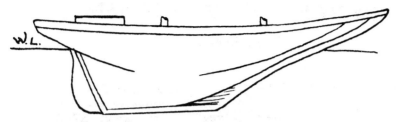

KNOCKABOUT SCHOONER— GENERAL LINES

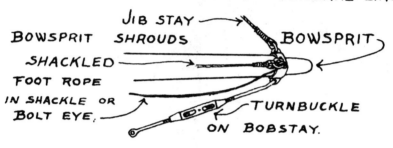

JIB STAY

BOWSPRIT SHROUDS

BOWSPRIT

SHACKLED

FOOT ROPE

IN SHACKLE OR
BOLT EYE.

TURNBUCKLE
ON BOBSTAY.

Plate 116

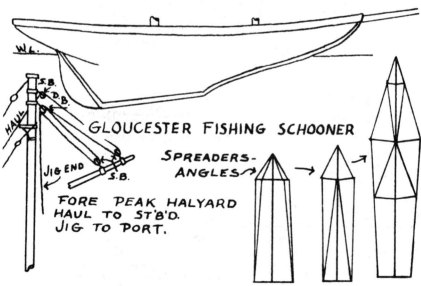

W.L.

S.B.

D.B.

HAUL

GLOUCESTER FISHING SCHOONER

SPREADERS-
ANGLES

JIG END

S.B.

FORE PEAK HALYARD
HAUL TO ST'B'D.
JIG TO PORT.

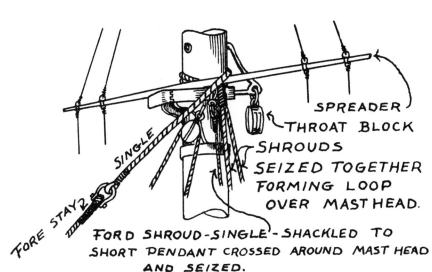

SPREADER
THROAT BLOCK
SHROUDS
SEIZED TOGETHER
FORMING LOOP
OVER MAST HEAD.

FORE STAY? SINGLE

FORD SHROUD-SINGLE-SHACKLED TO
SHORT PENDANT CROSSED AROUND MAST HEAD
AND SEIZED.

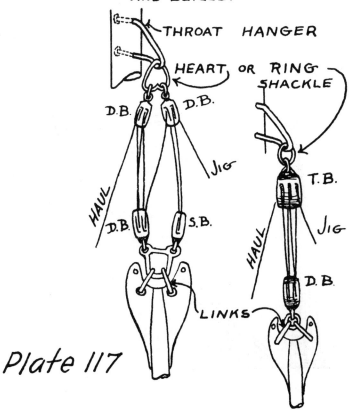

THROAT HANGER

HEART, OR RING
SHACKLE

D.B.   D.B.

JIG

HAUL

D.B.   S.B.

T.B.

JIG

HAUL

D.B.

LINKS

Plate 117

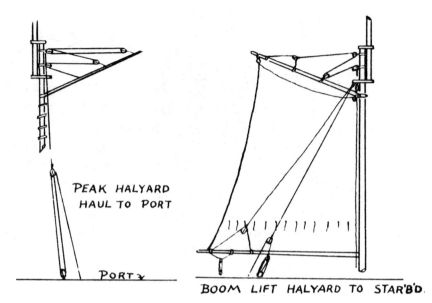

PEAK HALYARD
HAUL TO PORT

PORT

BOOM LIFT HALYARD TO STAR'B'D.

Plate 118

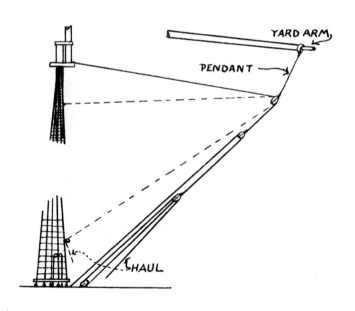

YARD ARM

PENDANT

HAUL

Plate 119

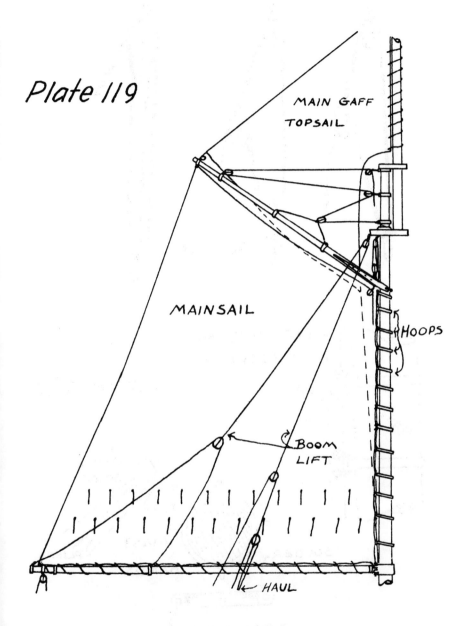

MAIN GAFF
TOPSAIL

MAINSAIL

HOOPS

BOOM
LIFT

HAUL

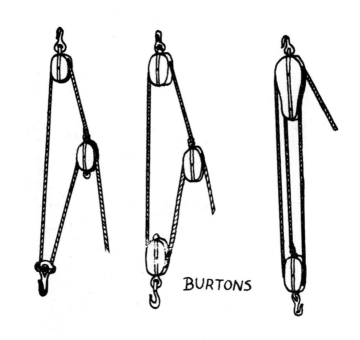

BURTONS

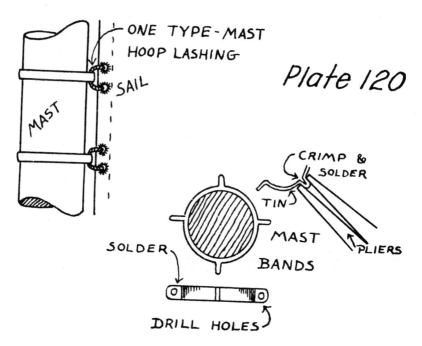

ONE TYPE - MAST
HOOP LASHING

SAIL

MAST

Plate 120

CRIMP &
SOLDER

TIN

MAST
BANDS

PLIERS

SOLDER

DRILL HOLES

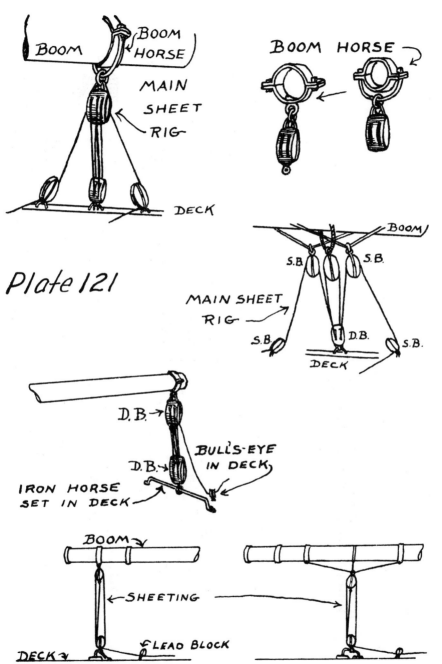

BOOM

BOOM
HORSE

MAIN

SHEET

RIG

DECK

BOOM HORSE

Plate 121

BOOM

S.B.   S.B.

MAIN SHEET
RIG

S.B.   D.B.   S.B.

DECK

D.B.

BULL'S-EYE
IN DECK

D.B.

IRON HORSE
SET IN DECK

BOOM

SHEETING

DECK   LEAD BLOCK

207

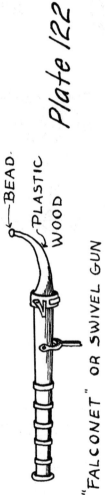

EARLY TYPE GUNS.

BEAD
PLASTIC WOOD

"FALCONET" OR SWIVEL GUN

Plate 122

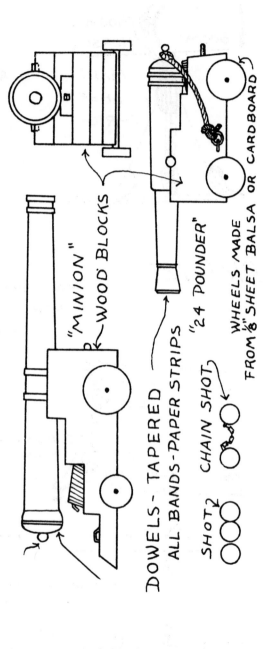

"MINION"
WOOD BLOCKS

DOWELS - TAPERED
ALL BANDS - PAPER STRIPS

"24 POUNDER"

SHOT   CHAIN SHOT

WHEELS MADE
FROM 1/8" SHEET BALSA OR CARDBOARD

Many armed sailing vessels of the 15th century, and later, were equipped with swivel guns called "falconets." Usually they were mounted amidship, with possibly one aft on the poop deck. Some 16th and 17th century ships mounted "saker" and "minion" guns, or cannons; they were forerunners of the 12- and 24-pounders and larger guns, such as served the *Constitution*. Modern warships bristle with guns of various calibres that are used for both offensive and defensive purposes: 16" guns in turrets, anti-aircraft weapons, heavy machine-gun emplacements, etc.

To make a falconet, use a very small dowel piece, tapered slightly. The curved handle end can be shaped from plastic wood and finished off at the tip with a small bead. The bands can all be made from glued paper strips. Use a shackle, soldered to a wire, for the mounting, and attach at the balance point of the gun barrel.

The sakers, minions, carronades, and the 12- to 68-pounders are similar to each other in construction. The guns can be made from tapered and slightly shaped dowels. If you want to make the trunnions, that is, the side projections, or pivot pieces, drill a hole through the barrel just forward of the balance point and insert a wire or a bamboo splinter. The carriage for the cannon can be made from a small block of wood which is hollowed out sufficiently for the gun to fit into it. A series of steps—generally three—is cut into one end. The wheels may be wooden or cardboard disks cemented into place. Use paper bands and a bead for finish, as before. Carronades and the 12- to 68-pounders were mounted on trucks with small wheels, and were rolled to and from the gun port by various kinds of tackle. The rings, eyes, staples, etc., necessary for these may be made from wire, soldered and then imbedded in the carriage with cement.

ARABIAN DHOW.

English 50-gun ship. A typical English ship of the class built at Deptford in 1686. Here ship ornamentation reached its greatest height. (Crabtree Collection, The Mariners' Museum, Newport News, Va.)

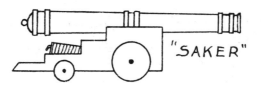

"SAKER"

Plate 123

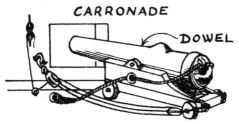

CARRONADE

DOWEL

WHEELS-WOOD OR CARDBOARD

24-32 POUNDERS

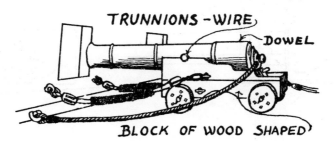

TRUNNIONS-WIRE

DOWEL

BLOCK OF WOOD SHAPED

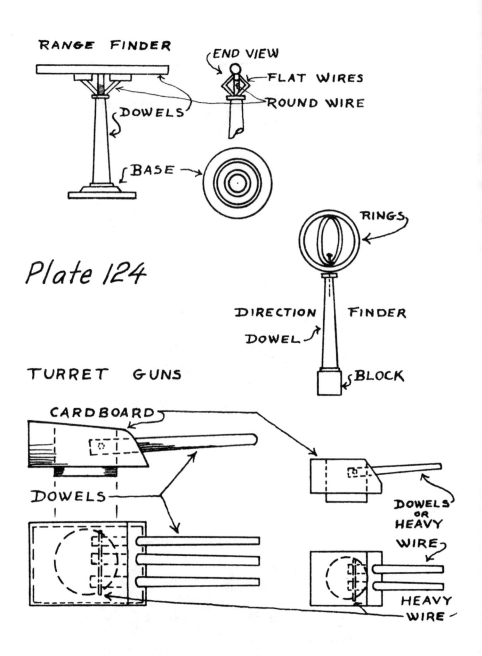

RANGE FINDER

END VIEW

FLAT WIRES

ROUND WIRE

DOWELS

BASE

RINGS

Plate 124

DIRECTION FINDER

DOWEL

BLOCK

TURRET GUNS

CARDBOARD

DOWELS

DOWELS
OR
HEAVY
WIRE

HEAVY
WIRE

If your ship is a modern man-of-war you will need, on the bridge or at some other good observation point, a range finder, and also a radio direction finder. The former might be made from small dowels, some wire or bamboo strips, and two tiny accessory blocks. Mount on a base of wood or cardboard. The direction finder consists of a dowel pedestal mounted on a small block or on a circular base of wood or cardboard. Two vertical metal rings, one fitting within the other, are cemented to the top of the dowel. Scale will hardly permit this piece to be workable, so the rings might be flattened at the bottom, and a pin driven through to secure them to the pedestal.

The large multiple-gun turret structures vary slightly in form: some are angular, others curvilinear. Unless very small, cardboard is the best construction material. None of these turrets and guns—workable or stationary—is particularly difficult to make, but when completed they look surprisingly dangerous.

It is a good idea to complete the guns and center mount first; then fit the turret around them. The guns, usually two or three to a turret, are wired together through holes drilled in the after parts of the barrels so that they are parallel with each other. The wires continue through to attach the barrels to the center mount, or base. This mount is an upright cylinder made of cardboard.

Lay out the turret top, side and ends as you would a deck cabin. Allow tabs for gluing and cut holes for the guns to penetrate. Assemble and glue to the top of the cylinder mount and glue the mount, in turn, to the deck. If you want your turret to be workable, cement a wooden disk (over which the cardboard cylinder should fit) to the deck; then set the mount over it so that the turret revolves.

If scale prevents detail a simple turret setup can be carved out of a small block of wood.

A type of hoist peculiar to armed vessels has a firm pedestal set on a wooden or cardboard base. The crane-neck may be shaped from wood and cemented into place. Attach the tackle to the top. All necessary trim can be painted on.

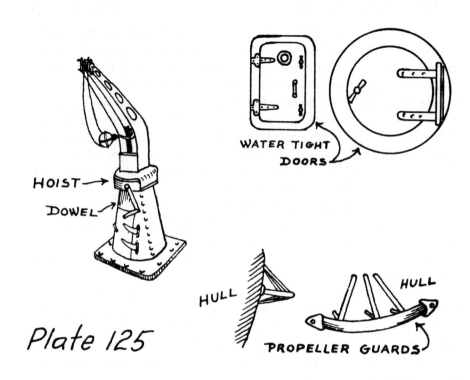

HOIST

DOWEL

WATER TIGHT
DOORS

HULL

HULL

PROPELLER GUARDS

Plate 125

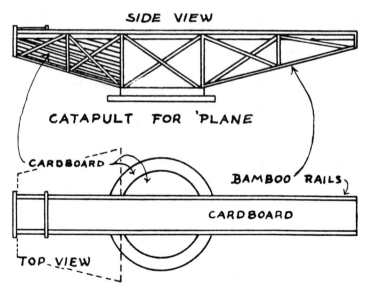

SIDE VIEW

CATAPULT FOR 'PLANE

CARDBOARD

BAMBOO RAILS

CARDBOARD

TOP VIEW

Watertight doors for fighting craft may be drawn in ink or painted on where needed.

Some warships have propeller guards attached to both sides of the vessel's stern between the deck and the water line. Such guards are easily made from bamboo strips bent to shape and cemented into position. The braces may be made from bamboo strips or splinters.

The building of a catapult for seaplanes should be an interesting undertaking from the standpoint of contrast, at least. It is quite easily constructed. Lay out the top and after-side pieces of thin cardboard. Cut out and fold side pieces down. Use bamboo splinters to form lattice-work frame and top with bamboo tracks and carriage rest. The two end pieces and the base on which the catapult is mounted may also be of thin cardboard.

The following pieces of artillery need not be workable:

1) Single machine guns. May be made of scrap balsa or other wood pieces, slightly shaped. The mounts may be of small dowels, the handles of wire.

2) Multiple machine guns or "Pom-Poms." Will have to be simulated by gluing together small blocks of wood, dowels and wire. Use discretion when adding the trim—try not to make them too elaborate.

3) "Y" guns, which shoot depth charges to port or starboard. They are shaped from single pieces of wood or made from dowels of different sizes, one for the main body and two smaller pieces for the arms of the Y. Mount on a circular cardboard base.

A depth-charge rack with its load of "ash cans" may be cut and shaped from a solid piece of wood, or the base may be of cardboard and very small dowels glued to it. Bamboo splinters or wire make realistic looking enclosures.

The main carriage of the deck gun illustrated in PLATE 128, #1, is made from three small pieces of wood mounted on a cardboard base. The gun barrel—a small, tapered dowel (from now on take it for granted that all good little gun barrels are made from tapered dowels), is cemented to the center block. The two pieces of recoil mechanism (also tiny dowels), supported by wedges, are glued in place, as shown, in line with the barrel. Trim may be of cardboard or painted on. There are several other ways of making deck guns—some even simpler than this.

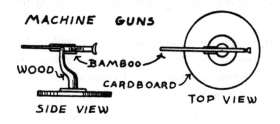

MACHINE GUNS

WOOD

BAMBOO

CARDBOARD

SIDE VIEW

TOP VIEW

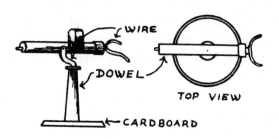

WIRE

DOWEL

TOP VIEW

CARDBOARD

Plate 126

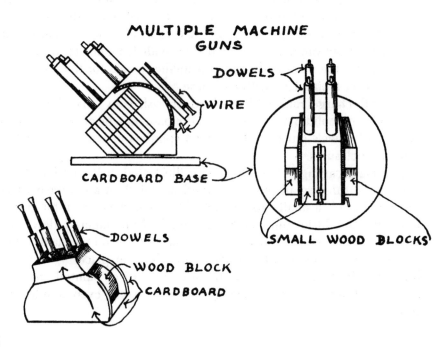

MULTIPLE MACHINE GUNS

DOWELS

WIRE

CARDBOARD BASE

SMALL WOOD BLOCKS

DOWELS

WOOD BLOCK

CARDBOARD

A deck gun which is more modern than the one described above is illustrated in PLATE 128, #2. Pieces of balsa wood, dowels, wire, and cardboard may be utilized to make it. The gun part is made up of barrel and recoil. Set into a shaped wooden block that has been cut to receive them. This piece, in turn, is glued to a squat, slightly tapered dowel mounted on a circular cardboard base. The barrel is topped by a small, shaped piece of balsa, pierced by a short wire. The sight is of wire. (*See detail sketch in* PLATE *130 of the Oerlikon.*) Keep the trim inconspicuous on these pieces.

To simulate a torpedo tube, shape a thin cardboard piece into a lengthwise half-cylinder with one end angle-cut and the other closed by a half-disk of cardboard or wood. Or use a dowel. Make the center mount of a cardboard cylinder or a slice of a wooden dowel. Cement a cylinder head of shaped wood to the top of the tube.

A torpedo battery generally consists of a unit of three tubes with a single central mount.

Turrets of single- or double-gun construction may be made of solid blocks of wood, slightly shaped, with the gun barrels inserted. Whatever trim you consider advisable may be made of cardboard. The entire turret setup is mounted on a disk cut out from a good-sized dowel.

The barrels of the Bofors anti-aircraft cannon shown have short sections wound with thin wire. These two barrels rest in a niche cut in a block. A sturdy, tapered dowel forms the base for the mechanism. A shaped piece of wood is glued to the loading end of the gun. The sight is made of wire. (*See again illustration of Oerlikon,* PLATE *130.*)

The Oerlikon, another anti-aircraft gun, is set into a carved piece of wood which in turn is glued to a tapered stand. On one side, near the top of the barrel, is the ammunition cylinder. Two vertical cardboard pieces, one on each side of the barrel, serve as the armor plates protecting the gunner. The handles, or butts, are of heavy wire, soldered; on the actual guns these are curved to fit a man's shoulders.

The sight is made of wire, and fastened to the top of the barrel. The detail drawing shows how several pieces of wire are soldered together to form the sighting apparatus. This feature may be simplified, as shown in the very small sketch.

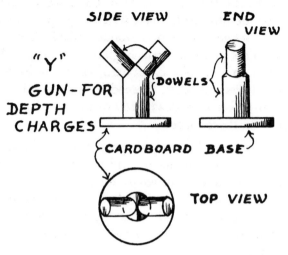

SIDE VIEW   END VIEW

"Y" GUN-FOR DEPTH CHARGES

DOWELS

CARDBOARD BASE

TOP VIEW

Plate 127

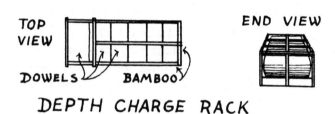

TOP VIEW

END VIEW

DOWELS   BAMBOO

DEPTH CHARGE RACK

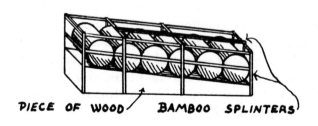

PIECE OF WOOD   BAMBOO SPLINTERS

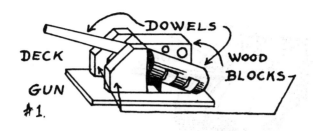

DECK
GUN
#1.

DOWELS

WOOD
BLOCKS

DECK
GUN
#2

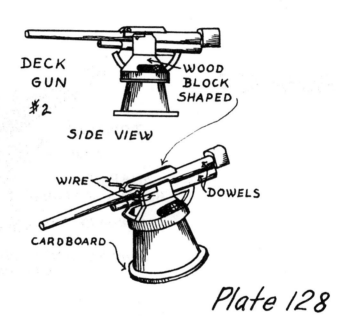

WOOD
BLOCK
SHAPED

SIDE VIEW

WIRE

DOWELS

CARDBOARD

Plate 128

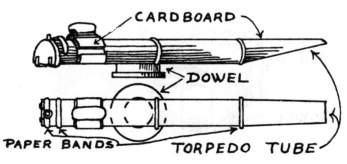

CARDBOARD

DOWEL

PAPER BANDS

TORPEDO TUBE

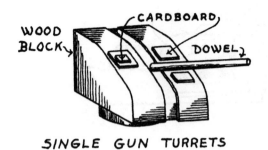

SINGLE GUN TURRETS

Plate 129

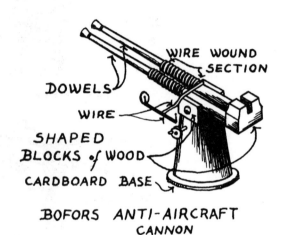

DOWELS

WIRE WOUND SECTION

WIRE

SHAPED BLOCKS of WOOD

CARDBOARD BASE

BOFORS ANTI-AIRCRAFT CANNON

WOOD BLOCK

DOWEL

DOWEL

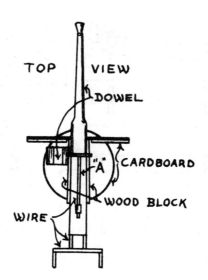

TOP VIEW

DOWEL

CARDBOARD

"A"

WOOD BLOCK

WIRE

Plate 130

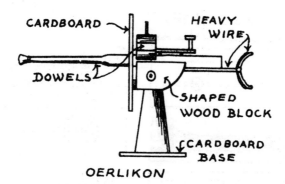

CARDBOARD

HEAVY WIRE

DOWELS

SHAPED WOOD BLOCK

CARDBOARD BASE

OERLIKON

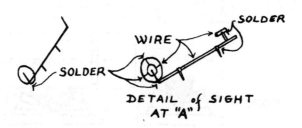

SOLDER

WIRE

SOLDER

DETAIL of SIGHT AT "A"

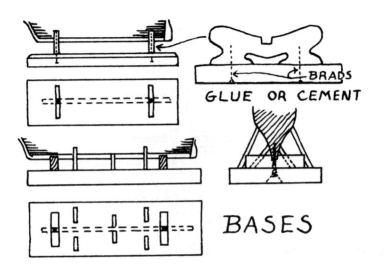

BRADS

GLUE OR CEMENT

BASES

Plate 131

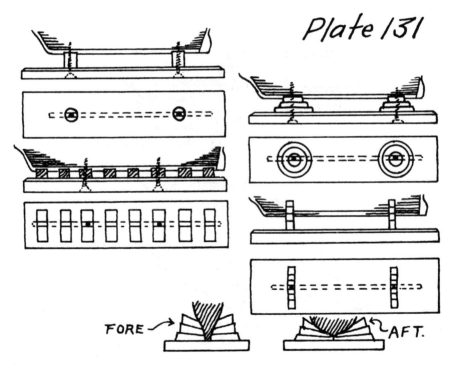

FORE

AFT.

A completed ship model, to be set off properly, should be mounted on a neat, trim base. Many people mount them on detachable cradles, but these make rather unsteady supports for good pieces; family members feel constrained to tiptoe past them. A few standard types of mountings are illustrated. The base of each is a horizontal plank of wood, usually with bevelled upper edges, and is as long, at least, as the model it supports.

On each the model is seated in some sort of shoring, and through this is attached to the base by means of holding screws—two are sufficient for the average size ship. Drill holes through the base piece; countersink them in the bottom enough to bury the screw heads. Drill holes also through the shoring pieces, then smaller ones into the keel at the proper places.

Before assembling, apply finish, usually shellac and varnish over the natural wood, to the base and connecting pieces. The hull bottom (and top, if you wish) should also be painted before joining. (*See page 225, Hull Painting.*)

A more fanciful method of mounting is very effective if well done. The base is covered with a Plaster of Paris sea surrounding the model, which has been cut off at, or slightly below, the water line and screwed or cemented in place. It is important to decide on the pitch, or angle, of the ship before beginning work on the hull; naturally, the amateur should not go in for typhoon effects. It would be a good idea to experiment a bit first. After the plaster waves have dried, paint the surface in various shades of blue, green and violet, with white crests and surges around the model.

A felt or leatherette pad should be glued to the bottom of each base to protect furniture; fill in the countersunk holes with plastic wood before applying.

Protection of the model from grime, dust, atmospheric changes, etc., presents a problem. Frequent dusting with a soft brush is helpful; nevertheless, grime does penetrate the surface, the rigging becomes furry and, in the course of years, much detail work is lost or brushed away. Whenever you do a model that you are proud of, protect it with a glass case if possible. If you change your mind about its merits as time goes by, replace it with your current best effort, and be glad that you are making progress.

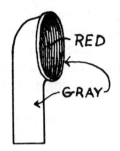

RED

GRAY

Plate 132

TUBES *of* METAL-WOOD OR
CARDBOARD

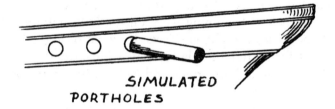

SIMULATED
PORTHOLES

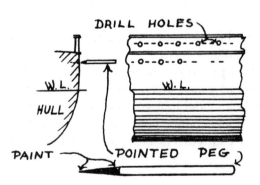

DRILL HOLES

W.L.

HULL

W.L.

PAINT

POINTED PEG

Before painting the ship model or any part of it, examine it to see if any spot has been overlooked during the shellacking process. Be sure that all wood, cardboard, thread, or any other absorbent material has been coated. This is most important for a neat appearance; another advantage is that the paint goes on more easily. Check the hull and parts for roughness—shellac raises the grain of the wood slightly and seems to have a way of luring all the dust in the vicinity to it while wet. Fill all pinholes with plastic wood, and allow to dry. Sandpaper the surface with fine paper, using a light touch.

Use quick-drying colors. Apply to the hull with a large (approximately 1″ in diameter) brush; in addition, have on hand one or two very small brushes for striping and detail work.

HULL. The hull top, that is, the section from cap rail to water line, should be painted first; it may be gray, black, or brown. Allow the top paint to overlap the water line. Allow to dry before applying the bottom paint, which is almost always red, and covers the entire area from the water line down, including the keel. A vertical scale, subdivided into feet to indicate the ship's draught, is conspicuously painted on all commercial carrying vessels. A safe load line, called Plimsoll's line or Plimsoll's mark, is shown on this scale.

WATER LINE. May be any color contrasting with the top paint. This can be painted directly on the hull with a fine brush; another method is to use a string or thread which has been painted and then stretched out to dry. Glue the colored string to the hull in a neat straight line between the top and bottom colors.

DECKS. Decks are shellacked, and sometimes followed by a thin wash of brown paint. This should be rubbed down with a clean cloth to remove all excess paint and leave a warm, tinted surface.

RAILINGS. Railings, as a rule, are painted entirely black, gray, or white. Some are black, with white, brown, or gray supports; the rail supports, in this case, should be painted first. Cap rails may be painted white or brown, or left natural, with only a coat of shellac.

STAIRWAYS. They are painted brown, white, or gray. Sometimes a combination of colors is used, for example: white for the side, or stair pieces, with brown treads and risers; or brown treads and black risers. If colors are combined, paint treads and risers first.   *225*

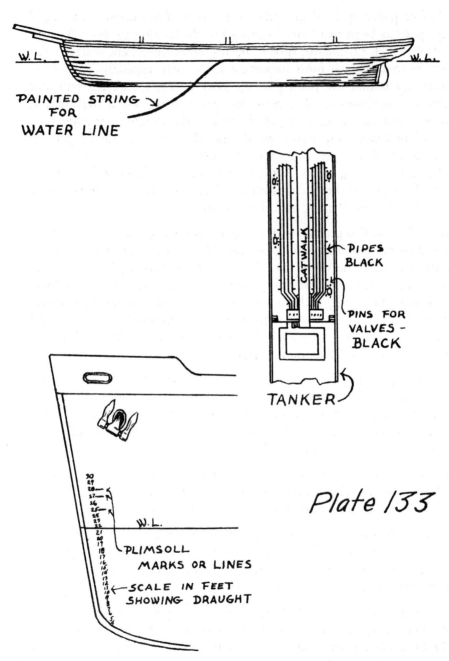

W.L.

W.L.

PAINTED STRING
FOR
WATER LINE

CATWALK

PIPES
BLACK

PINS FOR
VALVES -
BLACK

TANKER

Plate 133

W.L.

PLIMSOLL
MARKS OR LINES

SCALE IN FEET
SHOWING DRAUGHT

226

MASTS AND BOOMS. Masts, booms and spars are almost always left natural. Apply a coat or two of shellac, and sandpaper. Add a coat of varnish if you wish. Occasionally a model may call for painted masts; the color is generally brown or white; but the doublings are left natural.

FUNNELS. Unless the colors of the funnels are already established according to tradition or rule, the choice is left to your own discretion. The background might be black, with a contrasting band of bright red; or brown with yellow; red and blue; white and green; orange with white or black; and so on. Emblems or initials are, as a rule, painted in the band. The inside of the stack should be black.

VENTILATORS. Almost without exception, ventilators are gray or white, with mouth, or opening, red. To obtain a neat finish allow the outside color to overlap the inner red color just a trifle.

ROOFS. Roofs, or decks, as they are sometimes called, are left natural, or painted light tan or brown.

PLATFORMS. Platforms, or bases for winches and other deck fixtures, may be painted brown, tan, gray, or black.

HATCHES. As a rule, the sides are white or brown, with gray, brown, or black hatch covers. If a tarpaulin is used or simulated, paint it light brown.

SKYLIGHTS. Should be painted the same as deckhouses or cabins—gray with white trim is usual. Guard rails should be black.

LIFEBOATS. All white, except in a few cases where a colored band is run around each. If the lifeboat has a cover, paint that gray or brown, but paint the body first.

PORTHOLES. If the portholes have trim around them it may be painted black, dark brown, or gold. Where portholes are to be simulated, as on solid hull, deckhouses, etc., a transfer marker should be used. For this purpose, get a circular, open-ended metal rod, cardboard tube, or wooden ring; more than one size may be needed for a model. To make sure that the portholes are of uniform height, draw a faint horizontal guide line on the hull. Dip the end of the tube lightly into the paint—be careful not to get too much paint on it—then press it against the hull.

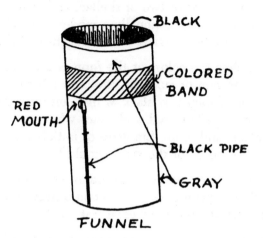

- BLACK
- COLORED BAND
- RED MOUTH
- BLACK PIPE
- GRAY
- FUNNEL

Plate 134

PLACE NAME OF SHIP ON BOW & STERN

> ॰ॄ **NEW YORK CITY** ॰ॄ

⌐CLOTH, MENDING TAPE OR SCOTCH
TAPE. MAKE STENCIL FOR BOW ᴏʀ
USE STRING GLUED IN PLACE.

SCOTCH TAPE ⌐

NEW YORK CITY

MAKE STENCIL FOR STERN ᴏʀ
USE STRING GLUED IN PLACE

Drill or pierce holes for portholes that are extremely small in scale. Dip the end of a pointed matchstick or round toothpick into the paint, and force it into the hole; turn it around once, and remove.

WINCHES. May be painted gray or black; a spot or two of red may be added to the end of the sheaves, the lever handles, or as a striping line somewhere. Such spots enliven the entire deck area.

LETTERING. The final touch—the ship's name—should appear on both sides of the bow, and on the stern. There are many styles of lettering and methods of application to choose from, depending on the ship's size, period or type, and, to some degree, on the model builder's skill.

The lettering may be painted—in gold or contrasting color—directly on the hull, or cut into a tape stencil. For small models, it may be inked or painted on strips of tape or paper whose background color is the same as that of the hull. Another method is to make raised letters of string, glued into place and ends cut off with a razor blade as the work progresses.

Period ships almost invariably have their names and surrounding embellishments displayed in gold.

MISCELLANEOUS.

Anchors: always painted black.

Deck fixtures black or gray. If the base of the fixture is light in color, use black.

Horns and whistles: black or gold.

Pipes: black, as a rule; also gray or brown on some tankers. Sometimes a set of pipes is black, with a central pipe or two gray.

Propellers: black or gold. The gudgeon straps and trim on the rudder may also be black. Shafts may be painted black, or same as the bottom paint.

Ships of countries at war are painted dull gray, or, as in the first World War, are camouflaged with broken designs in several colors. Navy vessels, as a rule, are all gray—"battleship" gray. Many auxiliary ships (tenders, hospital ships, etc.) are white.

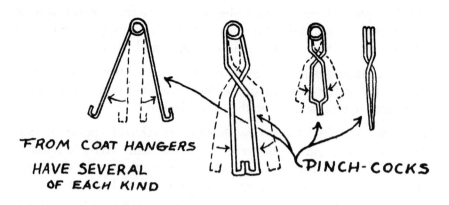

FROM COAT HANGERS
HAVE SEVERAL
OF EACH KIND

PINCH-COCKS

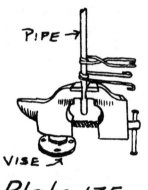

PIPE →

VISE

Plate 135

CLOTHES PIN

BULWARKS

PINS

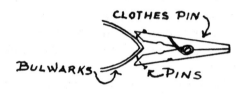

TWO HARDWOOD ADDITIONS

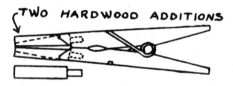

MAKE LONG NOSE CLAMP - HAVE

SEVERAL
of
VARYING
LENGTHS

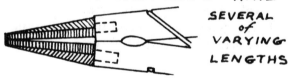

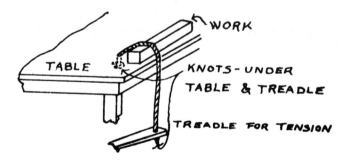

WORK

TABLE

KNOTS-UNDER
TABLE & TREADLE

TREADLE FOR TENSION

At this time it would be a good idea to make a few tools that are particularly helpful and time-saving.

Pinch cocks are easily made from old wire coat hangers. Straighten out the wire after cutting off the twisted ends. For an average size—outward pressure—pinch cock, measure off approximately 6″ from one end of the wire; from this point begin to wind around a small pipe. Make 1½ turns so that the two arms are parallel. Mark second arm the same length as the first, and cut off excess wire. Blunt both ends. You may wish to bend the ends back on themselves, thus avoiding any sharp or ragged edges. To make an inward-pressure pinch cock proceed as before, but cut the arms longer, and cross them. You will need several of both kinds in various lengths. This is a marvelous tool for holding together pieces that have been glued and set in place.

The spring type of clothespin, with a few additions, can also be used to good advantage as a holder. Heavy pins or small nails driven through the jaws at an angle will give you a fine holder for small pieces, and for pieces that are difficult to hold without some sort of pointed projecting grip. With the addition of hardwood strips you can have a series of long-nosed clamps. It is best to remove the spring from the jaws for this work, and replace it after the added pieces have dried and set firmly.

A *rope and treadle vise,* or holder, is very useful for holding small work that is to be carved and shaped, and which you may need to turn or move frequently. It can be of rope or thin cord, which is strung through a hole bored into a drawing board, table or other working surface, then knotted or otherwise fastened. It should be long enough to reach the treadle, which has one end resting on the floor. A slight foot pressure on the treadle will hold any object placed under the cord. For delicate work the cord can be covered with something soft, so the pressure will not mar the surface.

A *small V-shaped gouge* is a tool you can make which will repay you for the effort by saving time in later work. Drive a nail (pick your own size, depending on the scale of the model you are working on) into a small block of wood which you will later shape into a handle. Cut off the head of the nail and file the long "V" shape down the center. The two outer sides will have to be filed slightly in order to give a cutting edge. Sharpen on a hone to a keen edge. (*See* PLATE *14, page 29.*)

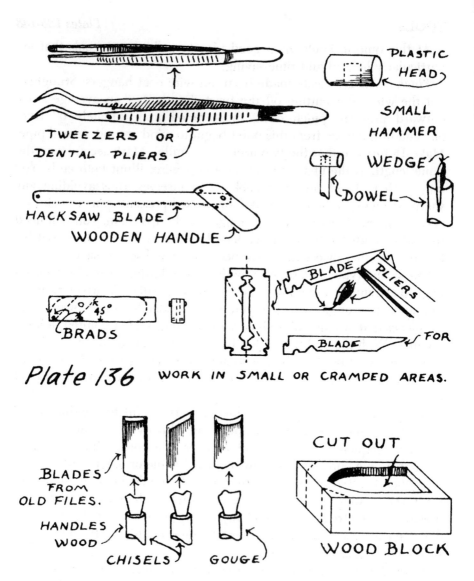

TWEEZERS OR
DENTAL PLIERS

PLASTIC
HEAD

SMALL
HAMMER

WEDGE

DOWEL

HACKSAW BLADE
WOODEN HANDLE

BRADS

BLADE

PLIERS

BLADE

FOR

Plate 136   WORK IN SMALL OR CRAMPED AREAS.

BLADES
FROM
OLD FILES.

HANDLES
WOOD

CHISELS   GOUGE

CUT OUT

WOOD BLOCK

OLD FLATIRON

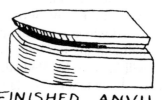
FINISHED ANVIL

A *small saw* can be made from a hack-saw blade and a small piece of wood, as illustrated. Cut a slit in the wood for the saw blade, and drill a hole for a small bolt to hold the blade and handle together. A small nail on each side of the blade will keep it firmly in place.

Chisels of two or three sizes and shapes are easily made from old files or other pieces of good scrap steel. Shape on an emery wheel, but don't burn the metal by holding it against the wheel too long at one time. Fit on wooden handles and sharpen on a hone to get a keen edge.

A *small hammer* for woodwork is easily made from an old umbrella handle of plastic. Cut as long a cylinder as possible and drill a hole at the center for the handle; a dowel can be used for the handle. Cut a half-inch slit at one end of the dowel, in which set a small wedge. Drive wedge end of dowel into the hole.

Thin, pointed knives can be made from old double-edged razor blades. Break blade into two halves; with a pair of pliers grip one half near the end, at an angle, and break off by pressing down on a flat hard surface. This gives you an excellent blade for fine work. These blades can be held in a pin vise or (but less satisfactorily) in a regular razor-blade handle.

Tweezers are necessary, so get a couple of them in different sizes. Try to get one pointed pair, because it will be perfect for rigging work. All the smaller pieces will have to be handled with tweezers, rail supports, chocks, cleats, blocks, railings, ratlines, deadeyes, etc.—to mention a few other uses, also in placing of all small, glued pieces of wood or cardboard, pins, beads and placing of all the rigging—standing and running.

A *small anvil* will be useful to you in many instances. Sink an old flat-iron base, or other piece of good steel having a flat surface, into a wooden block, and you will have a fine anvil. A flatiron is especially good because of its shape. It has sharp angles, curves, and a point; almost any kind of work can be handled on it.

A *power drill* is more complicated to make, but worth the effort. Any old or broken-down kitchen utensil having a small electric motor in good condition will furnish your power supply. Dismantle enough of it so you can fasten a handle, equipped with a switch, in such a position that it can be operated by the hand holding the handle. Over the original shaft place a short nipple or pipe length, threaded at one end for the chuck. Drill a hole through both to take a small metal pin. Clinch in

233

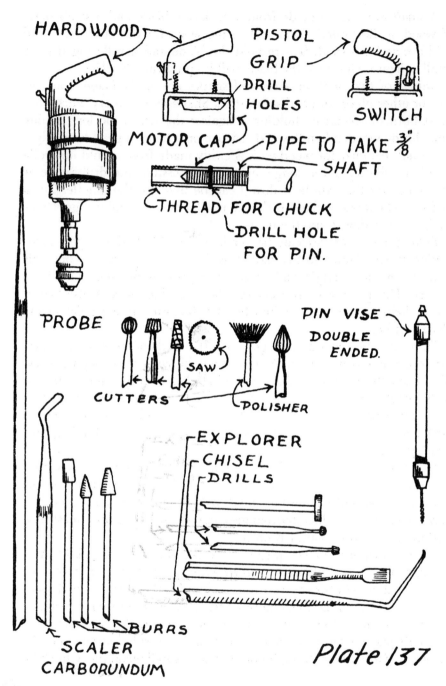

HARDWOOD

PISTOL
GRIP
DRILL
HOLES

SWITCH

MOTOR CAP

PIPE TO TAKE ⅜"
SHAFT

THREAD FOR CHUCK

DRILL HOLE
FOR PIN.

PROBE

PIN VISE
DOUBLE
ENDED.

SAW

CUTTERS

POLISHER

EXPLORER
CHISEL
DRILLS

BURRS

SCALER
CARBORUNDUM

Plate 137

234

place, making a solid shaft of the two. The chuck should be a size to hold a variety of drills ranging down to 1/16". You will have to buy this chuck at a hardware store, or use one from an old hand or breast drill. Your power unit will be complete with the addition of a few cutters and shapers. Of course, no really heavy work can be done with this size motor, but for model making it is adequate.

As you progress, there are other tools that you will acquire if you do not already have them. Following is a suggested list. Most of them can be obtained at the ten-cent stores.

Files—Of various shapes and sizes, for wood and metal.
Screw drivers—Various sizes.
Hammers—Carpenter's and jeweler's.
Small spoke shave.
Chisels and gouges—Various sizes.
Small set of wood-working tools—Modeling tools, small.
Nail set—Center punch—Paper punch.
Long-nosed pliers—Cutting pliers.
Pointed scissors.
Reamer—Countersinker.
Coping saw—Small hand saw—Jeweler's saw—Hack saw.
Wood clamps—Small metal clamps.
"T" square—Right-angle triangle—Carpenter's try square.
Oil stone or hone.
Paint brushes 1", ½", and smaller.
Breast or hand drill—Drills of various sizes.
Small table or bench vise.
Awls or piercing instruments.
Small modelmakers' planes—Large plane.
Tap and die set—Small.
Tin snips—Soldering iron.
Rasps.

For special tools I also want to suggest the use of discarded dental instruments. Any dentist has an assortment of tools that are helpful to model builders. I am lucky enough to have a close friend who is a dentist; he has given me many instruments which after slight alterations are among my best tools for model making. There are tweezers of various shapes and sizes, probes, scalers, chisels, explorers, and some I don't know the name of—all of them ideal for my purposes. There are also

CABINET *for* TOOLS & MATERIALS

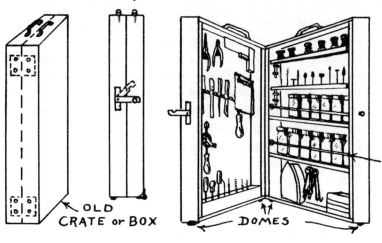

OLD CRATE or BOX

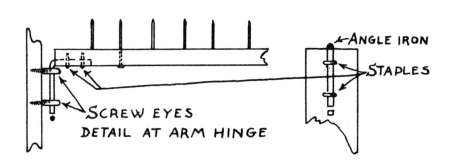

DOMES

ANGLE IRON

STAPLES

SCREW EYES
DETAIL AT ARM HINGE

Plate 138

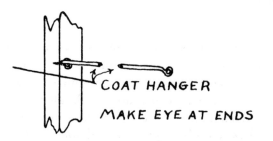

COAT HANGER

MAKE EYE AT ENDS

ROUND
or
SQUARE
BOTTLES

cutters, burrs, drills, saws, sanding disks, etc., that give unlimited possibilities in shaping and carving. If your dentist is your friend, you might ask him what he does with his discarded instruments. Tools with broken points—rusted or otherwise—of no value to him, can be resurrected and made into chisels, knives, piercing tools, etc. The burrs and cutters that are too dull for his particular work are sharp enough for the work the model builder will have them do; cutting soft woods, cardboard and thin metal.

Pin vises (single- or double-ended) are hand pieces with chucks at one or both ends, and will take the smallest of drills. Very useful in tight spots, and for drilling of small holes where the power unit would be too cumbersome and where the speed and weight of it might do damage.

With your growing accumulation of tools, materials, and odds and ends, there is a decided need for a place to keep them all. The cabinet illustrated is much like one I built for myself, which surprised me by the number of things it eventually accommodated. Such a cabinet not only conserves space but it puts everything right at the worker's finger tips. The jars are transparent so the blocks, gear, beads, and miscellaneous odds and ends can be picked out at a glance. The tool space is adequate if the tools are arranged well. The swinging arm equipped with nails, can hold spools of wire, thread, chain, etc. If you want to, in place of the outer nail, pad the section into a small pincushion for holding needles and pins. Pins are a necessity, and you will use a good many of them.

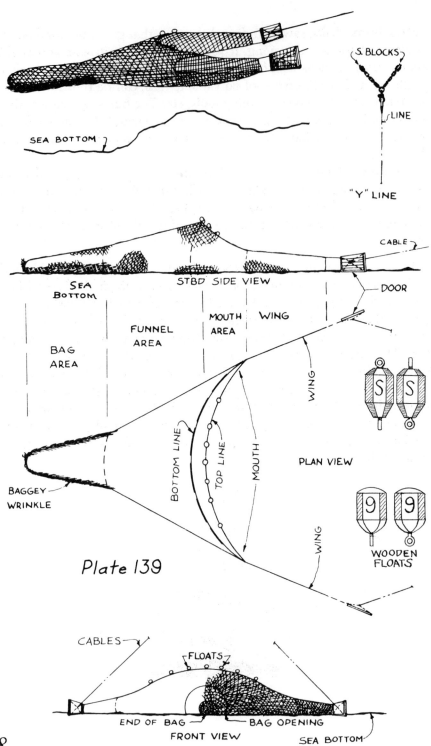

S. BLOCKS

LINE

"Y" LINE

SEA BOTTOM

CABLE

STBD SIDE VIEW

SEA BOTTOM

DOOR

MOUTH AREA

WING

FUNNEL AREA

BAG AREA

WING

BOTTOM LINE

TOP LINE

MOUTH

PLAN VIEW

S   S

BAGGEY WRINKLE

9   9

WOODEN FLOATS

WING

Plate 139

CABLES

FLOATS

END OF BAG

BAG OPENING

FRONT VIEW

SEA BOTTOM

238

Drag nets come in various sizes, depending on the size and power of the trawlers handling them; one of them will hold a ton or more of fish. The one pictured here is part of the equipment of the vessel on page 21, which is now made up into a working plan accompanying this book. Most beam trawlers and draggers use this type.

A drag net, when in operation, looks somewhat like a flexible funnel. Attached to each side, and extending diagonally forward approximately thirty feet, are lengths of netting, called wings. Secured by ropes to the forward ends of these wings are spreader vanes, or "doors." These are much larger than the average door of a house, for instance, and are constructed usually of heavy oak planking, reinforced on three sides by heavy bolted metal frames. Besides giving the doors necessary weight, the metal withstands the abuse of dragging along a rough and sometimes rocky sea bottom.

A cable is attached to each door a short distance aft of exact center, and leads through a series of blocks to a large winch on the vessel. By this off-centering, the doors—each one trying to escape the rush of water—are made to yaw outwards at an angle, thus opening the net to its fullest capacity.

The bag at the opposite end of the funnel is partly covered with shredded rope, called "baggey wrinkle." When the bag is full of fish, this stuff skids along the sea bottom like slippery runners. The tail end of this bag is closed by a purse rope run through a series of rings attached to the netting. After the haul is made, the bag is suspended above the deck, the knot of this purse rope is loosened, and the fish spill out.

In the mouth area, the edge of the lower netting is weighted with lengths of chain to keep it on or near the bottom; the upper line is buoyed with the help of floats; if increased buoyancy is needed, floats are added and sections of chain removed until the net operates in the desired level, depending upon the species of fish wanted.

In constructing a scale model of a drag net, fine mesh veiling net, buckram or crinoline (with the sizing soaked out), may be used. Select some shade of brown if possible, or dye the material, because the real article is always dipped in a tar solution for durability. Make the bag, funnel, mouth and wing sections separately, and sew them together.

239

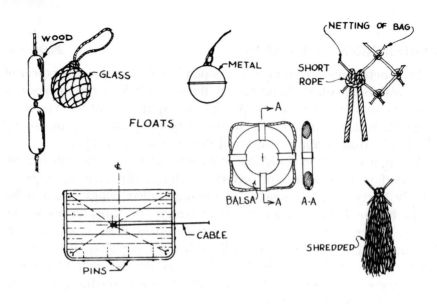

WOOD

GLASS

METAL

NETTING OF BAG

SHORT ROPE

FLOATS

A

BALSA

A-A

SHREDDED

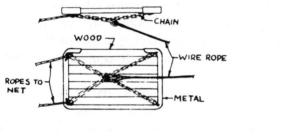

CABLE

PINS

NETTING

CHAIN

WOOD

WIRE ROPE

ROPES TO NET

METAL

BAGGEY WRINKLE
(SHREDDED ROPE)

DOORS

Plate 140

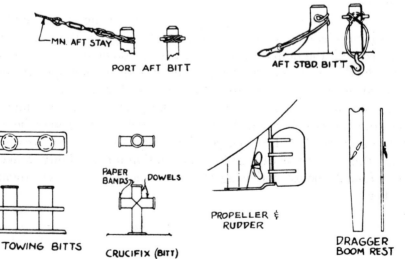

MN. AFT STAY

PORT AFT BITT

AFT STBD. BITT

PAPER BANDS

DOWELS

PROPELLER &
RUDDER

TOWING BITTS

CRUCIFIX (BITT)

DRAGGER
BOOM REST

For the doors, use thin pieces of wood, and simulate planking with a "V" gouge.

Narrow strips of thin tin, with small pins simulating bolts, may be used for the frames. Represented here are two types. The simpler one, called a runner, is merely a ribbon of tin "bolted" to and running flush with the edges on three sides of the door. The other is a wider strip, which folds down over the edges about ⅛ of an inch on each side. It should also be long enough to extend a short distance beyond each corner along the fourth edge. The corners are rounded, and there will be some inevitable bunching, but this can be tapped down gently until neat and trim.

Cut two lengths of chain for each door, allowing about ¼ of an inch slack at the points where they will cross, which would be about ⅛ of an inch aft of the exact center. Drill two small holes at each corner, then attach the chains as indicated, to the *inside* of the doors.

For floats, use beads. They can be of wood, glass, plastic, metal, paste—almost anything, just so the scale is right. You may want to cover these floats with netting, which should be of even finer quality than that used for the drag net. Sew in place, and attach a short length of thread to each float, and tie in position. Your floats may be of any color you choose, but of course all should be alike.

It may be of interest to many that by mutual pre-arrangement in fishing communities, each fisherman's equipment is recognizable by its color and markings. One man's rowboat, floats, etc., may be yellow, for example, with red stripes, borders, dots, circles, or other selected symbols.

For a suggestion on how to display your drag net effectively, please consult the detail drawings on the plan sheet.

"Y" LINE AND MORE ABOUT DRAG NETS *Plate 139*

The "Y" line gets its name from its shape, although I have often wondered if the fishermen call it that because people ask so many questions about it. Its function is to control the action of the drag net cables.

As this is a part of the rigging of a fishing vessel unfamiliar to many and perhaps seems a little complicated until understood, it might be a good idea at this point to have the rigging sheet open before you.

The "V" part of the Y line consists of two short chains terminating in single block fittings, and joined to the line at the base by a ring

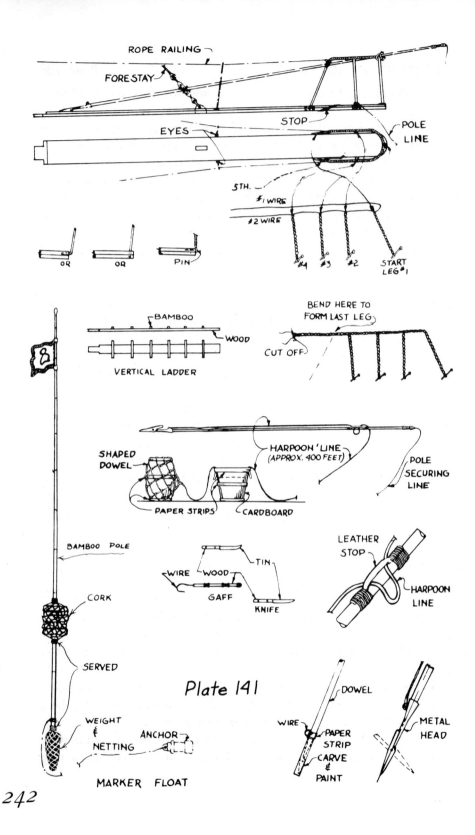

ROPE RAILING

FORESTAY

EYES

STOP

POLE LINE

5TH.

#1 WIRE

#2 WIRE

OR   OR   PIN

#1   #3   #2   START LEG #1

BAMBOO

WOOD

VERTICAL LADDER

BEND HERE TO FORM LAST LEG

CUT OFF

SHAPED DOWEL

HARPOON LINE (APPROX. 400 FEET)

POLE SECURING LINE

PAPER STRIPS   CARDBOARD

BAMBOO POLE

CORK

SERVED

WIRE   WOOD   TIN

GAFF   KNIFE

LEATHER STOP

HARPOON LINE

Plate 141

DOWEL

WEIGHT & NETTING   ANCHOR

WIRE   PAPER STRIP CARVE & PAINT

METAL HEAD

MARKER FLOAT

242

and shackle fitting. For your model, you might use a single length of chain, catching the ring fitting into the middle link.

As mentioned in the previous section, the drag net cables are regulated by a winch on the main deck. From this winch they are reeved through blocks on the deck and next through blocks suspended from the cross trees; without the Y line they would trail the vessel from this great height, sweeping from side to side and endangering men, wheel house, or other deck fixtures. So they must be reeved once more, this time through the blocks of the Y line, which is belayed to the aft starboard bitt; here they are confined and controlled;—the net follows obediently, and all is well.

The rest of this chapter has nothing to do with actual construction details, but I firmly believe that anyone can make a better model if he senses as much as possible of the smells, sounds and feeling of the original—have more fun doing it too. Therefore I would like to give a brief description of the activities connected with hauling in the net.

The speed of the vessel is cut to idling, and the wheel "put over," that is, turned three to five degrees to starboard. This shifts the cables slightly from astern toward the starboard side. The winch begins to retrieve the cables, and when the net is sighted the Y line is released from the bitt, allowing the cables to swing off. the starboard side, amidship. Just before the doors come aboard, heavy wire servings on the cables carry the Y line aloft, out of the way. The doors are temporarily stowed aft at the rail, the cables belayed to the aft starboard bitt, and the net is hauled aboard by hand and carefully arranged to prevent snarling. When all but the bag is aboard, a rope is passed around it and it is hauled up by the hoisting tackle and swung inboard. The purse line is opened and the fish spill out and flop around in the deck bins. The purse rope is retied.

If a new drag is to continue on the same run, the bag is lowered into the water and released. Its weight pulls the net overboard, the winch raises the doors enough to clear the rail, and they disappear. The Y line is refastened to the bitt, and the vessel put on its course.

The second run has started, but the deck work is waiting. The catch must be sorted, cleaned, packed and iced. A white cloud of squawking sea gulls is already surrounding us, looking for a free meal. The unmarketable portion of the catch—quite often the greater part of the haul—is shovelled overboard. (Most of these survive.)

243

American frigate of 1797 *Constitution*. Ship was rebuilt and restored completely in the 1930's. (In the collection of the Mariners' Museum, Newport News, Va.)

Finally, decks are washed down, portable bin boards replaced, and all is in readiness for the next catch. "Better luck this time," the men say.

MARKER FLOAT *Plates 140, 141*

Fishermen never drag the same course twice in a day. To prevent doing so on foggy or extremely hazy days they use floating markers, or marker floats, as they call them. When the net is put over, one of these markers is thrown over also. The shaft is weighted at the lower end and has an anchor line attached to it.

A compass course is held for a two hour run (average), after which the net is hauled aboard and another marker put over. The vessel turns, and while the crew is sorting and cleaning and readying the ship the skipper returns to the first marker, turns, and another drag begins—on the same compass course, but to the right or left of the former run.

A long narrow bamboo strip or shaped dowel may be used for the pole. To simulate the cork floats cut four balsa disks into roughly square shapes—or carve one piece, if you would rather. Drill holes through the center of each and place them about one-fourth of the way up the shaft. Cover with a double layer of netting, gathered at the ends, and trimly served as near the cork as possible. Top the marker with a flag bearing the fisherman's colors. It may bear a number, your initials, monogram, or any chosen symbol.

For the weight, wind narrow strips of paper somewhat roughly around the lower end, and paint it black.

BITTS *Plate 140*

The bitts used on this dragger are sturdy little fellows, and should give you no trouble. (See p. 96)

As mentioned previously, the Y line is belayed to the aft starboard bitt when the net is overboard. When net and doors are unrigged, however, the cable ends are anchored to the bitt by a hook which is attached to a rope loop around the bitt.

The aft port bitt is used as a permanent anchorage for the main after stay. The fitting for this is a small chain loop encircling the bitt under the pin and terminating in a shackle fitting. The shackle will take the after stay turnbuckle. (shackles, stays, turnbuckles, etc., pp. 140-143)

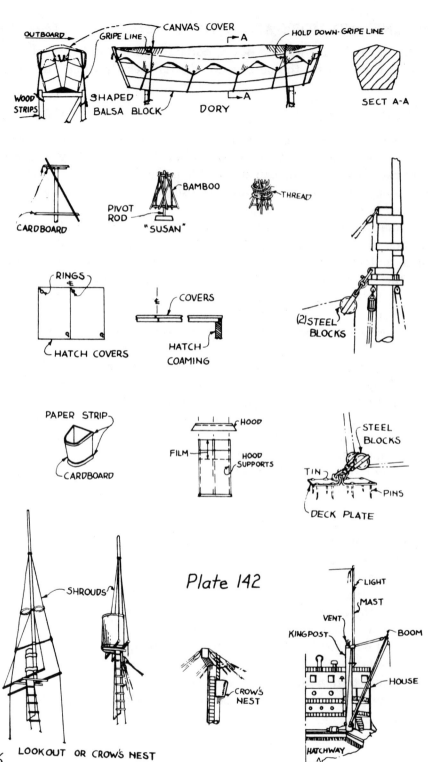

OUTBOARD

GRIPE LINE

CANVAS COVER

A

HOLD DOWN · GRIPE LINE

A

WOOD STRIPS

SHAPED BALSA BLOCK

DORY

SECT A-A

CARDBOARD

BAMBOO

PIVOT ROD

"SUSAN"

THREAD

RINGS

HATCH COVERS

COVERS

HATCH COAMING

(2) STEEL BLOCKS

PAPER STRIP

CARDBOARD

HOOD

FILM

HOOD SUPPORTS

STEEL BLOCKS

TIN

PINS

DECK PLATE

SHROUDS

Plate 142

CROW'S NEST

LIGHT

MAST

VENT

KINGPOST

BOOM

HOUSE

LOOKOUT OR CROW'S NEST

HATCHWAY

A harpooner operates from a "pulpit," which is a long, narrow plat-form overhanging the bow of the fishing vessel.

The walk is made from a thick plank, or, if this is not available, two thin ones. The inboard end is fitted between and secured to the for-ward bitts. Rope hand rails extend from the shroud lines to the sturdy forward enclosure where the harpooner stands.

Use thin pieces of wood for the plank—tongue depressers provide good material, and I believe they can be purchased in most drug stores. Cut to desired length and round the forward end. A little slot should be cut in the plank to accommodate the forestay fitting.

The rail enclosure may be of wire. Legs ♯ 1 and ♯ 5, as you see, are continuations of the rail bent to an angle; the other three legs are spaced between them and soldered to the rail. Curve your piece to conform to the plank line, then glue and insert the legs into pre-drilled holes in the planking in any one of the methods shown.

For those not equipped with soldering material, here is another method of making rail enclosures. Fold a long piece of thin wire (similar to tie wire), and for practical purposes call the upper length Wire ♯ 1, and the lower one ♯ 2. Using a common pin as a twisting lever, twist up four legs on Wire ♯ 2. Then return to leg ♯ 1, and from there, twist Wire ♯ 1 neatly around Wire ♯ 2 to form the hori-zontal railing plus leg ♯ 5. It would be a good idea to peg the work down to a board. Cut off excess wire and insert legs into planking as described.

In both types, the horizontal railing should be finished with a "serving" of cotton thread. (P. 135)

The rope rail may be of stout cotton thread. About midway of the plank's length, place a screw eye fitting in the edge on each side. Run a short thread line from each eye up to the rail, and adjust till neces-sary tautness is achieved.

A thin strip of leather or simulated leather may be glued to the outer edge of the plank near leg ♯ 5. This is called a stop, and is used to hold a loop of the harpoon line. More about stops and their purpose in the next section.

HARPOON AND GEAR *Plate 141*

The harpoon is a very long spear with a detachable barbed metal head. A securing line running from the opposite end of the pole to a

247

English royal yacht *Katherine*, one of several yachts of Charles
II. They had luxurious carvings and fittings. (Crabtree Collection,
The Mariners' Museum, Newport News, Va.)

leg of the rail enclosure retrieves the pole after action has taken place. The harpoon, or warp line, as it is sometimes called, extends from the metal head to a "stop" on the pole, from there through two or more stops on the vessel to a warp tub on the forward deck, where about 400 feet of line are coiled; the end of the line is tied to a water-tight keg standing alongside.

The first stop is a narrow strip of leather lashed to the pole, which grips a loop of the harpoon line, keeping it taut and preventing snarling. The second stop, as described in the previous section, is on the pulpit, and the third on the rail near the bow of the vessel; location of the warp tub would determine if more are necessary.

When a fish is hit, he darts violently off, trying to rid himself of the harpoon. He gets rid of the pole, but the barbed end with its attached harpoon line remains. The line whips itself free of the stops and rapidly begins to play out from the tub. One of the "hands" stands by, ready to heave the keg overboard when the end of the line is reached. The keg then serves as an easily discerned buoy.

Pole and head can be made all in one from a long thin dowel. Carve the barbed head and finish neatly with two or three windings of narrow paper, catching in a wire loop to accommodate the harpoon line. Paint the head to simulate metal.

The warp tub can be made from cardboard, and the keg from a shaped dowel, which if you wish, may be covered with netting of the same scale as that used for floats. Neatly glued paper bands add much to the realistic appearance of both pieces. To save a lot of unnecessary coiling of line in the warp tub, you might glue in a dummy bottom near the top.

"SUSAN" *Plate 142*

I am sure that the "Susan" must have derived its name from the Lazy Susan. Anyway, it revolves, and is a large sort of spool for dispensing twine for mending fishermen's nets.

To make the Susan, cut three cardboard disks as indicated, two of them with center holes to accommodate the rotating rod, which would be a small dowel or piece of bamboo. Glue diagonal strips of bamboo to the top and bottom disks at approximately a sixty degree angle. Set the pivot rod into a small wooden base. Your model may be far too small to rotate and be actually workable, but if your fingers are nimble, go ahead and try it.

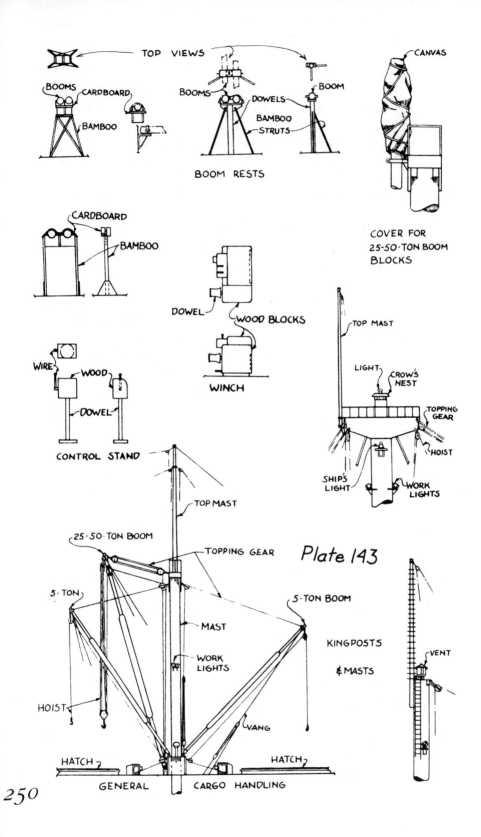

TOP VIEWS

BOOMS
CARDBOARD
BAMBOO

BOOMS
DOWELS
BAMBOO
STRUTS

BOOM

BOOM RESTS

CANVAS

COVER FOR
25·50·TON BOOM
BLOCKS

CARDBOARD
BAMBOO

DOWEL
WOOD BLOCKS
WINCH

WIRE
WOOD
DOWEL
CONTROL STAND

TOP MAST

LIGHT
CROW'S
NEST
TOPPING
GEAR

HOIST

SHIP'S
LIGHT
WORK
LIGHTS

TOP MAST

25·50·TON BOOM

TOPPING GEAR

Plate 143

5·TON

5·TON BOOM

MAST

WORK
LIGHTS

KINGPOSTS
& MASTS

VENT

HOIST

VANG

HATCH

HATCH

GENERAL   CARGO HANDLING

Wind some thread on your piece now, and it will look quite authentic. For its location on the vessel, see the deck arrangement plan of the dragger.

VERTICAL LADDERS *Plate 141*

This portable ladder leads from the deck down into the fish hold. It is merely a plank with cross members of wood set a foot apart. Near the upper end, cut away a small rectangular piece out of each side—this section fits into a slot in one of the deck support members. On the floor of the hold, make a recess of strips of wood to take the lower end of the ladder.

GAFFS AND KNIVES *Plate 141*

Gaffs are short handled picks used for sorting out the fish for market use. They have huge metal hooks which are barbless but have very sharp points. A thin dowel will serve as a handle; drill a hole in one end and insert a shaped wire head.

If you want to dress your gaff up, wind servings at top and bottom ends, and also at center, if you wish. In actual service the top serving helps prevent splitting of the wood, and the others assist a gloved hand to a better grip on a slimy surface.

During the day's activities knives are kept in constant use—for cleaning fish, repairing nets and rigging, cutting rope, etc.—therefore they must be easily accessible. Two large knives are kept in stops on the forward wall of the after house structure, and at least one on the mast. Make your stops as directed in the harpoon gear section. The knife blades may be shaped from tin, and the handles from wood.

Here is a good test for finger dexterity: if any of your knives are large enough, try extending the metal of your blade into the handle. Sandwich between two pieces of wood, drill two tiny holes through the sandwich and rivet together, using small pins as rivets. Carefully shape the handle of your masterpiece with a file.

DECK PLATE *Plate 142*

The deck plate for the lower steel blocks through which the drag cables are reeved can be made from a narrow strip of tin. Fold it double, and about $\frac{1}{16}$ of an inch from the folded edge and half an inch apart, drill two small holes for the shackles.

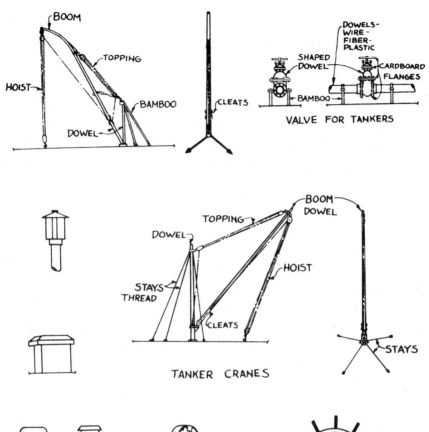

BOOM

TOPPING

HOIST

BAMBOO

DOWEL

CLEATS

DOWELS-
WIRE-
FIBER-
PLASTIC

SHAPED
DOWEL

CARDBOARD
FLANGES

BAMBOO

VALVE FOR TANKERS

BOOM
DOWEL

TOPPING

DOWEL

HOIST

STAYS
THREAD

CLEATS

STAYS

TANKER CRANES

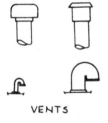

SPACER

PADDLE

BOOK

SECT. A-A

BOOK

VENTS

DOWELS OR CARDBOARD

Plate 144

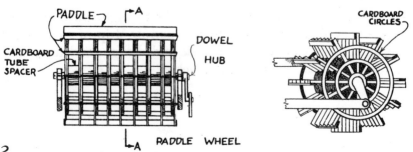

PADDLE

A

CARDBOARD
TUBE
SPACER

DOWEL
HUB

CARDBOARD
CIRCLES

A

PADDLE WHEEL

DECK PLATE

Plate 142

Draw a line parallel with the folded edge and about $\frac{3}{16}$ of an inch from it. Place the folded edge in a vise on the $\frac{3}{16}$ line and bend both sides to right angles of the fold. Remove from the vise, drill a few holes along the edges, and fasten the plate to the deck, using cut-off pins to simulate bolts.

THE DORY AND ITS STOWAGE

Plate 142

The life boat on the dragger is a dory stowed aft near the wheel house on a high rack, where it is out of the way, leaving space beneath for stowing oil drums, marker floats, extra blocks, tools, fenders, etc. (Crewmen on small vessels are as bent upon utilizing space as housewives in a one-room apartment.)

The boom hoisting tackle is used for launching this dory from its lofty cradle, using a sling attached fore and aft. Nevertheless, a lot of physical brawn is needed to keep the boat from plunging forward when released.

Carve the dory from a solid block of balsa wood, and instead of hollowing it out, keep the center line from fore to aft level with the top bow and stern lines—then there will be no sagging of the cover. For the cover, use any cotton fabric which has a weave resembling canvas. Drape and fit it over the wood, allowing enough for a series of V cuts along the edges. Connect matching V's on both sides with threads passed under the dory; connect small flaps fore and aft, and it is ready for the stowage rack.

This rack is simply two tall pieces of wood framework resting on the deck and spaced to suit the dimensions of the dory. The inboard uprights are fastened to the walls of the after house structure, the outboard ones to the bulwark;—cut notches in the cap rail to recess them. A horizontal cross member is fitted between the uprights at the top, and an angle brace inserted for stability.

The ropes which bind the dory to the framework are called gripe lines.

BOOM REST

Plate 143

The portable boom rest for the dragger can be made from a narrow piece of thin wood. Taper the width of the lower one-third section slightly, and cut a curve in the top to fit the boom. The boom is held securely in the curve by the main sheet tackle.

U.S.S. *Atlanta*, 7,500-ton (light) cruiser. Saw action in Battle of Midway, Solomon Islands, Santa Cruz Island, and finally damaged so badly at Guadalcanal that she had to be sunk. (Courtesy Gibbs & Cox, Inc. of New York.)

BOOM REST
Plate 143

The boom rest slips through a slot on the after house structure, and the lower end fits into a recess on the deck made from nailed down strips of wood. Attach a small cleat to the forward side of the boom rest about one-third the distance from the top—this is for securing the gaff peak halyard. (P. 197-207)

CROW'S NEST
Plates 142, 143

The lookout, or crow's nest, is, for obvious reasons, set as high as possible on the mast. Varying greatly in construction and style, they range from simple rope loops—used on most fishing vessels, to elaborately equipped cubicles furnished with heat, phones, mounted binoculars, etc., found on larger craft—liners, freighters, Navy vessels.

For the primitive type, make loops of wire or stiffened thread to simulate rope, and lash into position between the upper mast and the shroud lines on each side. At a proper distance below this air-conditioned nest, fasten a foot-rope, also between mast and shrouds.

Another type, a step higher in comfort but usually several steps lower on the mast, is this semi-circular enclosure of arm pit height, whose platform rests on the cross trees or on a bracket fastened to the front of the mast. You might make this enclosure and the platform of cardboard. Paper strips glued around the top and base will give a finished and realistic appearance.

The more elaborate type is not difficult to construct. Make a small tube from thin cardboard or Bristol board, and use the same material for the platform, circular overhanging hood and the flat top. A piece of film or thin plastic will serve as window material. Glue to the inside of the tube, allowing a narrow section to project above it. Glue four tiny cardboard or bamboo supports inside after the film has been placed, then glue the top in place.

One of the ship's lights is sometimes mounted on the top of the hood at the forward edge.

TANKERS
Plate 144

Tankers have such a maze of pipes, valves, manifolds and vents on the main deck that to provide easy access to all parts of the ship, a catwalk runs along the center from fore to aft; stairs and ladders lead from it to the main deck. The cranes on these vessels are designed to handle and control huge fuel lines which connect the valves from ship to ship or from ship to shore installations.

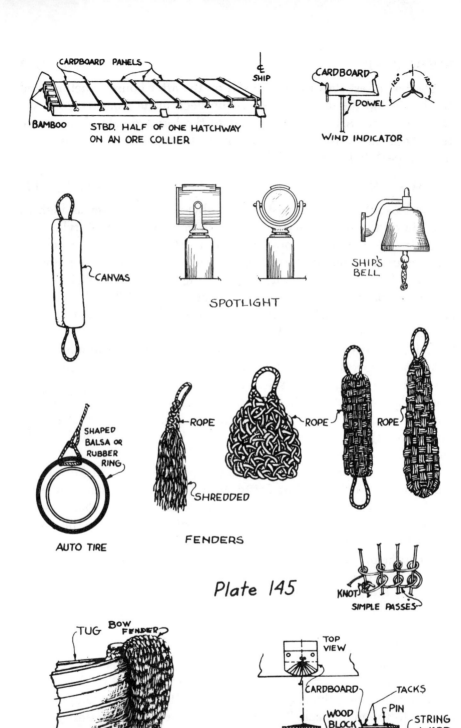

CARDBOARD PANELS

BAMBOO

STBD. HALF OF ONE HATCHWAY
ON AN ORE COLLIER

℄ SHIP

CARDBOARD

DOWEL

120°

WIND INDICATOR

CANVAS

SPOTLIGHT

SHIP'S
BELL

SHAPED
BALSA OR
RUBBER
RING

AUTO TIRE

ROPE

SHREDDED

ROPE

ROPE

FENDERS

Plate 145

KNOT

SIMPLE PASSES

TUG BOW FENDER

TOP
VIEW

CARDBOARD

TACKS

PIN

WOOD
BLOCK

STRING
WARP

KNOTS

PIN

FRONT

TABLE
TOP

SIDE
VIEW

Pipes can be made from any material that resembles pipes when painted. A good material—and a time saver for small models—is string or cord that has been thoroughly shellacked and allowed to dry taut between pins. It handles well—can easily be bent to follow a new run, or remain straight for long runs. Apply a little glue to freshly cut ends to keep them from fraying.

Valves for the small model may be made from pins with various head sizes. For larger models, the valves, bolt heads and nuts may be carved from balsa, and cardboard used for flanges.

FREIGHTERS *Plates, 143, 144*

Although all freighters have basic similarities, they vary in size, in types and arrangement of masts, king posts, hatches, winches, booms, etc. Generally speaking, the larger the ship the more cargo rigging she will carry. Vessels designed to handle and carry assorted heavy cargo or special cargo may be equipped with booms capable of handling up to fifty tons—"fifty ton booms," these are called.

The large booms are nearly always stowed perpendicularly alongside the mast, stowed to it at the cross trees. As they are put into service only occasionally, the heads of the booms and the upper blocks are protected from weather, rust, etc., by canvas bags, or hoods.

When not in use, the small booms are stowed in nearly horizontal positions in boom rests—brackets or special devices on the deck. In this location and position they offer minimum wind resistance. Shown here are a few of the many types of boom rests found on cargo vessels. Some house two booms, but there are many types that stow only one; some are portable, but most are welded to the deck, the hatch coaming, or to one of the houses. They are placed where they interfere least with cargo work or other activities on board.

WORK BOATS *Plates, 144, 145*

Some characteristic features of other types of work boats (besides fishing vessels) are included here for anyone who might be working from a kit unit, or from plans with incomplete details and instructions.

Models of work ships require the same amount of skill and painstaking attention to detail as those of ships loaded with sail and rigging —and sometimes more. The true craftsman is just as proud of a job well done on these really beautiful utilitarian vessels as on any famous-name ship. They add freshness, vitality and variety to any collection.

The *Constellation*, U.S. 38-gun frigate launched Sept. 7, 1797. First Commander was Captain Tomas Truxton. (In the collection of The Mariners' Museum, Newport News, Va.)

WORK BOATS

Plates, 144, 145

As in all model building, work for correct scale throughout, have patience in executing all the infinitesimal details, do a neat paint job, and you will be more than rewarded. Most important of all—*do not hurry.*

At this point, I should like again to remind anyone who loves to make ship models how helpful it is to keep a picture and information file on all kinds, shapes and sizes of ships and boats. It is surprising and gratifying how fast such a collection can grow. You might begin with a manila filing folder, graduating to alphabetical box files, accordion files, *loose leaf* scrap books, or whatever appeals. Certainly, library research will continue to be helpful and stimulating to the student, but occasions inevitably develop when having data of one's own on hand saves hours of time and frustration. A magnifying glass is a useful adjunct for picking out picture details.

TUG BOATS

Plate 145

A set of working plans for a typical harbor tug accompanies this book. These busy little boats remind me of scurrying water beetles on the look-out for some tid-bit. Several of them are sometimes called into service to dock a large liner or Navy vessel.

In general structure tug boats are basically alike. There are two distinct types: harbor tugs and ocean going tugs. Most people know that there are tugs that perform their duties along the seaboard, but it comes as a surprise to many to learn that there are tugs which tow cargo and craft across the ocean.

TUG BOAT FENDERS

Plate 145

All vessels carry protective buffers, or fenders on board, on some to be taken out and used when necessary, on others kept in constant service, as on tug boats and a few other work boats. Some fenders are purchased from nautical supply houses, some made by crew members.

Tug boat fenders are almost infinite in variety, but the large bow fender, which is such a characteristic feature of the tug, is basically similar on all. These huge mats of rope are shock absorbing cushions, which prevent surface damage to the ships which the tugs nudge and push in and out of their pier berths.

Making miniature fenders is fun. To weave a bow fender for a tug, cut a piece of cardboard for a jig so that it resembles somewhat a wide slice of bread. Cut notches in the "crust," and tack the piece to a

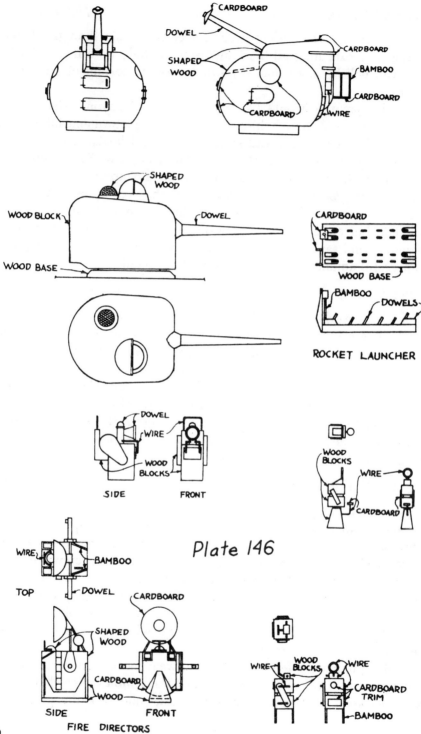

CARDBOARD

DOWEL

SHAPED WOOD

CARDBOARD

BAMBOO

CARDBOARD

WIRE

CARDBOARD

SHAPED WOOD

WOOD BLOCK

DOWEL

WOOD BASE

CARDBOARD

CARDBOARD

WOOD BASE

BAMBOO

DOWELS

ROCKET LAUNCHER

DOWEL

WIRE

WOOD BLOCKS

SIDE

FRONT

WOOD BLOCKS

WIRE

CARDBOARD

Plate 146

WIRE

BAMBOO

TOP

DOWEL

CARDBOARD

SHAPED WOOD

CARDBOARD

WOOD

SIDE

FRONT

FIRE DIRECTORS

WIRE

WOOD BLOCKS

WIRE

CARDBOARD TRIM

BAMBOO

260

block of wood about the height you want your fender to be, with the upper half of the "slice" extending beyond the block. Set the block on a table or drawing board so that the notched edge comes flush with the table edge. Drive a pin firmly through the cardboard into the center line of the block as shown, and one into the table edge, also at the center line.

For your middle warp thread, tie a string between the pins, making it as taut as possible. Next take the outside warp thread, tie it to the top pin, run it through the outside notch on one side, loop once around the lower pin, through the other outside notch, and back to the upper pin again.

Proceeding upward from the bottom, tie all the intermediate warp threads to the center warp thread in as even a series of knots as possible, continue through the proper notches over the top, and again tie to the center thread; because this top area is smaller, it will be a bit more difficult than the front. Remember always to allow *as little slack as possible* in all warp threads.

In the weaving, you do just the opposite, and try *not* to pull the thread tightly. Beginning at the bottom, tie a string to the outer left-hand warp thread, pass it around and under itself on the next thread, and so on. Notice that the winding begins from the *inside* on each new row, and continues as before, with the string coming around the warp *under* itself.

As you complete each row, push it down as far as possible so you will have a closely woven, compact mat. Continue over the top in the same manner. Remove pins and cardboard, and sew on a loop to go around the tug bitt. Sometimes an overlay of baggey wrinkle, prepared on netting, is sewn in place over the fender, reminding one irresistibly of a goat's beard. If the finished bow fender needs more bulk, pad the inside a little before mounting it. If it needs coloring, dip in coffee or strong tea.

The small fenders seen here (which are used in dozens of places) are quite easy to make. They can be woven, braided, plaited; or cores can be covered with coarsely woven fabrics which resemble rope weaves.

RIVER STEAMERS   *Plate 144*

River steamers and show boats, which add so much color and romance to any model fleet, are a joy for the model builder to make;—

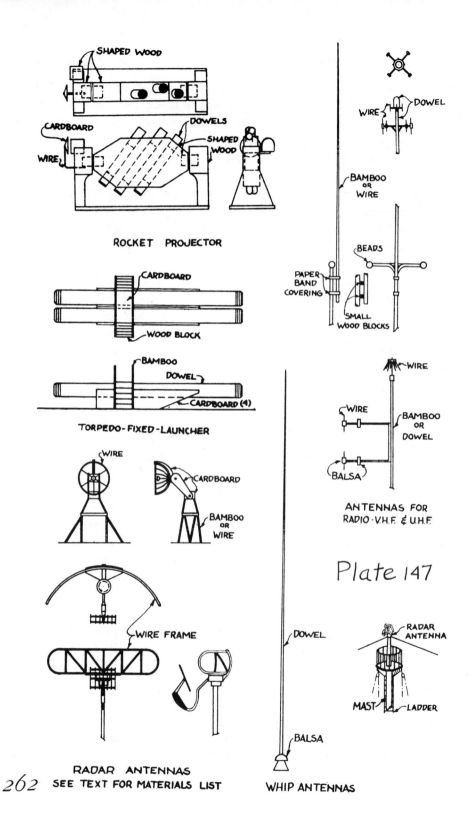

SHAPED WOOD

CARDBOARD
WIRE
DOWELS
SHAPED WOOD

ROCKET PROJECTOR

CARDBOARD
WOOD BLOCK

BAMBOO
DOWEL
CARDBOARD (4)

TORPEDO-FIXED-LAUNCHER

WIRE
CARDBOARD
BAMBOO
OR
WIRE

WIRE FRAME

RADAR ANTENNAS
SEE TEXT FOR MATERIALS LIST

DOWEL
WIRE

BAMBOO
OR
WIRE

BEADS
PAPER
BAND
COVERING
SMALL
WOOD BLOCKS

WIRE
WIRE
BAMBOO
OR
DOWEL
BALSA

ANTENNAS FOR
RADIO·V.H.F. & U.H.F.

Plate 147

DOWEL

BALSA

WHIP ANTENNAS

RADAR
ANTENNA

MAST LADDER

262

in their construction, about the only feature that might try one's patience is the paddle wheel.

For certainty of neatness, I suggest that you cut the wooden dowel hub and cardboard paddle pieces a little longer than you consider necessary; they can be trimmed when the job is finished.

The diagram shows one wheel unit ready for the assembly line, with a small and a large ring piece glued onto the spoke section, shown in black. Using a sharp razor blade, cut the necessary number of each from cardboard—if your model plan calls for nine wheel units, for instance, cut nine spoke sections, nine large and nine small rings. Drill a small hole in the center of each spoke section to fit the dowel hub. Next, cut the same number, minus one, of the spacers.

Roll and glue the spacers into tubes, and fold down the tabs; of course if you find ready-made tubes small enough, you can cut them into sections for spacers. Glue the circles to the spokes, remembering that on the outside wheels, the circles must be on the *outside*. Glue one end of each spacer to the center of a wheel, then line up all the sections on the dowel hub—here is where you will be grateful for its extra length, which allows comparative freedom of movement.

During this process, have the horizontal lines of spokes on both sides resting in a simple jig, or as illustrated, on the edges of two books large enough to allow the pieces to clear the table top. Glue all spacers and wheel units together and to the dowel. Allow to dry thoroughly. Cut paddle sections from cardboard.

Next, using the same jig contrivance, glue the paddles in place along one line of spokes, let dry, carefully shift the next line of spokes to the jig, glue on the next paddle, and so on. When thoroughly dry, trim paddle pieces and dowel hub as necessary.

GREAT LAKES ORE COLLIERS   *Plate 145*

In these powerful ore boats, the distance between the bridge in the forward superstructure area and the working quarters in the stern is so great that an Olympic sprinter could get a pretty good workout covering it. (See insert.)

The surface of this vast deck area is broken by innumerable hatchways, which gradually slope away from the center line outwards, and are bordered by long, narrow port and starboard aisles.

Each hatchway has a series of overlapping sliding covers or panels, which stack together at the outboard sides to permit loading or re-

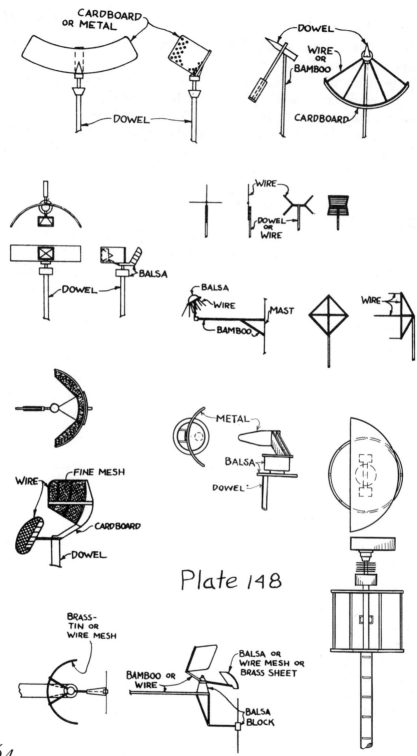

CARDBOARD OR METAL

DOWEL

DOWEL

WIRE OR BAMBOO

CARDBOARD

WIRE

DOWEL OR WIRE

DOWEL

BALSA

BALSA

WIRE

MAST

BAMBOO

WIRE

METAL

BALSA

DOWEL

FINE MESH

WIRE

CARDBOARD

DOWEL

Plate 148

BRASS-TIN OR WIRE MESH

BAMBOO OR WIRE

BALSA OR WIRE MESH OR BRASS SHEET

BALSA BLOCK

moval of ore cargo. When closed, the panels are held down by clamps attached to the hatch coamings.

A bright spot of interest, it seems to me, is that after unloading, a bulldozer is swung down by a crane to scrape the bottom clean.

The hatchways can be built up entirely of cardboard, or with balsa base and cardboard panels. Hinges and clamps may be of cardboard or bamboo.

ARMAMENT *Plates 146, 147*

There have been some revised and many new forms of armaments since this book first appeared in print. Many designs, of course, are top secret and will be for some time to come, but some of those released are illustrated here in sufficient detail to be practical for the model builder.

Their construction will be simplified if you have the following materials on hand:

Balsa wood blocks, sheets and strips. Carves more easily than any other kind of wood.

Cardboard. Is perfect trim material when neatly cut and glued. Still looks crisp and retains sharp edges after shellacking and painting.

Wire in various sizes. If you cannot obtain as fine a wire as you want, use stripped bamboo.

Bamboo. Will split into minutely fine sections which are perfect for struts, braces, and framework of all kinds. Can be used instead of wire in many instances. Bends easily, but still retains a certain amount of rigidity which fine wire lacks.

Dowels. Various sizes, ranging from ¼ of an inch diameter down to the minutest. Scout drug stores for applicators and tongue depressors, also Good Humor wagon for ice cream sticks and spoons.

ANTENNAS *Plates 147, 148*

In the field of electronics, wonderful new developments appear on the horizon in such rapid and steady succession, that one hesitates to include them in a volume of this kind;—it could be a case of, "This is a nice antenna—wasn't it?" But in they go, for when antennae become obsolete, they will begin to acquire historical value, together with wind jammers, World War II armaments, et al.

Therefore, illustrated here are a few current designs from the field of electronics—radio, radar, sonar, fire control, range finding and

U.S.S. *Juneau*, 7,500-ton (light) cruiser. Forward superstructure, port side, looking to starboard. Sunk by Jap submarine at Guadalcanal. (Courtesy Gibbs & Cox, Inc. of New York.)

relay systems, very high frequency (V H F), ultra high frequency (U H F).

For small models, do not include too many details in these installations, or suddenly the rest of your model will appear unfinished. Keep the scale right, do the simple assembly and painting carefully, and the finished product will be certain to appear effective and authentic. The vanes may be of solid material—metal, cardboard, plastic, etc.

Craftsmen whose models require more complicated detail work will discover a miniature world of possibilities in old radio tubes. But before breaking the glass envelope of the tube, put the tube in a paper bag or cover with some protective material; discard glass splinters with great care before taking apart the interior maze of wires, screens, etc.

WHALERS   *Plate 149*

Centuries ago, a whaler had a chance to be a homebody if he felt like it, for all hunting was close to the shore. But gradually, as the whales moved toward open and ice-infested seas, man followed, and the boats, the work, and the men became increasingly rugged. Voyages lasting three to four years were routine, as were savage storms, hard dangerous work, and poor food. It was a Norwegian whaler who, in 1894, was the first man to set foot on the Antarctic continent.

The first known human being born in Antarctica (1948) was the child of Soviet whalers—yes, there are even lady whalers now; the Russians broke the age-old "bourgeois," bad-luck superstition. At first, whalers from other countries did giant double-takes, but now they are becoming accustomed to it. There have been countless other changes in the industry, too. Now there are swift, powerful factory ships, with dentists, librarians, chemists, and technicians aboard, and there is an International Whaling Commission that strictly regulates seasons, hunting areas, sizes and species of whales. The old masters are turning over in their graves.

The plan view of a typical whaling ship deck arrangement, shown in PLATE *149*, will help acquaint the beginner with the way things are placed in relation to the ship. There are variances to this arrangement but, in general, this depicts the set-up of an average 19th-century whaler.

The vessel had to be well constructed from heavy timber throughout the hull in order to withstand heavy seas and nudging ice floes. Characteristic features are the large whaleboats and the method of

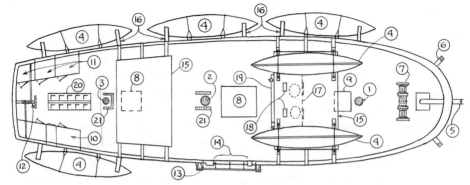

DECK ARRANGEMENT OF A TYPICAL WHALING SHIP

(1) FOREMAST	(8) HATCH	(15) SHELTER DECK
(2) MAINMAST	(9) COMPANIONWAY FWD.	(16) DAVITS
(3) MIZZENMAST	(10) CAPTAIN'S QUARTERS	(17) TRY WORKS
(4) WHALEBOATS	(11) 1st, 2nd & 3rd MATES' QUARTERS	(18) FLUES
(5) BOWSPRIT	(12) STEERING GEAR	(19) WORKBENCH
(6) CATHEAD	(13) "CUTTING-IN" STAGE	(20) SKYLIGHT
(7) WINDLASS	(14) GANGWAY AREA	(21) FIFE RAIL

Plate 149

DK.　　GANGWAY　　RAIL

PLAN VIEW OF
"CUTTING-IN" STAGE OR FRAME

HEAVY DUTY GEAR

FWD. TACKLE

WHALE

"CUTTING-IN" STAGE

AFT TACKLE

RAIL

BLUBBER HOOK & BEGINNING OF "BLANKET"

AFT TACKLE

PLANK

STANCHION

SAFETY RAIL

PLANK

FWD. TACKLE

PLANK

BRACE

stowing them. The davits are fixed, with the boats stowed outboard on keel rests, and with a warp line forward and aft securing each boat to her cradle. They are equipped and ready for instant launching at the call, "Thar she blows!" from the crow's nest.

"CUTTING-IN" STAGE   *Plates 149-150-151*

Most interesting of all the whaler details, in the author's opinion, is the "cutting-in" frame, or stage. This was installed on the starboard side, outboard of the "gangway," operated with block and fall tackle, so it could be raised and lowered to suit working conditions. It looks like a dangerous place to work, and it certainly was, especially during heavy weather. Sometimes, as many as five or six men would be on the stage at one time. Even in comparatively calm weather, the footboards were precarious, being slippery from both water and grease. In bad weather the men tied themselves to the rail with a length of rope. All "cutting-in" tools, spades, saws, etc., were anchored by ropes to some part of the frame, in case they might be wrenched from the men's hands, or inadvertently dropped.

A man had to balance himself on the slippery and constantly turning carcass of the whale whenever the blubber hook was inserted into a new "blanket." A "blanket" was the entire strip of blubber stripped from the carcass circumference. The flenser made a lengthwise cut in the carcass, then cut two slashes at right angles to it, each about eighteen inches long.

The blubber hook was then forced through the edge of one slash into and through the fat blanket, and out the other slash in the skin. The winch, or windlass, was started, pulling the hook upward and inboard. The cutting-in men then made two parallel cuts about three feet apart, and the blubber was stripped off as the whale's body revolved alongside the ship.

In other instances, chunks, or parts of the body, would be severed and hauled aboard for further reduction by the men on deck. A large piece of the whale to be "tried out" (or "rendered," or "boiled down") had to be cut into small pieces for easy handling, then put into the "trying-out" vats. The residue from this process was used for fuel, to keep the all-important fires going. It burned well and gave off considerable heat.

CUTTING-IN STAGE CONSTRUCTION. The planking may be made from thin balsa sheets cut to the required size. The rail and its stanchions may be of split bamboo, or the rail may be a thin dowel, and the

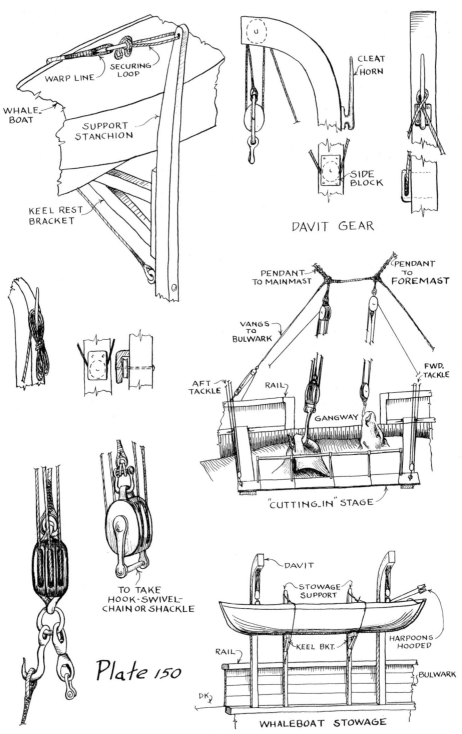

WARP LINE

SECURING LOOP

WHALE-BOAT

SUPPORT STANCHION

KEEL REST BRACKET

CLEAT HORN

SIDE BLOCK

DAVIT GEAR

PENDANT TO MAINMAST

PENDANT TO FOREMAST

VANGS TO BULWARK

AFT TACKLE

RAIL

GANGWAY

FWD. TACKLE

"CUTTING-IN" STAGE

TO TAKE HOOK-SWIVEL-CHAIN OR SHACKLE

Plate 150

DAVIT

STOWAGE SUPPORT

RAIL

KEEL BKT.

HARPOONS HOODED

BULWARK

DK?

WHALEBOAT STOWAGE

270

stanchions made from wire. The ship end of the planks is hinged; a simple arrangement is shown. The outboard corners have a ringbolt penetrating the planks; the block is fastened to this ringbolt. The aft tackle is attached directly to the mainmast, or to a pendant, which is fastened between the mainmast and the mainmast shroud lines. The forward tackle is fastened to the shelter deck supports.

The heavy-duty gear and triple blocks are secured to the mainmast crosstrees, and terminate in the large blubber hook. Sometimes double sets of blubber-stripping tackle are fitted, as shown in one of the sketches (the heavy-duty gear plus a smaller tackle for quicker handling of smaller odd portions of the whale).

CUTTING-IN STAGE HINGES. On the plank end, fasten a wire to simulate the pivotal rod and hold it in place with a wide piece of metal, as shown, or with two narrow straps. Rest the rod on two wooden blocks, and hold it in place with metal straps, one at each side of the plank, as shown in one of the sketches. These two sketches give you a choice. Both are easy to make, but if you have another idea that you think is good or better, go ahead and use it. There were many methods of hinging this end of the planks to the ship.

DAVITS   *Plate 150*

The davits may be shaped and carved from thick balsa pieces, or if you wish, you may rough-cut sheet balsa and then glue two or more pieces together, depending on the size of the model. When the glue has dried, shape them to finished form. The davit head contains triple sheaves, and the haul of the line is reeved through a block attached to the side of the davit.

Davits that are used as supports for shelter decks, etc., have an ordinary belaying pin at the rail for belaying the line, and to which the excess line may be hung when the boat is stowed. All others have a cleat horn, high up, for the same purpose.

The cradle, or stowage supports, are simple bracket-type outriggers secured to portable shaped stanchions. The stanchion has a ringbolt below the bracket to take the securing warp line, which ends in a ring. The top of the stanchion may be rigged with rings, or simply have a hole through which the securing loop of line penetrates. This double line, or loop, is fastened to the ring of the warp line in a buoy hitch, for ease in unfastening.

Some of the various types of blocks and fittings are shown in PLATE *151*, and a breakdown of how different blocks are reeved.

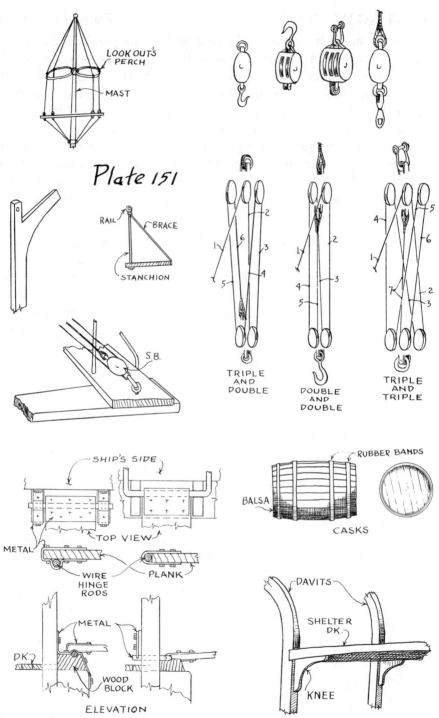

LOOK OUT'S PERCH

MAST

Plate 151

RAIL — BRACE

STANCHION

S.B.

TRIPLE AND DOUBLE

DOUBLE AND DOUBLE

TRIPLE AND TRIPLE

SHIP'S SIDE

TOP VIEW

METAL

WIRE HINGE RODS

PLANK

DK.

METAL

WOOD BLOCK

ELEVATION

RUBBER BANDS

BALSA

CASKS

DAVITS

SHELTER DK.

KNEE

No. 1 is the hauling end of the line, and it terminates on one of the blocks in a fastening, called a becket.

Preparations for the taking of whales and the arduous task of extracting the oil began almost as soon as the ship got under way. Harpoons and "cutting-in" instruments were sharpened to razor-edge, and the innumerable smaller pieces of tools and equipment were overhauled and made ready. Rope, sails and oars were checked and rechecked. The "try works" had to be built and reinforced against the dangers of dislodgment by storm and the ever-present hazard of fire. The overside "cutting-in" stage had to be assembled and rigged for easy and quick operation. The cooper was busy making up or assembling casks and barrels for storing the precious and hard-fought-for oil.

The lives of a boat crew, as well as the chances of capturing a whale, could hinge on the quality of preparation. The loss of a whale could add many toilsome days to the voyage.

TRY WORKS   *Plate 152*

"Try works," as mentioned before, is a condensed term for "trying-out works," or boiling down, or rendering paraphernalia. It is a stationary structure, built solidly on a brick or concrete base and secured firmly to the deck. It is perhaps the most important structure on board; it houses the fires and it has two apertures in the top to accommodate the "try pots," or cauldrons, which are situated directly above the fires. This is the heart of a whale ship during her hunting period. Here the fats are rendered into oil, which crew and owner hope will be abundant enough to give each man a good profit.

The body of the try works may be made from a balsa block, with sheet balsa strips simulating the base. Cut in the fire-door openings, but leave the holes for the try pots until you know their exact size. (All the extra appurtenances can be made.)

Flues, doors, apron (in front of fire doors), and the top should be made of thin metal—usually cigarette or cigar tin material will suffice. Again, leave try-pot holes until later. The doors are either hinged or are hung on a rod by two straps bent into guides. Hanging doors were the more common because of the ease in gaining access to the fires. Then all the men had to do was slide them to one side, replenish the fires, and slide them back into place again. Most try works had side supports of some kind. These were also anchored to the deck and solidly secured into the brickwork of the fireplaces.

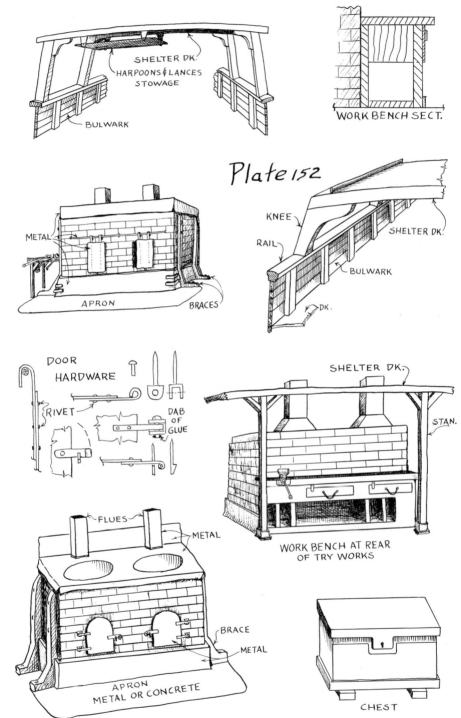

SHELTER DK.
HARPOONS & LANCES
STOWAGE

BULWARK

WORK BENCH SECT.

Plate 152

METAL

APRON   BRACES

KNEE

RAIL

SHELTER DK.

BULWARK

DK.

DOOR
HARDWARE

RIVET

DAB
OF
GLUE

SHELTER DK.

STAN.

WORK BENCH AT REAR
OF TRY WORKS

FLUES

METAL

BRACE

METAL

APRON
METAL OR CONCRETE

CHEST

274

The balsa block may be scored to simulate brick, or brick paper of proper scale may be glued to the block. All metal parts should be painted black.

The workbench that was often built directly behind the try works was merely a series of planks put together, but it also added to the support of the try works. On one side of the oven either a shelf was built, or a small barrel was placed and secured to hold the many tools of the men tending the fires and try pots. As the oil was rendered, it was ladled out into cooling vats and kept there for a short period of time before being barrelled.

TOOLS *Plate 153*

This plate is devoted to the miscellaneous items found on board a whaler. The bucket, cooper's devil base, and the half-barrel base of one of the grindstones may be shaped from balsa blocks. Score the stave lines and use thin paper strips glued in place for the hoops. Rubber bands glued in place serve very well, also, and here there is no problem about fitting them to the angle of the staves. When painted, they look authentic. The grindstone with cover may be shaped from a balsa block, or made up of cardboard.

The try pot shown presents a greater problem. Try to find either a thin metal or plastic cap or base of some sort which has the right scale. Roam around in the dime store—you will be sure to spot something that can be used.

Chests of various sizes may be shaped from a balsa block, with sheet balsa for bases and lids. For the locks, use pieces of sheet balsa fitted in place.

Blubber hooks may be shaped from heavy copper wire, flattened somewhat to give the necessary eye for a drilled hole to accommodate the fitting you intend to use.

The harpoons, lances, spades, etc., are shaped easily from flattened copper wire by filing. The spades should be fitted to dowels that have been split a short distance to take the metal cutter, and tapered slightly. After the spade head has been cemented in place and dried thoroughly, continue to shape the dowel carefully until it forms part of the head, as shown. A slight sanding around the dowel at a given line will give the demarcation between handle and metal head. For the other tools—harpoon, lance, etc., insert the wire directly into the dowel. Using thin strips of paper, build up a tapered joint between

BUCKET

COOPER'S
DEVIL

GRINDSTONES

COVER

TRYING-OUT VAT

METAL

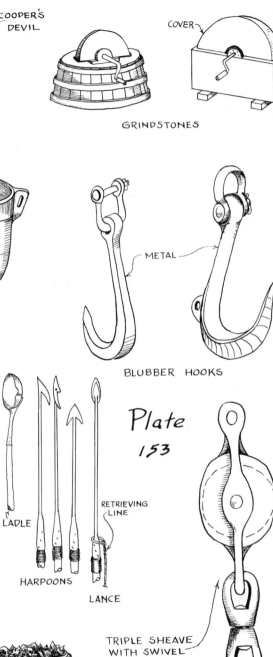

BLUBBER HOOKS

Plate
153

CUTTING
SPADES

GRAINS
FOR BLUBBER
HANDLING

LADLE

HARPOONS

RETRIEVING
LINE

LANCE

TRIPLE SHEAVE
WITH SWIVEL

SMALL BARREL
WITH TRY-WORK
TOOLS

FUEL PAN

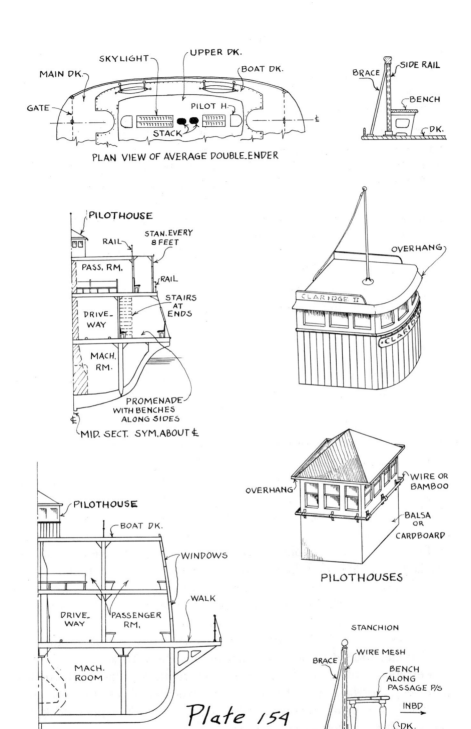

MAIN DK.
SKYLIGHT
UPPER DK.
BOAT DK.
GATE
PILOT H.
STACK

PLAN VIEW OF AVERAGE DOUBLE-ENDER

BRACE
SIDE RAIL
BENCH
DK.

PILOTHOUSE
RAIL
STAN. EVERY 8 FEET
PASS. RM.
RAIL
STAIRS AT ENDS
DRIVE-WAY
MACH. RM.
PROMENADE WITH BENCHES ALONG SIDES
MID. SECT. SYM. ABOUT ₵

OVERHANG
CLARIDGE II
CLARID

PILOTHOUSE
BOAT DK.
WINDOWS
WALK
DRIVE-WAY
PASSENGER RM.
MACH. ROOM
SECTION

OVERHANG
WIRE OR BAMBOO
BALSA OR CARDBOARD
PILOTHOUSES

STANCHION
WIRE MESH
BRACE
BENCH ALONG PASSAGE P/S
INBD
DK.

Plate 154

277

the metal and the dowel, giving the appearance of one fitting into the other.

The odd-looking tools in the barrel may be shaped from thinner wire, using split bamboo on some, for handles. Some are of metal throughout, such as fire stokers and some of the gaff hooks. Other tools are: a ladle, bristle brush, wire brushes, axes, scraping knives, and various lengths of gaffs. These are used at the try works.

Sometimes a metal basin, or metal-lined box, was used as a fuel pan, or box. This held the residue of the rendered-out blubber and skin and would be used for fuel, as needed.

The block is shown as another weird type of fitting. The swivel, even small ones, may be made from flattened copper wire, shaped, drilled and assembled by riveting. Place a small sheet of paper as a spacer between the halves before riveting. Remove the paper after the assembly is completed.

FERRYBOATS   *Plates 154-155-156*

Ferryboat: A vessel for conveying passengers, merchandise, etc., across a river or other narrow water. (Webster)

There are ocean-going ferries—one for rail travelers between Paris and London, where the passengers may, if they wish, travel across the Channel without stirring from the train. A powerful ferryboat from the mainland to Prince Edward Island, Canada, is an icebreaker, as well. At the other extreme, there are flat-bottomed barges fording inland streams by means of a chain. In fact, one could do a whole book on the varieties, but here we will confine ourselves to average sizes and types.

PLATE *154* shows a plan view (top view) of an average double-decked, double-ended boat, together with several sectional views. The lower deck is for cars, trucks and freight, and the upper one (and sometimes there are more) for passenger use. Many of these have snack bars and/or luncheonettes.

PLATES *155 and 156* show a few of the construction details the author has noticed in ferries in and around New York.

Ferryboat hulls may be of block construction or built up (review PLATES *1, 2 and 3*). For above-deck construction, sheet balsa is a good material, or a combination of balsa and cardboard. Upper deck and house sides are best formed from cardboard.

Two characteristic types of pilothouses are shown—one square, and one with rounded front. A pilothouse requires many windows; when you have cut them out, back them with plastic or transparent film to simulate glass.

Most of the ship structure stanchions (those that help support overhead decks, etc.) may be made from small-diameter dowels, and any square stanchions from square balsa strips.

The side rails have intermittent stanchions approximately eight feet apart; these may be made from dowels, balsa, or wire, flattened a bit at the points where the handrails join them. Sometimes these stanchions rise straight up to the overhead deck; others, as in one of the sketches, are supported by braces from the upper deck. Yet another variety, as you see, has added brace supports from the deck edge extending outside the rail.

Railing construction is rather tedious, but if carried out with patience, it will aid immeasurably in gaining a professional look. Split bamboo is best for the upright rails. Cut them in a jig for accurate length and ease in assembling. The upper and lower rails should be made of balsa strips. It is better to make the railings in sections to fit between the stanchions rather than in long strips sliced to fit.

For mesh railings on smaller models, use scrim or fine netting. Make these in sections, also, to fit between the stanchions. To save time and energy, tape a piece of scrim or net to a board or cardboard sheet. Then, as shown in the illustration on PLATE *155*, glue several cardboard frames of the proper size to it. Cover all with cardboard and a weight until dry. Remove tape, turn the whole thing over and repeat the original gluing process with duplicate frames.

When thoroughly dry, remove your framed sections carefully and neatly with a sharp razor blade. You will find them quite sturdy and most effective in appearance. Loops of linen thread encircling stanchions and frame corners will help to hold them in position during the installation. Leave the loops there when dry, cutting off excess thread, because the painting-over will make it part of the structure. (Other variations of jigs and handrails are on *page 45*).

Benches on all ferries are basically similar in structure, but there must be hundreds of various types. The majority have back rests, but many extend along the full length of the decks, using the railings as back rests. The feet, or supports, are sometimes of wood, sometimes of metal.

The gates that close off the forward and aft passageways are of great and interesting variety. Only the herringbone, or extension type, is shown here. This may be made of split bamboo and should be

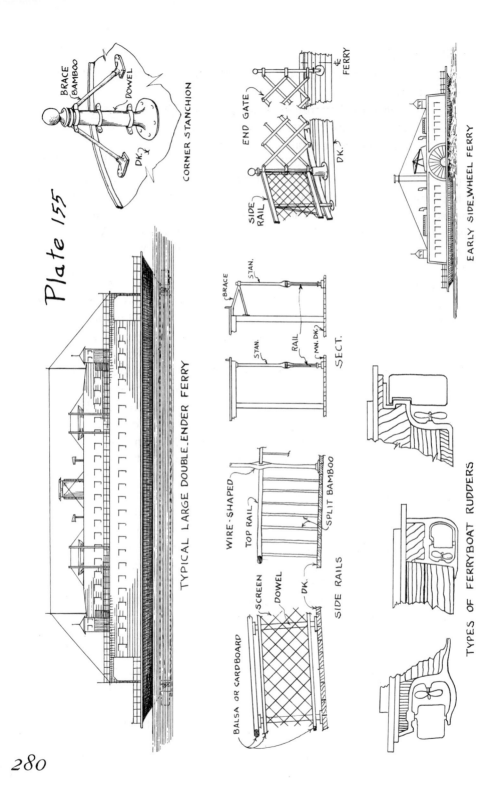

Plate 155

BRACE BAMBOO

DOWEL

DK.

CORNER STANCHION

END GATE

SIDE RAIL

DK.

℄ FERRY

EARLY SIDE WHEEL FERRY

TYPICAL LARGE DOUBLE-ENDER FERRY

BRACE

STAN.

STAN.

RAIL

MN. DK.

SECT.

WIRE-SHAPED

TOP RAIL

SPLIT BAMBOO

SIDE RAILS

BALSA OR CARDBOARD

SCREEN

DOWEL

DK.

TYPES OF FERRYBOAT RUDDERS

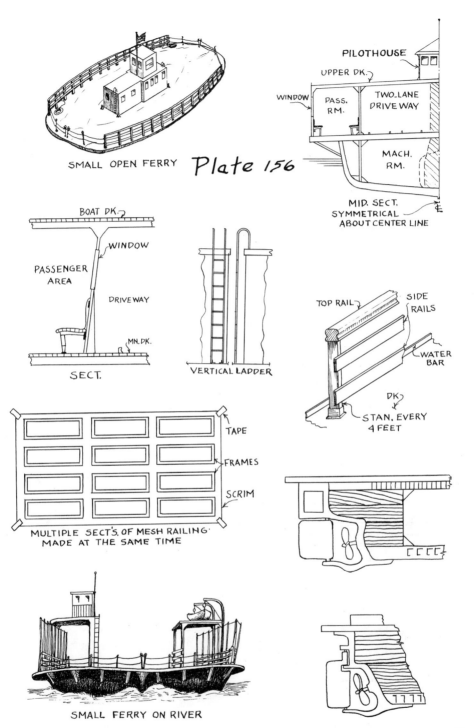

SMALL OPEN FERRY   *Plate 156*

PILOTHOUSE

UPPER DK.

WINDOW   PASS. RM.   TWO-LANE DRIVE WAY

MACH. RM.

MID. SECT.
SYMMETRICAL
ABOUT CENTER LINE

BOAT DK.

WINDOW

PASSENGER AREA

DRIVEWAY

MN. DK.

SECT.

VERTICAL LADDER

TOP RAIL   SIDE RAILS

WATER BAR

DK.

STAN, EVERY 4 FEET

TAPE

FRAMES

SCRIM

MULTIPLE SECT'S. OF MESH RAILING
MADE AT THE SAME TIME

SMALL FERRY ON RIVER

281

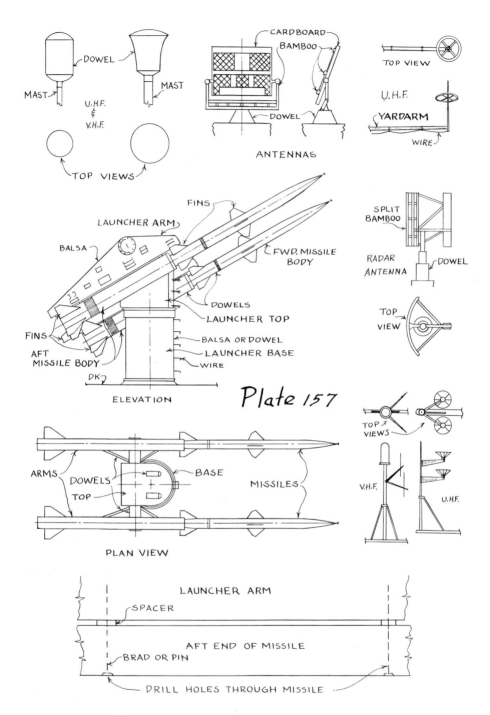

MAST · DOWEL · MAST

U.H.F. & V.H.F.

TOP VIEWS

CARDBOARD · BAMBOO · DOWEL

ANTENNAS

TOP VIEW

U.H.F. · YARDARM · WIRE

FINS · LAUNCHER ARM · FWD. MISSILE BODY

BALSA

SPLIT BAMBOO · RADAR ANTENNA · DOWEL

DOWELS · LAUNCHER TOP

FINS · AFT MISSILE BODY · BALSA OR DOWEL · LAUNCHER BASE · WIRE

DK

ELEVATION

TOP VIEW

Plate 157

TOP VIEWS

ARMS · DOWELS · TOP · BASE · MISSILES

PLAN VIEW

V.H.F. · U.H.F.

LAUNCHER ARM

SPACER

AFT END OF MISSILE

BRAD OR PIN

DRILL HOLES THROUGH MISSILE

METHOD OF SECURING MISSILE TO LAUNCHER ARM

shown extended. There are two parts, which meet at the boat's center line, where a chain loop or a clasp holds them together. It is best to assemble your herringbone pieces on a sheet of wax paper. A ruled sheet of paper placed underneath, marked with spacing joints at top and bottom, will help considerably in the gluing assembly job. For the centerline posts, use pieces of balsa, or dowels, if you can find any small enough; top each with an infinitesimal bead, and glue a tiny cardboard wheel to the bottom.

The corner stanchions for all gates have to be very strong and firmly braced; a few types are shown. Use dowels, gluing on a bead for the cap and a cardboard disk for the base, filling in the glued joints with gesso or a whiting-and-glue mixture (*pages 22-24*). Use the same paste treatment for the brace bases. The braces may be of split bamboo, tops inserted into the dowel, bases made of sheet balsa. With narrow strips of paper, encircle stanchions at points of contact with side rails, gates, and braces, if used.

Another type of gate (not shown) consists of three and four upright rods, to which parallel lengths of chain are stretched across. Another uses wire rope instead of chain. Some have hinged folding sections of regular railing, all these with wheeled stanchions.

The next time you board a ferryboat, study the details—it may lead to your making a collection to remind you of your travels.

If you construct one of the small open ferries, remember that the railings, always of wood, are on the inboard side of the stanchions and that they run almost the full length of the boat.

A few varieties of ferryboat rudder and propeller arrangements are shown. Consult the index for basic construction details.

MISSILES AND MISSILE LAUNCHERS *Plate 157*

A cursory glance at the illustrations may give the impression that missiles and missile launchers are difficult to construct. Actually, they are very simple.

The launcher here consists of (1) a body, or base, (2) a top, and (3) two arms, or outriggers.

Each missile consists of a forward and an after section, plus several fins: four at each forward section, four at each after section, and four at intermediate, varying in size and design, as is shown.

The launcher body is a circular, spool-like piece, and the top is rectangular, with a rounded front. The body and the launcher arms may be constructed of balsa wood. Join the arms to the launcher top by dowels running at right angles to them, and add small dowel braces.

U.S. 32-gun frigate *Raleigh*. One of the original 13 ships built for the first American navy. Captured by the British in 1778. (In the collection of The Mariners' Museum, Newport News, Va.)

Fit all the units of the launcher very carefully, and remember that the assembly and gluing should be done in sections—first, the base and the top glued together; second, support and braces glued to each arm; then, when everything is dry, glue the arm supports into the top. Be sure to align the launcher arms at exactly the same angle. When finally installed on your ship, any misalignment will give the impression that something has slipped.

The entire length of each missile body, minus the fins, may be made from one dowel, with the forward section shaped to a slightly smaller diameter than the after section. The fins may be shaped from sheet balsa and glued into place. For even alignment of the fins, draw lines around the dowels. Attach the missiles to the launcher arms by brads, as shown, leaving a narrow space between arms and missiles.

The ladder rungs may be made by bending thin wires into the shape pictured, or, if you have wire staples in scale, use them.

The entire launcher should be painted gray, except for the ladder rungs and other parts labeled as metal in the sketches. These should be painted black. The missile bodies may be painted a bright yellow and decorated with a couple of narrow bands of contrasting colored paper strips.

ANTENNAS. The antennas illustrated here are a few more examples of the ever-changing electronics developments. The two large antennas are for radar and they revolve. The other sketches are of units used for V.H.F. and U.H.F. For materials used in their construction, *see* PLATES *147-148.*

THE *MONITOR* AND THE *MERRIMAC*   *Folded Plan*

Various conceptions and stages of ironclad ship designs had been on inventors' drawing boards almost from the beginning of the 19th century, but as is customary, the bureaucrats of the day pronounced them crackpot. So for decades they gathered dust, while ships that had changed very little in hundreds of years carried on the business of warfare.

Early in the Civil War there came a time when the Confederate forces became desperate enough to try almost anything. They salvaged a frigate, the *Merrimac*, that had been scuttled when the Federals abandoned the Norfolk vicinity, and constructed from it one of those weird dreams, renaming her the *Virginia*. (But the old name stuck to her and probably always will.)

One morning this ironclad ship, without ever having had trial runs, tests, or practice of any kind, lumbered, wheezing and sputtering, out of her yard, with most of her brave crew frightened out of their wits. You know the rest, of course—how they disposed of two enemy frigates in a matter of hours and set about the next day to finish off a third that had run aground. They were absolutely amazed to find it guarded by an ugly, bristling, little bulldog, named the *Monitor*. This ironclad had been put together in New York with wild haste and had wallowed down here, almost foundering twice, with a crew of volunteers. What followed is known as "the most momentous drawn battle in history." The battle had world-wide significance. Suddenly, all wooden fighting ships had become obsolete.

These ironclads make interesting models; the construction of either the *Monitor* or the *Merrimac* is quite simple. And just for a change, the angular lines of the hull structure might be welcome. Hulls, pilot-houses, casemate, and turret may be shaped from solid balsa. The plating joints may be simulated by small V-grooves cut into whatever material is used. The guns for casemate and turret may be shaped from dowels.

The turret of the *Monitor* may be made to revolve, if desired. For the base of the turret, use a flat circular disk of balsa with a central dowel for the pivoting post. The *Merrimac* presents no difficulties.

Basic details common to ships in general, if not on your *Monitor* and *Merrimac* Insert Sheet Plans, are given in other sections of this book.

APPENDIX

MARINE, MARITIME AND NAVAL MUSEUMS
IN THE UNITED STATES AND CANADA

All of the museums, historical sites, etc., listed have material on display of interest to ship model builders. For a complete list of "Marine Museums of the World" refer to *Popular Boating* magazine of January 1966. In this issue the specialties of each museum are described.

CALIFORNIA
National City: Museum of American Treasures
Palos Verdes Estates: Marineland of the Pacific
Port Hueneme: Seabee Museum
San Francisco: San Francisco Maritime Museum
San Francisco Maritime State Historic Park
San Pedro: Cabrillo Beach Marine Museum

CONNECTICUT
Mystic: Mystic Seaport
Groton: Submarine Library and Museum
New London: United States Coast Guard Academy

DELAWARE
Lewes: Zwaanendael Museum

DISTRICT OF COLUMBIA
Exhibit Room, United States Treasury Building
Maritime Administration, U. S. Dept. of Commerce
Naval Historical Display Center—Building 76, Washington Navy Yard
Smithsonian Institute—Naval History Hall
Truxton-Decatur Naval Museum

FLORIDA
Clearwater: Sea-Orama
Miami: University of Florida, Marine Laboratory Museum
Key West: Martello Gallery and Museum
Pensacola: United States Naval Air Aviation Museum
St. Petersburg: HMS *Bounty* (Replica)
Stuart: House of Refuge

GEORGIA
Sapelo Island: University of Georgia Marine Institute

HAWAII
Honolulu: Bernice P. Bishop Museum

ILLINOIS
Chicago: Chicago Historical Society
Waukegan: Johnson Motors

INDIANA
Jefferson: Steamboat Museum

MAINE
Kennebunk: Brick Store Museum
Searsport: Penobscot Marine Museum

MARYLAND
Annapolis: United States Naval Academy Museum
Baltimore: Maryland Historical Society
U. S. Frigate *Constellation*
Landover Hills: Nautical Research Guild
St. Michaels: Chesapeake Bay Maritime Museum

MASSACHUSETTS
Andover: Addison Gallery of American Art
Boston: Boston Marine Society
      Bostonian Society
      Museum of Fine Arts
      Museum of Science
      U.S.S. *Constitution* (Old Ironsides)
Cambridge: Francis Russell Hart Nautical Museum, Massachusetts Institute of Technology
Cape Cod: Nauset Lifesaving Museum, Cape Cod National Seashore
Cohasset: Cohasset Maritime Museum
Falmouth: Historical Society
Fall River: Historical Society
Gloucester: Cape Ann Scientific, Literary and Historical Society
Mattapoisett: Historical Society Museum
Nantucket: Nantucket Whaling Museum
New Bedford: Whaling Museum, Old Dartmouth Historical Society
Plymouth: *Mayflower* (Replica)
Martha's Vineyard: Thomas Cooke House and Museum, Edgartown
Rockport: Sandy Bay Historical Society and Museum
Salem: Peabody Museum
      Salem National Historic Site

MICHIGAN
Detroit: Dossin Great Lakes Museum, Great Lakes Maritime Institute, Belle Isle

MISSOURI
Hermann: Historic Hermann Museum

NEW YORK
Buffalo: Buffalo and Erie County Historical Society
Centerport: Vanderbilt Museum
Cold Spring Harbor: Whaling Museum
Mapleview: Putnam's Antique Museum
New York City: Marine Museum of the Seaman's Church Institute
      Museum of the City of New York
      New York Historical Society
      Seaman's Bank for Savings
Sag Harbor: Suffolk County Whaling Museum
Stony Brook: Suffolk Museum and Carriage House
Staten Island: Sailor's Snug Harbor
Whitehall: Skenesborough Museum

NORTH CAROLINA
Manteo: Museum of the Sea, Cape Hatteras National Seashore
Wilmington: Fort Fisher State Historical Site
      USS *North Carolina* (Battleship)

OHIO
Fairport Harbor: Fairport Marine Museum
Marietta: Ohio Historical Society, Campus Martius Museum
Vermilion: Great Lakes Historical Society

OREGON
Astoria: Columbia River Maritime Museum

PENNSYLVANIA
Erie: USS *Niagara*
Philadelphia: Franklin Institute
      Philadelphia Maritime Museum

RHODE ISLAND
East Greenwich: Varnum Military and Naval Museum
Newport: New England Naval and Maritime Museum
      Newport Historical Society
Providence: Providence Public Library
West Barrington: Steamship Historical Society of America

VERMONT
    Northfield: Norwich University Museum
    Shelburne: Shelburne Museum

VIRGINIA
    Newport News: Mariners Museum
    Portsmouth: Norfolk Naval Shipyard Museum
    Yorktown: Colonial National Historical Park

CANADA
    Dawson City, Yukon Territory: S.S. *Keno* National Historic Site
    Halifax, N.S.: Maritime Museum of Canada
    Amherstburg, Ont.: Marine Museum
    Toronto, Ont.: Marine Museum of Upper Canada
    Vancouver, B.C.: Vancouver Maritime Museum
    Victoria, B.C.: Maritime Museum of British Columbia
    Wasaga Beach. Ont.: HMS *Nancy* Museum
    Whitehorse, Yukon Territory: S.S. *Klondike*

For information about other museums with supplementary marine exhibits, and for privately owned collections, inquire at libraries, tourist bureaus, Chambers of Commerce, etc.

For the systematic ones among you, here is a sample form of a model builder's log, which you may want to use as a basis for your own records for future reference.

LOG OF MODEL "＿＿＿＿＿＿＿＿＿"

LENGTH＿＿＿＿＿ MAX. BEAM ＿＿＿＿＿ DRAFT＿＿＿＿＿
SAILING VESSEL ＿＿＿ STEAM-SHIP＿＿＿＿ MOTOR SHIP＿＿＿＿

CONSTRUCTION – TIME EXPENDED

HULL
SOLID＿＿＿＿ PARTIALLY SOLID＿＿＿＿ KEEL & RIBBED＿＿＿＿
HULL FITTINGS - EXTERNAL ＿＿＿＿＿＿＿＿＿＿
DECK HOUSES＿＿＿ BULWARKS＿＿＿＿＿ HATCHES＿＿＿＿＿
DECK FITTINGS＿＿＿＿＿＿＿＿＿＿＿＿＿＿＿＿
FOREMAST＿＿＿ MAINMAST＿＿＿ MIZZENMAST＿＿＿＿ OTHERS＿＿
YARDS＿＿＿＿＿SPARS＿＿＿＿＿＿ BOOMS＿＿＿＿＿ OTHERS＿＿
FULL SAILS＿＿＿PARTIALLY REEFED＿＿＿ FURLED＿＿＿＿ OTHERS＿＿
CRADLE＿＿＿＿ WAYS＿＿＿＿＿＿ BASE＿＿＿＿ ASSEMBLY＿＿

PAINTING – FINISHING
HULL＿＿＿＿＿＿ DECK HOUSES＿＿＿＿＿ DECK FITTINGS＿＿＿＿＿
WAYS & BASE＿＿＿ MASTS & YARDS＿＿＿SPARS & BOOMS＿＿OTHERS＿＿

ASSEMBLY
HULL & BASE＿＿＿ BOWSPRIT＿＿＿＿ EXTERNAL FITTINGS＿＿＿＿＿
JIB BOOM＿＿＿＿FOREMAST＿＿MAINMAST＿＿MIZZENMAST＿＿OTHERS＿＿

STANDING RIGGING – SHROUDS & BACK-STAYS
FOREMAST＿＿＿＿ MAINMAST＿＿＿ MIZZENMAST＿＿＿＿＿ OTHERS＿＿
" TOPMAST＿＿＿＿ " TOPMAST＿＿＿ " TOPMAST ＿＿＿＿ "   ＿＿
" TOPGALLANT＿＿＿ " TOPGALLANT＿＿" TOPGALLANT＿＿＿＿ "   ＿＿
" ROYAL & SKYSAIL＿＿" ROYAL & SKYSAIL＿" ROYAL & SKYSAIL＿＿＿ "   ＿＿
BOWSPRIT＿＿＿＿＿ JIB BOOM＿＿＿ FLYING JIB BOOM＿＿＿ "   ＿＿

STANDING RIGGING – FORE-AND-AFT
ALL STAYS FROM JIB BOOM AFT＿＿＿＿＿＿＿＿＿＿＿＿＿＿

YARDS - SPARS - BOOMS
ALL MAINMAST＿＿ ALL MIZZENMAST＿＿ ALL FOREMAST＿＿＿ OTHERS＿＿

RUNNING RIGGING
MAINMAST＿＿＿ FOREMAST＿＿＿ MIZZENMAST＿＿＿＿＿ OTHERS＿＿
" TOPMAST＿＿＿ " TOPMAST＿＿＿ " TOPMAST ＿＿＿＿＿ "   ＿＿
" TOPGALLANT＿＿" TOPGALLANT＿＿" TOPGALLANT＿＿＿＿ "   ＿＿
" ROYAL & SKYSAIL＿ " ROYAL & SKYSAIL＿ " ROYAL & SKYSAIL＿＿＿ "   ＿＿

LIFTS & BRACES - PORT & STARBOARD
ALL MAINMAST＿＿＿ ALL MIZZENMAST＿＿＿ ALL FOREMAST＿＿＿＿＿ OTHERS＿＿

SAILS - IF USED
ALL MIZZENMAST＿＿＿ ALL MAINMAST＿＿ ALL FOREMAST＿＿ ALL JIBS＿＿
STAY SAILS＿＿＿ SPANKER＿＿＿ STUN-SAILS＿＿＿＿ OTHERS＿＿

COMPLETE CHECK OF VESSEL
ALIGNMENT OF ALL YARDS＿＿＿ TOUCHING UP＿＿＿＿＿＿＿＿＿
PLASTIC ENCLOSURE FOR MODEL＿＿＿＿＿＿＿＿＿＿＿＿＿＿

LOG OF MODEL "_ _ _ _ _ _ _ _ _"

LENGTH_ _ _ _ _ _ MAX. BEAM _ _ _ _ _ _ _ DRAFT_ _ _ _ _ _

SAILING VESSEL _ _ _ STEAM-SHIP_ _ _ _ MOTOR SHIP_ _ _ _

CONSTRUCTION – TIME EXPENDED
HULL

SOLID_ _ _ _ PARTIALLY SOLID _ _ _ _ KEEL & RIBBED _ _ _ _ _

HULL FITTINGS - EXTERNAL _ _ _ _ _ _ _ _ _ _ _ _ _ _ _

DECK HOUSES_ _ _ _ BULWARKS _ _ _ _ _ HATCHES _ _ _ _ _

DECK FITTINGS_ _ _ _ _ _ _ _ _ _ _ _ _ _ _ _ _ _

FOREMAST_ _ _ _ MAINMAST_ _ _ _ MIZZENMAST_ _ _ _ OTHERS_ _

YARDS_ _ _ _ _ SPARS _ _ _ _ _ BOOMS _ _ _ _ _ OTHERS_ _

FULL SAILS _ _ _ PARTIALLY REEFED_ _ _ FURLED_ _ _ _ OTHERS_ _

CRADLE_ _ _ _ WAYS_ _ _ _ _ _ BASE _ _ _ ASSEMBLY_ _

PAINTING — FINISHING

HULL _ _ _ _ _ _ DECK HOUSES _ _ _ _ _ DECK FITTINGS_ _ _ _

WAYS & BASE _ _ _ MASTS & YARDS _ _ _ SPARS & BOOMS _ _ OTHERS_ _

ASSEMBLY

HULL & BASE _ _ _ BOWSPRIT_ _ _ _ EXTERNAL FITTINGS_ _ _ _

JIB BOOM _ _ _ _ FOREMAST_ _ MAINMAST_ _ MIZZENMAST_ _ OTHERS_ _

STANDING RIGGING - SHROUDS & BACK-STAYS

FOREMAST_ _ _ _ MAINMAST_ _ _ MIZZENMAST_ _ _ _ OTHERS _ _

" TOPMAST_ _ _ " TOPMAST _ _ _ " TOPMAST _ _ _ _ " _ _

" TOPGALLANT_ _ " TOPGALLANT_ _ " TOPGALLANT _ _ _ _ " _ _

" ROYAL & SKYSAIL _ _ _ " ROYAL & SKYSAIL _ " ROYAL & SKYSAIL _ _ _ " _ _

BOWSPRIT_ _ _ _ _ JIB BOOM _ _ _ FLYING JIB BOOM_ _ _ " _ _

STANDING RIGGING — FORE-AND-AFT

ALL STAYS FROM JIB BOOM AFT _ _ _ _ _ _ _ _ _ _ _ _

YARDS - SPARS - BOOMS

ALL MAINMAST_ _ ALL MIZZENMAST_ _ ALL FOREMAST_ _ _ OTHERS_ _

RUNNING RIGGING

MAINMAST_ _ _ FOREMAST_ _ _ MIZZENMAST_ _ _ _ _ OTHERS_ _

" TOPMAST_ _ _ " TOPMAST _ _ _ " TOPMAST _ _ _ _ " _ _

" TOPGALLANT_ _ " TOPGALLANT _ _ " TOPGALLANT_ _ _ _ " _ _

" ROYAL & SKYSAIL _ " ROYAL & SKYSAIL _ " ROYAL & SKYSAIL _ _ _ " _ _

LIFTS & BRACES - PORT & STARBOARD

ALL MAINMAST_ _ _ ALL MIZZENMAST_ _ _ ALL FOREMAST_ _ _ _ OTHERS_ _

SAILS - IF USED

ALL MIZZENMAST_ _ _ ALL MAINMAST_ _ ALL FOREMAST_ _ ALL JIBS_ _

STAY SAILS _ _ _ SPANKER _ _ _ _ STUN-SAILS _ _ _ _ OTHERS_ _

COMPLETE CHECK OF VESSEL

ALIGNMENT OF ALL YARDS_ _ _ TOUCHING UP_ _ _ _ _ _ _ _

PLASTIC ENCLOSURE FOR MODEL _ _ _ _ _ _ _ _ _ _ _ _ _

LOG OF MODEL "_____"

LENGTH_____ MAX. BEAM_____ DRAFT_____
SAILING VESSEL___ STEAM-SHIP_____ MOTOR SHIP____

CONSTRUCTION – TIME EXPENDED
HULL
SOLID_____ PARTIALLY SOLID_____ KEEL & RIBBED_____
HULL FITTINGS - EXTERNAL_____
DECK HOUSES____ BULWARKS_____ HATCHES_____
DECK FITTINGS_____
FOREMAST____ MAINMAST____ MIZZENMAST____ OTHERS__
YARDS_____ SPARS_____ BOOMS_____ OTHERS__
FULL SAILS____ PARTIALLY REEFED____ FURLED____ OTHERS__
CRADLE_____ WAYS_____ BASE____ ASSEMBLY__

PAINTING — FINISHING
HULL_____ DECK HOUSES_____ DECK FITTINGS_____
WAYS & BASE____ MASTS & YARDS____ SPARS & BOOMS___ OTHERS__

ASSEMBLY
HULL & BASE___ BOWSPRIT_____ EXTERNAL FITTINGS_____
JIB BOOM_____ FOREMAST__ MAINMAST__ MIZZENMAST__ OTHERS__

STANDING RIGGING – SHROUDS & BACK-STAYS
FOREMAST____ MAINMAST____ MIZZENMAST_____ OTHERS___
" TOPMAST_____ " TOPMAST____ " TOPMAST_____ "   __
" TOPGALLANT____ " TOPGALLANT___ " TOPGALLANT_____ "   __
" ROYAL & SKYSAIL____ " ROYAL & SKYSAIL__ " ROYAL & SKYSAIL_____ "   __
BOWSPRIT_____ JIB BOOM___ FLYING JIB BOOM____ "   __

STANDING RIGGING – FORE-AND-AFT
ALL STAYS FROM JIB BOOM AFT_____

YARDS - SPARS - BOOMS
ALL MAINMAST__ ALL MIZZENMAST__ ALL FOREMAST____ OTHERS__

RUNNING RIGGING
MAINMAST____ FOREMAST____ MIZZENMAST_____ OTHERS__
" TOPMAST____ " TOPMAST____ " TOPMAST_____ "   __
" TOPGALLANT___ " TOPGALLANT__ " TOPGALLANT_____ "   __
" ROYAL & SKYSAIL__ " ROYAL & SKYSAIL__ " ROYAL & SKYSAIL____ "   __

LIFTS & BRACES - PORT & STARBOARD
ALL MAINMAST____ ALL MIZZENMAST___ ALL FOREMAST_____ OTHERS__

SAILS - IF USED
ALL MIZZENMAST____ ALL MAINMAST___ ALL FOREMAST___ ALL JIBS___
STAY SAILS____ SPANKER____ STUN-SAILS_____ OTHERS__

COMPLETE CHECK OF VESSEL
ALIGNMENT OF ALL YARDS___ TOUCHING UP_____
PLASTIC ENCLOSURE FOR MODEL_____

LOG OF MODEL "_ _ _ _ _ _ _ _"

LENGTH_ _ _ _ _ MAX. BEAM _ _ _ _ _ _ DRAFT_ _ _ _ _ _

SAILING VESSEL _ _ _ STEAM-SHIP_ _ _ _ _ MOTOR SHIP_ _ _ _

CONSTRUCTION — TIME EXPENDED
HULL
SOLID_ _ _ _ PARTIALLY SOLID _ _ _ _ KEEL & RIBBED _ _ _ _

HULL FITTINGS - EXTERNAL _ _ _ _ _ _ _ _ _ _ _ _ _ _

DECK HOUSES_ _ _ BULWARKS _ _ _ _ HATCHES _ _ _ _ _

DECK FITTINGS_ _ _ _ _ _ _ _ _ _ _ _ _ _ _ _

FOREMAST_ _ _ MAINMAST_ _ _ MIZZENMAST_ _ _ OTHERS_ _

YARDS _ _ _ _ SPARS _ _ _ _ _ BOOMS _ _ _ _ OTHERS_ _

FULL SAILS _ _ _ PARTIALLY REEFED_ _ _ FURLED_ _ _ _ OTHERS_ _

CRADLE_ _ _ _ WAYS_ _ _ _ _ _ BASE _ _ _ ASSEMBLY_ _

PAINTING — FINISHING
HULL _ _ _ _ _ DECK HOUSES _ _ _ _ DECK FITTINGS_ _ _ _

WAYS & BASE _ _ _ MASTS & YARDS _ _ _ SPARS & BOOMS _ _OTHERS_ _

ASSEMBLY
HULL & BASE_ _ _ BOWSPRIT_ _ _ _ EXTERNAL FITTINGS_ _ _ _

JIB BOOM _ _ _ _ FOREMAST_ _ MAINMAST_ _ MIZZENMAST_ _OTHERS_ _

STANDING RIGGING – SHROUDS & BACK-STAYS
FOREMAST_ _ _ MAINMAST_ _ _ MIZZENMAST _ _ _ _ OTHERS_ _

" TOPMAST_ _ _ " TOPMAST_ _ _ " TOPMAST _ _ _ _ " _ _

" TOPGALLANT_ _ " TOPGALLANT_ _ " TOPGALLANT _ _ _ _ " _ _

" ROYAL & SKYSAIL _ _ " ROYAL & SKYSAIL _ " ROYAL & SKYSAIL _ _ _ " _ _

BOWSPRIT_ _ _ _ JIB BOOM_ _ _ FLYING JIB BOOM _ _ _ " _ _

STANDING RIGGING – FORE-AND-AFT
ALL STAYS FROM JIB BOOM AFT _ _ _ _ _ _ _ _ _ _ _ _ _

YARDS - SPARS - BOOMS
ALL MAINMAST_ _ ALL MIZZENMAST_ _ ALL FOREMAST_ _ _ OTHERS_ _

RUNNING RIGGING
MAINMAST_ _ _ FOREMAST_ _ _ MIZZENMAST_ _ _ _ _ OTHERS_ _

" TOPMAST_ _ _ " TOPMAST_ _ _ " TOPMAST _ _ _ _ " _ _

" TOPGALLANT_ _ " TOPGALLANT_ _ " TOPGALLANT_ _ _ _ " _ _

" ROYAL & SKYSAIL _ " ROYAL & SKYSAIL _ " ROYAL & SKYSAIL _ _ _ " _ _

LIFTS & BRACES - PORT & STARBOARD
ALL MAINMAST_ _ _ ALL MIZZENMAST_ _ _ ALL FOREMAST_ _ _ _ OTHERS_ _

SAILS - IF USED
ALL MIZZENMAST_ _ ALL MAINMAST_ _ ALL FOREMAST_ _ ALL JIBS_ _

STAY SAILS _ _ _ SPANKER _ _ _ STUN-SAILS _ _ _ _ OTHERS_ _

COMPLETE CHECK OF VESSEL
ALIGNMENT OF ALL YARDS_ _ _ TOUCHING UP_ _ _ _ _ _ _ _

PLASTIC ENCLOSURE FOR MODEL _ _ _ _ _ _ _ _ _ _ _ _

INDEX

INDEX

Note: For clarity and simplification, items in the drawings are indexed according to their page numbers, not plate numbers.

TEXT-BOOK

of

SEAMANSHIP

The Equipping and Handling of
Vessels Under Sail or Steam

for the use of the

UNITED STATES NAVAL ACADEMY

by

REAR ADMIRAL S. B. LUCE, U. S.

revised by

Lieutenant W. S. Benson, U. S. N.

with illustrations drawn by

Lieutenant S. Seabury, U. S. N.

CORNELL MARITIME PRESS
CAMBRIDGE, MD.
1950

AN OUTSTANDING REFERENCE
FOR THE SERIOUS
SHIP MODEL BUILDER'S LIBRARY

Luce's TEXT-BOOK OF SEAMANSHIP, first published in 1862, was a success from its inception. It was the text for the study of seamanship at the U.S. Naval Academy and, as others learned of its existence, it became a reference manual for practical seamen everywhere. From the time it was first published in 1862, edition followed edition. This reprint is of the last (1898) edition.

Today's ship model builder will find "Luce's Seamanship" a most valuable reference on the masting and rigging of sailing ships and early steam vessels. Illustrated by 122 full-page plates containing in excess of 1000 illustrations depicting and fully describing the methods and gear of masting and rigging of the period. Here is a truly fine book that will be an excellent and practical addition to the library of the ship model builder.

The 32 chapters and 14 appendices in "Luce's Seamanship" cover every phase of seamanship. The emphasis throughout is on the equipping and handling of ships. This emphasis is what makes Luce's TEXT-BOOK OF SEAMANSHIP such an ideal reference volume for the serious ship model builder.

720 Pages,   122 Full Pages of Plates   6" x 9" $10.00

(Reprint of the 1898 Edition)

Published by

CORNELL MARITIME PRESS, INC.
Cambridge   **Maryland**

Order from:
Your bookseller or hobby supply dealer